高等学校试用教材

建筑类专业英语

暖通与燃气

第三册

周保强　张少凡　主编
师湧江　冀桂娥
陈星星　管继顺　编
颜景台
王　鸣　　　　主审

中国建筑工业出版社

《建筑类专业英语》编审委员会

总 主 编　徐铁城
总 主 审　杨匡汉
副总主编　（以姓氏笔划为序）
　　　　　王庆昌　乔梦铎　陆铁镛
　　　　　周保强　蔡英俊
编　　委　（以姓氏笔划为序）
　　　　　王久愉　王学玲　王翰邦　卢世伟
　　　　　孙　玮　李明章　朱满才　向小林
　　　　　向　阳　刘文瑛　余曼筠　孟祥杰
　　　　　张少凡　张文洁　张新建　赵三元
　　　　　阎岫峰　傅兴海　褚羞花　蔡慧俭
　　　　　濮宏魁
责任编辑　刘茂榆

前　言

经过几十年的探索,外语教学界许多人认为,工科院校外语教学的主要目的,应该是:"使学生能够利用外语这个工具,通过阅读去获取国外的与本专业有关的科技信息。"这既是我们建设有中国特色的社会主义的客观需要,也是在当前条件下工科院校外语教学可能完成的最高目标。事实上,教学大纲规定要使学生具有"较强"的阅读能力,而对其他方面的能力只有"一般"要求,就是这个意思。

大学本科的一、二年级,为外语教学的基础阶段。就英语来说,这个阶段要求掌握的词汇量为2400个(去掉遗忘,平均每个课时10个单词)。加上中学阶段已经学会的1600个单词,基础阶段结束时应掌握的词汇量为4000个。仅仅掌握4000个单词,能否看懂专业英文书刊呢?还不能。据统计,掌握4000个单词,阅读一般的英文科技文献,生词量仍将有6%左右,即平均每百词有六个生词,还不能自由阅读。国外的外语教学专家认为,生词量在3%以下,才能不借助词典,自由阅读。此时可以通过上下文的联系,把不认识的生词猜出来。那么,怎么样才能把6%的生词量降低到3%以下呢?自然,需要让学生增加一部分词汇积累。问题是,要增加多少单词?要增加哪一些单词?统计资料表明,在每一个专业的科技文献中,本专业最常用的科技术语大约只有几百个,而且它们在文献中重复出现的频率很高。因此,在已经掌握4000单词的基础上,在专业阅读阶段中,有针对性地通过大量阅读,扩充大约1000个与本专业密切有关的科技词汇,便可以逐步达到自由阅读本专业科技文献的目的。

早在八十年代中期,建设部系统院校外语教学研究会就组织编写了一套《土木建筑系列英语》,分八个专业,共12册。每个专业可选读其中的三、四册。那套教材在有关院校相应的专业使用多年,学生和任课教师反映良好。但是,根据当时的情况,那套教材定的起点较低(1000词起点),已不适合今天学生的情况。为此,在得到建设部人事教育劳动司的大力支持,并征得五个相关专业指导委员会同意之后,由建设部系统十几所院校一百余名外语教师和专业课教师按照统一的编写规划和要求,编写了这一套《建筑类专业英语》教材。

《建筑类专业英语》是根据国家教委颁发的《大学英语专业阅读阶段教学基本要求》编写的专业阅读教材,按照建筑类院校共同设置的五个较大的专业类别对口编写。五个专业类别为:建筑学与城市规划;建筑工程(即工业与民用建筑);给水排水与环境保护;暖通、空调与燃气;建筑管理与财务会计。每个专业类别分别编写三册专业英语阅读教材,供该专业类别的学生在修完基础阶段英语后,在第五至第七学期专业阅读阶段使用,每学期一册。

上述五种专业英语教材语言规范,题材广泛,覆盖相关专业各自的主要内容:包括专业基础课,专业主干课及主要专业选修课,语言材料的难易度切合学生的实际水平;词汇以大学英语"通用词汇表"的4000个单词为起点，每个专业类别的三册书将增加1000～1200个阅读本专业必需掌握的词汇。本教材重视语言技能训练，突出对阅读、翻译和写作能力的培养，以求达到《大学英语专业阅读阶段教学基本要求》所提出的教学目标："通过指导学生阅读有关专业的英语书刊和文献，使他们进一步提高阅读和翻译科技资料的能力，并能以英语为工具获取专业所需的信息。"

《建筑类专业英语》每册16个单元，每个单元一篇正课文（TEXT），两篇副课文（Reading Material A&B），每个单元平均2000个词，三册48个单元，总共约有十万个词，相当于原版书三百多页。要培养较强的阅读能力，读十万词的文献，是起码的要求。如果专业课教师在第六和第七学期，在学生通过学习本教材已经掌握了数百个专业科技词汇的基础上，配合专业课程的学习，再指定学生看一部分相应的专业英语科技文献，那将会既促进专业课的学习，又提高英语阅读能力，实为两得之举。

本教材不仅适用于在校学生，对于有志提高专业英语阅读能力的建筑行业广大在职工程技术人员，也是一套适用的自学教材。

建设部人事教育劳动司高教处和中国建设教育协会对这套教材的编写自始至终给予关注和支持；中国建筑工业出版社第五编辑室密切配合，参与从制定编写方案到审稿各个阶段的重要会议，给了我们很多帮助；在编写过程中，各参编学校相关专业的许多专家、教授对材料的选取、译文的审定都提出了许多宝贵意见，谨此致谢。

《建筑类专业英语》是我们编写对口专业阅读教材的又一次尝试，由于编写者水平及经验有限，教材中不妥之处在所难免，敬请广大读者批评指正。

《建筑类专业英语》
编审委员会

Contents

UNIT ONE
Text   Heat Transmission and Distribution Systems ·· 1
Reading Material A   Infiltration Heat Loss ··· 5
Reading Material B   Cast-iron Radiators ·· 7

UNIT TWO
Text   Exhaust Hoods ··· 9
Reading Material A   Ceiling Diffusers ··· 15
Reading Material B   Infiltration Measurement ··· 16

UNIT THREE
Text   Heat Transmission Through Glazing ··· 19
Reading Material A   The Factors Affecting Thermal Comfort ··············· 25
Reading Material B   Effect of Shifting Sun Load on Different Zones of Building ··· 27

UNIT FOUR
Text   Fluid Bed Technology is in Transition ·· 29
Reading Material A   Draft of Boiler ·· 33
Reading Material B   Safety Valves ·· 34

UNIT FIVE
Text   Compressor Failure ··· 37
Reading Material A   Compressor Overheating Due to Electrical Problems ············ 42
Reading Material B   District Heating and Cooling Systems ··················· 44

UNIT SIX
Text   Injection Odorization System Design ··· 47
Reading Material A   Safer Repair of Plastic Pipe ································· 52
Reading Material B   Computers Analyze Odorant Concentration ············ 54

UNIT SEVEN
Text   Floor Heating: Achieving Thermal Comfort in Artificial
            Environments ·· 57
Reading Material A   Floor Heating Design Criteria ································ 62
Reading Material B   System Economics and Design Optimisation of Floor
                                 Heating System ··· 63

UNIT EIGHT
Text   Fabric Filters ·· 67
Reading Material A   Particle Removers ·· 72
Reading Material B   Dust Classification ··· 74

UNIT NINE

Text	Introduction to VAV Systems	78
Reading Material A	Test Method of the Air Conditioning Plant	83
Reading Material B	Air Conditioning Water System Characteristics	85

UNIT TEN

Text	Horizontal-Return-Tubular Boilers	87
Reading Material A	Blueprints in the Fire	91
Reading Material B	Coil Watertube Boilers	92

UNIT ELEVEN

Text	Absorption Heat Pumps	95
Reading Material A	Operating Characteristics and Design Considerations of the Refrigeration system	100
Reading Material B	Absorption Chiller Controls	102

UNIT TWELVE

Text	New Emphasis on Natural Gas Storage	105
Reading Material A	SCADA Cuts Pipeline	110
Reading Material B	Flow Measurement up Grade Enables Cost-effective Monitoring	112

UNIT THIRTEEN

Text	Design of District Heating Networks	115
Reading Material A	Pipe Sizing for Steam Heating Systems	120
Reading Material B	Hot and Chilled Water Pipe Sizing	122

UNIT FOURTEEN

Text	Operation and Maintenance of the Airconditioning Plant	124
Reading Material A	Design Factors Affecting Outdoor Air Quantity	129
Reading Material B	Methods of Varying Fan Volume	131

UNIT FIFTEEN

Text	Gas Gathering and Transport	133
Reading Material A	Gas-Water Systems and Dehydration Processing	137
Reading Material B	Gas and Liquid Separation	139

UNIT SIXTEEN

Text	The Volumetric Behavior of Natural Gases Containing Hydrogen Sulfide and Carbon Dioxide	141
Reading Material A	How to Estimate Size Cost of Producing Equipment	145
Reading Material B	Foam Insulation Reduces Gathering System Costs	147
Appendix I	Vocabulary	150
Appendix II	Translation for Reference	156
Appendix III	Key to the exercises	179

UNIT ONE

Text   Heat Transmission and Distribution Systems

[1]   Heat is transported from the heat production plant to the heat demand centre, which may be some distance away, in the heat transmission pipeline.① Transmission system costs are a function of distance and the quantity of heat transmitted, which in turn is determined by the temperature difference and the flow rate of the heat transmission medium. The quality (thickness) of the piping is a function of the water pressure, while the pipe diameter at a given heat load is a function of the flow rate and the temperature difference.

[2]   Many large power stations are located remote from the centres of population for reasons of economy, environmental protection, fuel (such as coal) accessibility and storage etc. Thus, while the heat available at large power stations may technically be recovered for district heating and may match the heat demand of a large city, the cost of the transmission line can be prohibitive. At present the maximum economically viable transmission distance is up to 30 km for hot water and 3-5 km for steam, depending on the heat load and fuel prices. Some studies have shown that hot water transmission over distances above 30 km can be economically attractive. Because of the load and demand limitations already referred to, on an economic basis the number of potential applications is limited. In many circumstances it may be more economic to construct new heat production units at short distances from the demand centre than to construct a long transmission line.②

[3]   Depending on the terrain covered by the water transmission line, pumping stations may be required to maintain the pressure drop between the supply and return pipelines. Where possible the piping is constructed above ground to reduce costs.

[4]   To date, the most common piping systems have involved steel piping laid inconcrete ducts, although steel pipe-in-pipe systems or steel-in-plastic piping systems have been used in special cases. Pre-fabricated pipes, using polyurethane foam as insulation, can be cost-effective, but must be utilized within certain temperature constraints. Insulation material can be rock, mineral or glass wool, fibre glass, polyurethane foam (sometimes combined with glass wool), or calcium silicate.

[5]   Heat is distributed from the main transmission line to the consumer, sometimes directly to the consumer's in-house heat distribution system and sometimes through a heat exchanger to the consumer's in-house distribution system. In some cases the primary distribution grid is interfaced through a heat exchanger with a secondary distribution grid which feeds directly to consumer installations.

[6]   The cost of hot water heat distribution, which includes pumping as well ascontrol systems in the local heat network, depends on a number of factors, in cluding: the heat demand density; the supply and return temperatures; the charac teristics of the terrain and

the local infrastructure; and whether the development is new or involves retrofitting.③

[7]   The temperature in the piping system has an important influence on the cost of distribution per unit length. Generally, the lower the temperature range within which the system operates, the lower the cost of piping. This arises simply because less costly piping and insulation materials are required. At the same time cost is heavily dependent on the heat demand density. The greater the heat density the lower the distribution cost.

[8]   Lower return temperatures can be achieved by serial connection of space heating and hot water devices, by use of low-temperature heating devices and particularly by using thermostatic valves on the in-house heating devices. The latter control the temperature of hot water leaving the radiator or other heating device. In these cases the in-house heating surface may, however, need to be increased, at some cost.

[9]   Increasing supply temperatures and pressures result in thicker gauge pipes, sturdier valves and higher insulation levels and therefore lead to increased costs. Installation costs also tend to be greater. A further factor with an extraction turbine system is that electricity output decreases as the extraction temperature (i.e., the district heating supply temperature) increases, resulting in greater fuel consumption to provide the same energy output.④ This is an important consideration in determining the overall economic attractiveness of a combined production system.

[10]   One of the most important factors is whether the district heating system is being constructed as a new development or as a retrofit development. For the former, costs are much lower and disruption of traffic, pedestrians etc., can be minimized. For a retrofit situation, particularly in older towns and cities, costs can be prohibitive and the degree of disruption can be significant.

New Words and Expressions

accessibility [æk͵sesi'biliti]	n.	可及性
prohibitive [prə'hibitiv]	a.	过高的而不能
viable ['vaiəbl]	a.	有生存力的，可行的
terrain ['terein]	n.	地形
duct [dʌkt]	n.	管，沟（波道）
pre-fabricated [pri:'fæbrikeitid]	a.	预制的
cost-effective ['kɔstə'fektiv]	a.	成本可行的
polyurethane * [͵pɔli'juəriθein]	n.	聚氨酯
foam [fəum]	n.	泡沫
constraint [kən'streint]	n.	限制范围，约束
calcium * ['kælsiəm]	n.	钙
silicate ['silikit]	n.	硅酸盐
grid [grid]	n.	线路网，管网

interface ['intə(:)feis]	v.	连接	
infrastructure ['infrəˌstrʌktʃə]	n.	下部（低层）结构	
thermostatic [θə:məs'tætik]	a.	恒温的	
retrofit * ['retrəfit]	n.	重建，式样翻新	
sturdy * ['stə:di]	a.	坚实的	
valve [vælv]	n.	阀门	
extraction [iks'trækʃən]	n.	抽出	
turbine * ['tə:bin]	n.	涡轮机	
minimize ['minimaiz]	vt.	使…成极小	
pedestrian [pi'destriən]	n.	步行者，行人	

Notes

① which 引导一个非限制性定语从句，修饰 heat demand centre；本段另一…which…同样引出非限制性定语从句，which 的先行词是 the quantity of heat transmitted。

② In many … a long transmission line. 句中 than 引出比较状语，是 to construct new heat production units at short distances 与 to construct a long transmission line 比较。

③ The cost of …, depends on … retrofitting. 句中 depends on 是谓语动词；the heat demand density；the supply and return temperatures；the characteristics of the terrain and the local infrastructure；三个短语以及 whether the development is new or involves retrofitting 从句并列作 including 的宾语。

④ with an extraction turbine system 介词短语做定语修饰前面的 factor；that 从句是表语从句；resulting in … 分词短语是结果状语。

Exercises

Reading Comprehension

I. Say whether the following statements are true (T) or false (F) according to the text.

1. Many large power stations are located very near to the center of population for many reasons. ( )
2. In many circumstances it may be more expensive to construct new heat production units at short distance from the demand centre than to construct along transmission line. ( )
3. Heat is distributed from the main transmission line directly to the consumer's in-house distribution system or through a heat exchanger to the consumer's in-house distribution system. ( )
4. The greater the heat density the less the cost of heat distribution. ( )

5. For a district heating system retrofitting a development costs less than con-structing a new development in. ( )

II. Fill in the table with the information given in the text.

Items	Relations
1. Transmission system costs are	a function of
2. The quality of the piping is	a function of
3. The pipe diameter at a given heat load is	a function of

III. Find out the factors that influence the cost of hot water heat distribution.

1. _____
2. _____
3. _____
4. _____
5. _____

Vocabulary

I. Find words in the text which mean almost the same as the following.
1. the state or quality being able to be reached or got
2. able to exist, capable of living
3. mechanical device for controlling the flow of air, liquid, or gas through a tube or a pipe by opening or closing a passage
4. reduce to smallest possible amount or degree
5. being forbidden or too expensive

II. Now use the words you have found to fill in the gaps in the sentences. Change the form if necessary.
1. The inferior products can be _____ if the workers work carefully.
2. They are going to make a survey of the _____ of raw materials for the nearly-built plant.
3. Do you think this small creature is _____ under such a low temperature?
4. A boiler of high pressure usually has a safety _____ on it.
5. Smoking is _____ in most public places.

III. Choose one of the four choices that best completes the following definitions.
1. _____ is a kind of engine or motor whose driving-wheel is turning by a cur-rent of water.
 a. Fan   b. Wind-wheel   c. Motor-bike   d. Turbine
2. _____ means hard or firm.
 a. Study   b. Sturdy   c. Sticky   d. Still

3. Calcium silicate is a kind of _____ compound.
   a. technical   b. physical   c. metal   d. chemical
4. Retrofit means _____.
   a. renovate   b. retire   c. retreat   d. return
5. Polyurethane foam is called _____ in Chinese.
   a. 聚酯皂   b. 泡沫聚酯   c. 聚酯泡沫   d. 聚氨酯泡沫

Writing   Selecting the Key Words (1)

Ⅰ. Key words are informative words that can give the information about what a piece of writing is mainly talking about. They are often nouns and verbs, etc. For Example:
Read the following text and find out the key worlds:

With the rapid industrialization of the States, air pollution is posing a problem. Fertilizer and steel plants, thermal power plants and paper mills are among the units which cause air pollution.

Automobiles also cause air pollution as they emit smoke which contains hydrocarbon, nitrous oxide and carbon monoxide.

The Air Act was passed in Congress 1982 and came into effect in 1983.

Key words:

Air pollution, Pollutant, Air Act

Directions: Read the text of this Unit and find out three to five key words.

Reading Material A

Infiltration Heat Loss

During the heating season, a portion of heat loss is due to the infiltration of cooler outside air into the interior of the structure through cracks around doors and windows and other openings that are not a part of the ventilating system.① The amount of air entering the structure by infiltration is important in estimating the requirements of the heating system, but the composition of this air is equally important.

A pound of air is composed of both dry air and moisture particles, which are combined (not mixed) so that each retains its individual characteristics.② The distinction between these two basic components of air is important because each is involved with a different type of heat: dry air with specific heat, and moisture content with latent heat.

The heating system must be designed with the capability of warming the cooler infiltrated dry air to the temperature of the air inside the structure. The amount of heat required to do this is referred to as the sensible heat loss, and is expressed in Btuh. The two methods used for calculating heat loss by air infiltration are: (1) the crack method and (2) the air-change method.

The Crack Method. The crack method is the most accurate means of calcu lating heat loss by infiltration because it is based on actual air leakage through cracks around windows and doors and takes into consideration the expected wind velocities in the area in which the structure is located.③ The air-change method(see below)does not consider wind velocities, which makes it a less accurate means of calculation.

Calculating heat loss by air infiltration with the crack method involves the following basic steps:

1. Determine the type of window or door.
2. Determine the wind velocity and find the air leakage.
3. Calculate the lineal feet of crack.④
4. Determine the design temperature difference.

The data obtained in these four steps are used in the following formula:

$$H = 0.018 \times Q(t_i - t_0) \times L$$

where H=heat loss, or heat required to raise the temperature of air leaking into the structure to the level of the indoor temperature (t_i) expressed in Btu per hour.

Q = volume of air entering the structure expressed in cubic feet per hour (Step 2 above).

t_i=indoor temperature

t_0=outdoor temperature

0.018=specific heat of air (0.240) times density of outdoor
air (approximately 0.075)

L=lineal feet of crack

Determine the infiltration heat loss per hour through the crack of a 3 ft. × 5 ft. average double-hung, non-weather-stripped, wood window based on a wind velocity of 20 mph. The indoor temperature is 70℉, and the outdoor temperature 20℉.

The air leakage for a window of this type at a wind velocity of 20 mph is 59 cu. ft. per foot of crack per hour. This will be the value of Q in the air infiltration formula.

Air-Change Method. In the air-change method, the amount of air leakage (i.e., infiltration) is calculated on the basis of an assumed number of air changes per hour per room. The number of air changes will depend upon the type of room and the number of walls exposed to the outdoors.

Notes

①在供热季节，部分热损失是由于外部较冷空气通过门窗缝隙以及其他不是通风系统组成部分的孔洞渗入建筑物内部而引起的。

②空气是由干燥空气和潮湿粒子构成,两者是结合(不是混合),这样各自保留自己的特征。
③缝隙法是通过渗透计算热损失的最精确的手段,因为它是以透过门窗周围缝隙的实际空气渗漏为基础的并考虑了建筑物所在区域的预期风速而求解的。
④lineal feet of crack:缝隙的线英尺。

Reading Material B

Cast-iron Radiators

A cast-iron radiator is a heat-emitting unit that transmits a portion of its heat by radiation and the remainder by convection. An exposed radiator(or freestanding radiator)transmits approximately half of its heat by radiation, the exact amount depending on the size and number of the sections. The balance of the emission is by conduction to the air in contact with the heating surface, and the resulting circulation of the air warms by convection.①

Cast-iron radiators have been manufactured in column and tubular types, Column and large-tube radiators (with 2.5-in. spacing per section) have been discontinued. The small-tube radiator with spacings of 7/4-in. per section is now the prevailing type.② Ratings for various cast-iron radiators are given in handbook of the American Society of Heating, Refrigerating and Air-Conditioning Engineers.

Wall and window radiators are cast-iron units designed for specific applications. Wall radiators are hung on the wall and are especially useful in installations where the floor must remain clear for cleaning or other purposes. Window radiators are located beneath a window on an exterior wall. The heat waves radiating from the surface of the unit provide a very effective barrier against drafts.③

Attempts to improve the appearances of cast-iron radiators by painting them, covering them, or recessing them in walls also succeed in reducing their heating efficiency.④ An unpainted, uncovered, freestanding radiator is always more efficient.

Radiator Piping Connections

The important thing to remember when connecting a radiator is to allow for movement of the risers and runouts. This movement is caused by the expansion and contraction resulting from temperature changes in the piping.

Radiator Efficiency

Radiator efficiency is important to the operating characteristics of the heating system. The following recommendations are offered as a guide for obtaining higher radiator operating efficiency:

1. A radiator must be level for efficient operation. Check it with a carpenter's level. Use wedges or shims to restore it to a level position.

2. Make sure the radiators have adequate air openings in the enclosure or cover. The openings must cover at least 40 percent of the total surface of the unit.

3. Unpainted radiators give off more heat than painted ones. If the radiator is painted, strip the paint from the front, top, and sides. The radiator will produce 10 to 15 percent more heat at a lower cost.

4. Check the radiator air valve, If it is clogged, the amount of heat given off by the radiator will be reduced. Instructions for cleaning air valves are given in "Troubleshooting Radiators".

5. Radiators must be properly vented, This is particularly true of radiators located at the end of long supply mains. Instructions for venting radiators are given in "Vents and Venting".

6. Never block a radiator with furniture or drapes. Nothing should block or impede the flow of heat from the radiator.

7. Placing sheet metal or aluminum foil against the wall behind the radiator will reflect heat into the room.

Notes

① 热量散发是通过向与散热表面接触的空气传热以及由此而引起的空气循环而达到的。
② 每节有 7/4 英寸间隙的小管散热器是现在盛行的样式。
③ 来自该装置表面的热波辐射提供了对气流非常有效的障碍。
④ 试图通过给它们上油漆、加罩来改善铸铁散热器的外观或者把它们放置于墙上凹处确实减少了它们的供热效率。

UNIT TWO

Text Exhaust Hoods

[1]   Exhaust hoods are collectors in local extraction systems, usually of pyramidal or conical shape, mounted above or at the side of the source of impurity.① They are very widely used, much more than they deserve, for it is exceptional to find one that is fully effective in operation.

[2]   With an extract hood there is always an unbounded space between the source of the impurity and the hood itself.② Hence the surrounding air can flow over the source and in certain conditions deflect the impurity away from the hood. Exhaust hoods therefore have a much greater air consumption than ventilated chambers.

[3]   The various kinds of hood may be classified as simple, active, individual and grouped (glazed frames suspended from the ceiling), Fig. 2-1 shows a simple individual hood (a), a hood above the charging port of a furnace (b), an active hood with slits around its perimeter (c), a hood with a supply of air on both sides of a work table (d), and a multiple hood with its glazed casement (e). Other kinds of hood will be mentioned in connection with local exhaust for dust removal. The system of extraction may be natural or mechanical. In either case the hood is brought as close as possible to the source of impurity. Hoods located above the source are usually placed 1.8 to 2 m from floor-level for clear head-room while being yet close to the breathing zone.③

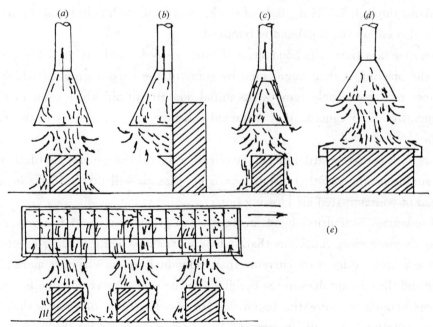

Fig. 2-1

[4]　　When more contaminated air collects under the hood than can be removed by it, the air flows from under the brim and contaminates the work area. ④ In this case it would be much better if there were no hood at all because if the density of the contaminated air were less than that of the surrounding air, it would rise and when eventually it returns to the work area due to circulation, it would then be more diluted and less contaminated than when it left the over-filled hood. ⑤

[5]　　Exhaust hoods are effective when the rates of suction into the space between the source and the canopy are sufficient to trap all the impurity beneath the hood. The suction rate must also overcome the cross-currents of indoor air which could deflect the stream of impurity away from the hood. The suction rate should be quite uniform over the entire plane of the hood inlet. The effectiveness of a hood therefore depends essentially on its shape.

[6]　　In long low hoods it is impossible to achieve uniform suction. It was established in another chapter that for uniformity of suction the angle at the apex of the hood should not exceed 60°.

[7]　　When an ascending current of contaminated air forms above the source of the impurity it entrains with it a large volume of the surrounding air on its way into the canopy. For effective operation the quantity of air withdrawn should not be less than that of the rising stream of air, otherwise contaminated air must overflow from the hood into the building.

[8]　　One can illustrate this by the following example, which also shows the real difference between a hood and a chamber. Fig. 2-2 shows a rectangular chamber with a hood inside; a suction fan is connected to pipe 2, and only as much air enters through the opening 1 as is sucked out through 2. ⑥ If the base of the hood is flush with hole 1, all the air entering through 1 also enters the hood and is removed.

[9]　　Suppose we now move the hood some distance away from the inlet 1. The air entering through the opening is then augmented by some of the surrounding air which it entrains. But since pipe 2 will only remove the initial quantity of air which came in through the inlet, a quantity of air equal to that entrained will flow out of the entry to the hood into the chamber.

[10]　　Hoods with natural ventilation can be effective only if the general ventilation of the building is suitably arranged. Otherwise it is possible that air will flow into the hood from outside instead of contaminated air blowing out.

[11]　　The advantage of multiple hoods in the form of glazed casements hanging from the ceiling is that they are more capacious than individual hoods. Owing to their greater size, they are also less affected by cross-currents than individual hoods. They are more pleasing in appearance and they do not darken the building. At the time of maximum pollution, they are often large enough to store the impurities for short periods of time without overspill. This accumulation is eventually removed by a system designed for the average rate of contamination.

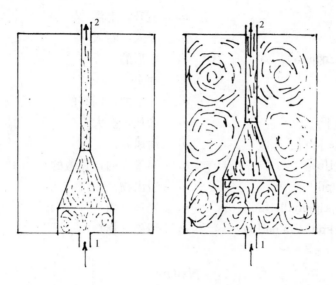

Fig. 2-2

New Words and Expressions

hood *	[hud]	n.	罩，挡风板（罩）
extraction	[iks'trækʃən]	n.	排出，抽出
pyramidal *	[pi'ræmidl]	a.	金字塔形的
conical	['kɔnikəl]	a.	圆锥形的
extract	[iks'trækt]	vt.	排出，抽出
deflect	[di'flekt]	vt.v.	（使）偏转，偏离
unbounded *	[ʌn'baundid]	a.	不受限制的
ventilate	['ventileit]	vt.	使通风，给…装通风设备
glaze *	[gleiz]	v.	装（配）玻璃
perimeter *	[pə'rimitə]	n.	边长，周长
casement *	['keismənt]	n.	窗扉
brim *	[brim]	n.	边缘
contaminate	[kən'tæmineit]	vt.	污染
circulation	[sə:kju'leiʃən]	n.	循环，环流
dilute	[dai'lju:t]	v.	变稀薄
overfilled *	['əuvəfild]	a.	过满的
uniformity	[,ju:ni'fɔ:miti]	n.	均匀
canopy *	['kænəpi]	n.	（排气）罩
cross-current *		n.	逆流
inlet	['inlet]	n.	入口，进口
apex *	['eipeks]	n.	顶（点，尖）

assend *	[əˈsend]	v.	上升，上浮
entrain *	[inˈtrein]	v.	吸入，卷入
rectangular	[rekˈtæŋgjulə]	a.	矩形的
suck out			抽出
flush	[flʌʃ]	a.	齐平的，同高的
augment	[ɔːgˈment]	vt.	增加，扩大
ventilation	[ventiˈleiʃən]	n.	通风
capacious *	[kəˈpeiʃəs]	a.	容量大的，宽敞的
overspill *	[ˈəuvəspil]	n.	溢出物
accumulation *	[əˌkjuːmjuˈleiʃən]	n.	聚集（物）
contamination *	[ˈkənˈtæmˈneiʃən]	n.	污染（物）

Notes

①Exhaust hoods …, usually of …impurity. usually of …介词短语和… mounted above or at … 过去分词短语 … 并列修饰 collectors 作定语。

②with 这里是对…；就…说来。

③Hoods … to the breathing zone. clear 这里词意是无障碍的，空旷的；while being＝while it is。

④When more …than can be removed …than 引出比较状语从句，同时 than 可以说是 can be removed 的主语。

⑤In this case … the over-filled hood. 句中 it would be much better if there were no hood at all 是全句的主句，后面带有 because … the over-filled hood 的从句，所以全句是带有原因状语从句的主从复合句；because 引出的从句中又有 and 引出的两个并列句，也就是 if the density … it would rise 和 when eventually … over-filled hood；这两个并列分句又是各自带有 if 和 when 从句的主从复合句。

⑥… as is sucked out through 2 中的 as 是关系代词，先行词是 air，as 本身还有"像…"的词义。

Exercises

Reading Comprehension

Ⅰ. Say whether the following statements are True (T) or False (F) according to the text, making use of the given paragraph reference number.

1. Exhaust hoods are very widely used, for it is difficult to find one that is more effective in operation than they are. (Para. 1)   ( )

2. If more contaminated air gathers under the hood than can be extracted by it, the air

will move beyond the hood and contaminate the work area. (Para. 4)   ( )

3. The suction rate should be constant over the entire surface of the hood inlet. The effectiveness of a hood therefore depends mainly on its suction rate. (Para. 5)   ( )

4. For effective operation the quantity of air removed should not be less than that of the rising air, otherwise contaminated air will spread from the hood to the building. (Para. 7)   ( )

5. Hoods with natural ventilation should be suitably arranged with the general ventilation of the building, otherwise it is impossible that air will flow into the hood from outside instead of contaminated air blowing out. (Para. 10)   ( )

II. Choose the best answer.

1. Exhaust hoods are collectors in local extraction systems, usually _____, fixed above or at the side of the source of impurity.

    A. of conical or rectangular shape

    B. of circular or conical shape

    C. of conical or pyramidal shape

    D. of pyramidal or rectangular shape

2. While the system of extraction may be natural or mechanical, the hood should be placed _____.

    A. as near as possible to the source of impurity.

    B. as far as possible to the source of impurity.

    C. placed 1.6 to 1.8m from floor-level.

    D. placed 2 to 2.2m from floor-lever.

3. When more contaminated air collects under the hood than can be removed by it, it would be much better if there were no hood because _____.

    A. if the density of the contaminated air were less than that of surrounding air, it would rise

    B. when the contaminated air eventually returns to the work area due to circulation, it would be more diluted and less contaminated than when it left the overfilled hood

    C. both A and B

    D. neither A nor B

4. The rates of suction into the space between the source and the canopy must overcome the cross-currents of indoor air which _____.

    A. could flow over the stream of impurity

    B. could cause the stream of impurity to turn away from the hood

    C. could entrain with them the stream of impurity into the hood

    D. could bring the stream of impurity to flow from under the brim of the hood

5. The advantage of multiple hoods in the form of glazed casements is that _____.

    A. they are more capacious than individual hoods.

B. they are less affected by cross-currents than individual hoods.
  C. they are more pleasing in appearance and they do not darken the building.
  D. all of the above

Ⅲ. Fill in the blanks with the information given in Para. 8 and Para. 9 and Fig. 2-1
  1.
    1) A hood is inside _____ .
    2) A suction fan _____ to pipe 2.
    3) If the base of the hood _____ , the air entering through the opening 1 also enters the hood _____ .
  2.
    1) If the hood _____ away from the inlet 1, the air entering through the opening _____ .
    2) A quantity of air _____ will flow _____ to the hood _____ .

Vocabulary

Ⅰ. Fill in the blanks with the words and expressions given below. Change the forms if necessary.

  | deflect, extraction, inlet, perimeter, dilute, suck out, ascend, entrain |

  1. The circular ceiling diffuser can be used for supply or _____ or a combination of both.
  2. Slot diffusers can be used to provide a continuous strip across a ceiling or on the _____ of a ceiling.
  3. An inert (惰形的) or nonreactive gas easily detected in _____ quantities is uniformly mixed in the atmosphere in the building.
  4. In certain conditions the surrounding air can _____ the stream of impurity away from the hood.
  5. They stood on the mountain and watched the mists _____ from the valley.
  6. The air _____ thought the pipe 2 is as much as that entering though the opening 1.

Ⅱ. Find the words in the text which mean almost the same as the following.
  1. para 2: without limits
  2. para 4: edge of a cup, bowl, glass, etc.
  3. para 7: draw in by suction
  4. papa 8: level with adjoining surface
  5. pare 9: make or become greater; increase
  6. para 11: material, etc. accumulated or collected

Ⅲ. Now use the words you have found to complete the following sentences. Change the form if necessary.
1. We must ensure a rational proportion between _____ and consumption.
2. The door of the old building is _____ with the pavement.
3. Their powers were practically _____.
4. He pulled the _____ of his hat down over his eyes and slept very badly.
5. These windows seem to _____ the dust outside.
6. The air entering the chamber through the inlet _____ by some of the surrounding air which it entrains.

Writing   Selecting the Key Words（2）

Directions: Read the text of Unit Two and find out 3 to 5 key words.

Reading Material A

Ceiling Diffusers

A ceiling is the most convenient surface for diffusing the initial high momentum of an air jet because it is outside the occupied zone of the room. Ceiling diffusers are probably the most common types of ATDs used for air distribution in commercial buildings.[①] There is a wide variety of ceiling diffusers to suit almost every application. Some of the more widely used types are briefly discussed here.

Circular multi-cone diffusers are used in applications requiring compact diffusers, for large volume flow rates. These are usually constructed from steel or aluminum spinnings and their core can be adjusted to produce horizontal (along the ceiling) or vertically downward flow patterns. The diffusers can be supplied with dampers for controlling the flow rate. The flow pattern is usually determined by the magnitude of the angle, ϕ, between the jet outlet and the ceiling. For $\phi < 30°$ a horizontal flow is produced due to the Coanda effect, but greater values of ϕ will produce a downward projection. For $\phi < 30°$, the decay of maximum jet velocity along the ceiling for a single cone diffuser is given by:

$$U_m/U_0 = 2.2 \sqrt{\{r_0 b \cos\phi/[r(r-r_0)]\}}$$

The circular ceiling diffuser can be used for supply or extraction or a combination of both. In the latter case, supply air is discharged through the outer cones and extract air is drawn through the inner cones. However, the extract air flow rate is usually limited to about 80% of the supply air to avoid short-circuiting of supply air to the extract duct.

Circular swirl diffusers with fixed or adjust able vanes are designed to generate radial air jets with a swirling action. The jets of air generated by the vanes merge on discharge and produce a swirling jet of air which attaches to the ceiling due to the Coanda effect. The swirling jet induces large air entrainment causing a rapid diffusion of the jet with room air. This type of ceiling diffuser is suitable for handing large air volumes without the risk of draughts in the occupied zone.

Square and rectangular ceiling diffusers are available in one-, two-, three- and four-way discharge and can be used for supply of extraction.② Diffusers are usually available to set ceiling tiles or panels of various sizes. Most of these devices have adjustable cores to give the system designer flexibility of size selection and flow patterns.

Although linear slot diffusers are usually designed for ceiling installations they can also be used for wall, sill or floor supplies. Ceiling slot diffusers normally have flexible vanes or other control elements for varying the jet direction, but wall, sill and floor diffusers are usually provided with fixed vanes. Slot diffusers are available as single or multiple slot outlets and can be used to provide a continuous strip across a ceiling or on the perimeter of a ceiling.③ They are usually made from extruded aluminum and can be provided with such accessories as plenum boxes, control dampers, flow equalizing grids, blanking-off strips and mitred corners. Slot diffusers are used for air supply and extraction usually without any changes being necessary. The main characteristics of the supply slot diffusers are high air-handling capacity, variable flow pattern capability and good performances at reduced flow rates, which makes them attractive for Variable Air Volume (VAV) systems.④ In integrated ceiling designs troffer diffusers can be incorporated with luminaries, which is particularly attractive for extract air where part of the lighting load is extracted at source before it enters the air-conditioned space.

Notes

①句中 ATDs＝air transport distributions。
②单向、双向、三向和四向排气。
③条缝型散流器有单条缝出口型或多条缝出口型，能连续排成条状横穿顶棚或沿顶棚周边布置。
④送风条缝形散流器的主要特性是具有高的空气输送能力，并在流速减少的情况下有改变流态的能力和良好的工作性能，这就使得这种散流器在变风量系统中有吸引力。

Reading Material B

Infiltration Measurement

Tracer gas measurements are a practical direct measure of infiltration. An inert or nonreactive gas easily detected in dilute quantities is uniformly mixed in the atmosphere in the building. If the tracer does not react and is not absorbed or adsorbed on building materials and furnishings, it tags the air within the building and permits measurements to show the difference between outside air leaking in and inside air currently present[1]. ASTM Standard E741-83 describes a standard tracer dilution method for infiltration measurement.

The tracer gas selected should be nontoxic and nonreactive and should behave like air as it flows through the structure. Gases used include coal gas, carbon dioxide, hydrogen, argon, krypton, nitrous oxide, helium, methane, ethane and sulfur hexafluoride. Ethane has a molecular weight nearly equal to air, while methane is somewhat lighter and diffuses rapidly. They are considered safe when used in concentrations 50 to 100 times less than the lower flammability limit. Sulfur hexafluoride, although much heavier than air, is popular because it can be readily measured in concentrations in the parts per billion range[2]. It does not settle out after it is dispersed in very dilute concentrations. The other gases are usually used in concentrations from 10 to 1000 parts per million.

Tracer gas measurements are based on the continuity equation. The rate of change of the amount of tracer gas in the test space, $V(dc/dt)$, is the difference between the gas injected into the space F, and the tracer gas leaving the space due to exfiltration Qc:

$$V(dc/dt) = F - Qc \qquad (1)$$

where

c = tracer concentration

V = space volume containing tracer gas, m^3

F = tracer injection rate, m^3/h

Q = exfiltration (or infiltration), m^3/h

t = time, h

Equation (1) is based on the assumption that exfiltration is the dominant process that removes the tracer gas from the space. Several procedures can be used to measure infiltration: (1) pulse injection followed by decay, (2) maintaining constant concentration of tracer gas in the space and (3) injection of tracer gas at a constant flow rate.

Tracer Decay Method[3]

The tracer decay method is the most common and requires the simplest apparatus. Tracer gas is initially injected into the test space long enough to give a safe but easily measured concentration. After injection stops, F is zero and the solution of the continuity equation is:

$$c(t) = c_0 e^{-(Q/V)t} \qquad (2)$$

where c_0 is the concentration at $t = 0$.

The ratio of the infiltration Q, to the volume sampled by the tracer gas V, has units of number of volumes/time (i.e., air changes per hour) and is called the air change rate

I. Therefore,

$$c(t) = c_0 e^{-It} \tag{3}$$

A plot of concentration vs. time on a semi-log graph gives a straight line if the concentration of tracer gas is well-mixed throughout the volume and the infiltration is constant. Several periodic injections give a group of straight lines. The slope of each straight section is the air infiltration rate for that time interval.

Constant Concentration Technique

The constant concentration technique is the simplest technique, conceptually. The injection rate of tracer gas is adjusted to keep the concentration within the space constant. When the concentration is constant, the left side of Eq. (1) becomes zero and the infiltration is simply

$$Q = F/c \tag{4}$$

where the terms have been defined in Eq. (1).

This technique has been used successfully by several researchers but requires a sophisticated automatic feedback stem to provide injection rates that maintain constant concentration conditions. This hardware limitation means that it ill likely remain a research tool rather than a technique that in be used widely for infiltration measurements.

Notes

①如果示踪气体不起反应，不被建筑材料和家具吸收或吸附，那么就尾随室内的空气，从而使测量成为可能，显示室外渗入的空气与室内现有空气的差异。
②六氟化硫虽然比空气重得多，却受欢迎，因为其成分浓度在十亿分之几就能容易地测出。
③示踪衰减法。

UNIT THREE

Text   Heat Transmission Through Glazing

[1]   Glass is formed from a molten mixture of 70% silica (SiO_2), 15% soda (Na_2O), 10% lime (CaO), 2.5% magnesia (MgO), 2.5% alumina (Al_2O_3) or other metallic elements to give it particular properties, such as gold(Au)and selenium(Se)to make it photosensitive. An oil-fired furnace liquefies the components at up to 1590℃ which are then floated on to a bath of molten tin and progressively cooled. This is the float-glass method in current use. ① Glass fibre and glass wool are made by passing the hot liquid through fine orifices (Encyclopaedia Britannica. 1980). Glass is manufactured in 4, 6, 10 and 12 mm thicknesses as clear float, modified float, toughened and laminated depending upon type, safety requirements and wind loading. ② Clear float glass is the most common but body-tinted grey, bronze, blue or green can be chosen for aesthetic, daylighting or thermal reasons. ③ Colour pigments are added during the molten stage and the full thickness of the glass is coloured. Metallic particles added to the surface during the fluid stage of production form a reflective surface on one side of the glass. The reflected light may give a silver colour rendering but transmitted light may appear as bronze. The low-emissivity surface improves the thermal insulation properties of the glass.

[2]   Glass is transparent to high-temperature, high-frequency solar irradiance but is poor at passing long-wave radiation from low-temperature surfaces within the building, thus creating the greenhouse effect. The glass surface that has the reflective coating is often located on the inner face of double-glazed units for protection. Body-tinted glass is good at absorbing solar irradiance and reducing heat flow into the building; however, increased glass temperature and thermal expansion are caused. Freon gas can be used to fill the space within sealed doubleglazing units as its reduced convection heat-transfer ability lowers the U value.

[3]   The area of glazing used may be limited by statutory regulations for energy-conservation reasons. Whether large or small areas are advantageous depends upon the annual balance between the adventitious solar heat gains, the internal heat generation from people, lights and equipment and the heat losses. ④ The availability of natural internal illumination through the glazing is an important part of the energy balance, with reductions in the electrical energy used for artificial lighting. Whether large glass areas are advantageous or not can be analysed from the net energy consumption of the whole building on a monthly and annual basis.

[4]   Fig. 3-1 shows the proportions of the solar energy flows through glass due to its three properties of transmissivity T, absorptivity A and reflectivity R. Glasses have different transmittances for direct and diffuse irradiance. Some irradiance that is absorbed by the

glass is radiated into the room and a total transmittance figure is given. These properties remain constant until the solar incidence angle exceeds about 45° when they rapidly diminish to zero at 90° incidence. Double glazing may consist of tinted or reflective glass in the exterior layer and a clear float inner pane. The outer glass is raised to a higher temperature by being insulated from the cooler interior of the building and sustains greater thermal expansion. The overall direct solar transmittance will be the multiplication of the two glass types such as 0.86 for the clear and 0.23 for the reflective, equalling 0.2. The outward view through tinted glass is not seriously affected and the effect may be hardly noticeable. Reflective glass provides a high degree of internal privacy for the occupants of the building.

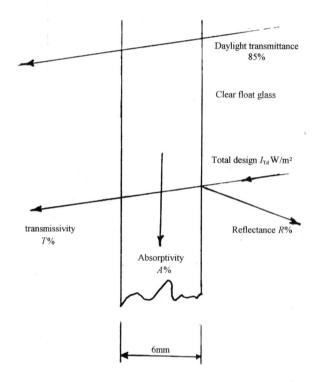

Fig. 3-1 Properties of glass

Table 3-1. Performance data for glass

Glass type	Light T	Direct solar irradiance			Total T
		T	A	R	
4mm clear	0.89	0.82	0.11	0.07	0.86
6mm tinted	0.5	0.46	0.49	0.05	0.62
6mm reflective	0.1	0.08	0.6	0.32	0.23

The exception is at night when interior lighting and external darkness cause the viewing direction to be reversed. The interior is then clearly visible from the street. Typical values are given in Table 3-1.

> EXAMPLE 3-1.
> A window facing southwest is 3 m long and 2.75 m high and has a shaded area of $0.2 m^2$. Solar altitude is $43.5°$, solar azimuth is $66°$ W of S. direct solar irradiance normal to the sun is $832 W/m^2$ and diffuse irradiance is $43 W/m^2$. The transmissibilities of direct and diffuse irradiances are 0.85 and 0.8. Calculate the solar heat gain transmitted through the glass.

Glass azimuth is $45°$ W of S, so

$\quad$ glass-solar azimuth $= 66° - 45° = 21°$

$\quad I_{DVd} = I_D \cos A \cos D = 832 W/m^2 \times \cos 43.5 \times \cos 21 = 563.4 W/m^2$

$\quad$ direct transmitted irradiance $Q_D = 0.85 I_{DVd} \times$ sunlit area W

$\quad$ diffuse transmitted irradiance $Q_d = 0.8 \times 43 \times$ glass area W

$\quad Q_D = 0.85 \times 563.4 \times [(3 \times 2.75) - 0.2] W = 3855.1 W$

$\quad Q_d = 0.8 \times 43 \times 3 \times 2.75 W = 283.8 W$

$\quad$ total transmitted heat gain $= Q_D + Q_d = 3855.1 + 283.8 W = 4138.9 W$

New Words and Expressions

silica * ['silikə]	n.	氧化硅
soda * ['səudə]	n.	苏打，碳酸钠
lime *	n.	氧化钙，石灰
magnesia * [mæg'ni:ʃə]	n.	氧化镁
alumina * [ə'lju:minə]	n.	氧化铝，矾土
selenium * [si'liniəm]	n.	硒
photosensitive *	a.	光敏的，(能)感光的
float-glass		浮法玻璃
liquefy * ['likwifai]	v.	液化，熔解
tin *	n.	锡
progressively * [prə'gresivli]	ad.	逐渐地
orifice ['ɔrifis]	n.	(管子等的)口，孔
toughened ['tʌfənd]	a.	坚韧的，有硬度的
laminated ['læmineitid]	a.	分层的，叠层的
tint	v.	给…(染)色
bronze ['brɔnz]	n.	青铜色，青铜
aesthetic * [i:s'θetik]	a.	审美的，美学的
pigment *	n.	颜料
metallic	a.	金属(性)的
render * ['rendə]	v.	打底，初涂

emissivity *		n.	辐射率，辐射能力
greenhouse effect			温室效应
irradiance	[i'reidiəns]	n.	辐射（度），辐照（度）
transparent	[træns'pɛərənt]	a.	透明的
freon *	['frion]	n.	氟利昂
statutory	['stætjutəri]	a.	法定的，法规的
adventitious	[ˌædven'tiʃəs]	a.	外来的
illumination	[iluːmi'neiʃən]	n.	照明，照明度
transmissivity *	[trænzmi'siviti]	n.	透射率
absorptivity *	[əbsɔːp'tiviti]	n.	吸收率
reflectivity *	[riflek‚tiviti]	n.	反射率
transmittance *	=transmissivity		
incidence	['insidens]	n.	发生（率），入射（角）
pane *		n.	窗格玻璃
multiplication		n.	乘，乘法，倍增
azimuth *	['æziməθ]	n.	方位角
occupant *	['ɔkjuːpənt]	n.	居住者

Notes

①float-glass 浮法玻璃。

②Glass is …loading. 句中 in 是按、以；type, safe requirements 和 wind loading 三者并列作 depending upon 的宾语。

③… but … 句中 but 并列连词连结两句分句，body-tinted grey, bronze, blue or green 是第二个分句的主语。

④whether … the heat losses. 句中 whether large or small areas are advantageous 是主语从句。

Exercises

Reading Comprehension

Ⅰ. Say whether the following statements are Ture (T) or False (F) according to the text, making use of the given paragraph reference number.

1. Clear float glass is the most common but body-tinted grey, bronze, blue or green can be chosen for type, safety requirements and wind loading. (Para. 1)　　　　（　）

2. Glass can transmit high-temperature, high-frequency solar irradiance but is poor at passing long-wave radiation from low-temperature surfaces within the building, and

so produces the greenhouse effect. (Para. 2)　　　　　　　　　　　　( )
3. Whether large or small areas have an advantage depends upon the annual balance between the heat gains from the sun, the heat generation from people, lights and equipment and the heat losses. (Para. 3)　　　　　　　　　　　　　　　　　　( )
4. Reflective glass provides a high degree of internal privacy for the occupants of the building but at night interior lighting and external darkness can make the viewing direction be reversed. (Para. 4)　　　　　　　　　　　　　　　　　　　　　( )
5. The properties of glass remain constant until the solar incidence angle is beyond about 90° when they rapidly lower to zero at 45° incidence. (Para. 4)　　　　　( )

II. Complete the following illustration, referring to Table 3-1 Performance data for glass.

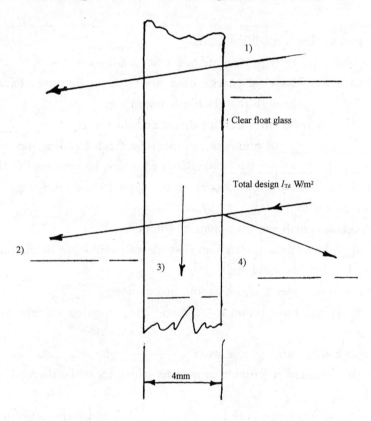

Fig. 3-2

III. Fill in the blanks with the information given in the text.
  1. During the fluid stage of glass production _____ added to the surface form a reflective surface one side of the glass.
  2. Body-tinted glass can absorb solar irradiance effectively and reduce heat flow into the building with the result of _____.
  3. The space within sealed double-glazing units can be filled with _____ as its reduced convection heat-transfer ability lowers the U value.

4. Whether large glass areas are advantageous or not can be analysed on a monthly and annual basis from _____ .

5. The outward view through tinted glass is not seriously affected and the effect may be _____ .

Vocabulary

I. Fill in the blanks with the words and expressions given below. Change the forms if necessary.

tinted, toughened, aesthetic, illumination, transmissivity, multiplication, irradiance, occupant

1. Manufacturing clear float, modified float, _____ and laminated glass depends upon type, safety requirements and wind loading.
2. With reductions in the electrical energy used for artificial lighting, natural internal _____ through the glazing is important.
3. Glasses have different transmittances for direct and diffuse solar _____ .
4. The _____ of numbers has made our club building too small.
5. These are the _____ standards to which he remained faithful.

II. Find the words in the text which almost mean the same as the following.
1. para 1: colour; give colour to
2. para 1: cover (glass) with the first layer of colour
3. para 2: allowing light to pass through so that object behind can be distinctly seen
4. para 3: coming by chance; accidental
5. para 4: person who occupies a house, room or position

III. Now use the words you have found to complete the following sentences. Change the form if necessary.
1. When the sun is bright some people wear _____ glasses.
2. Many systems are required to provide conditions which meet the thermal comfort conditions for the _____ .
3. The explorers to the Antarctic Pole got _____ aid and were out of danger.
4. The reflected light may give a silver colour _____ but transmitted light may appear as bronze.
5. It is marvellous that those _____ curtains will never keep the light out.

Writing   Outline Writing (1)

To write an outline of an article. You must first of all identify the main ideas in the paragraphs and then express them by using noun phrases (topic outline) or simplesentences (sentence outline).

Topic outline is one that uses incomplete sentences, e.g. nouns, noun phrases, etc. while sentence outline uses complete sentences.

For example

The Topic Outline:

a) Three Main Groups of Oil

b) Uses and Importance of Mineral Oil

c) History and Origin of Mineral Oil

The Sentence Outline:

a) Oil falls into three categories: animal, vegetable & mineral.

b) Of them mineral oil is the most useful and has changed our life.

c) The oil originated in the distant past and has formed from living things in the sea.

Directions: Now read the text of Unit Three again and then complete the outline by matching the paragraph numbers in Column A with their proper topic outline in Column B:

Column A (para. numbers)	Column B (main ideas)
1.	A. Properties of glass
2.	B. Factors determining the are of glazing used
3.	C. Making and tinting of glass
4.	D. The proportions of the solar energy through glassand the performance data for glass

Reading Material A

The Factors Affecting Thermal Comfort

When a building is to be air conditioned it will be necessary for the designer to decide the internal space conditions that should be maintained throughout the year when the building is occupied. Many systems are required to provide conditions which meet the thermal comfort conditions for the occupants; other systems provide conditions suitable for the efficient operation of machines and processes, the storage of food and artifacts. However, it will rarely be the case that air conditions have to be maintained at a constant levelvariations are usually permitted about an optimum level.① In this text, various aspects of these topics are examined, leading to a choice of appropriate indoor design conditions.

In normal health a man or a woman has an internal body temperature of about 37℃ and this temperature has to be supported for healthy living. Departures of a few degrees from normal body temperature are usually a sign of ill health, and even a danger to life itself; heat stroke and hypothermia are well known, if relatively rare, examples of high and low body temperatures.② When these conditions occur, precautions must be taken against a further deterioration in that temperature.

The body generates a certain amount of heat due to the oxidation of food and this has to be dissipated if the body temperature is not to rise. Conversely, if too much heat is lost to the surroundings the body temperature will fall. The amount of heat produced will depend on the amount of physical activity being undertaken, or rate of work. At rest the body produces about 100 watts of heat and during hard work about 500 watts. It is the body's physiological mechanisms which regulate the rate of heat production together with the rate of heat loss, arranging the balance which maintains constant body temperature.③ When the body temperature falls, more heat is generated by imperceptible tensing of the muscles, a further fall by the onset of shivering. A rise in body temperature is countered by increased perspiration.

The nude body can only cope with a small range of external conditions in maintaining its body temperature and clothing is therefore used as insulation. The amount of clothing will affect the rate of heat loss and this in turn will affect the feeling of warmth.

The feeling of warmth depends on a balance between the rate of heat production and the rate of heat loss, which in turn depends on the environmental conditions. Generally the body loses heat through convection, radiation and evaporation but it may also gain heat by convection and radiation when the surrounding air and surface temperatures are higher than the body's surface temperature. Evaporation heat loss consists of insensible perspiration from the skin together with the water vapour expired from the lungs. When rates of physical activity are low in a normal indoor environment, the proportion of heat loss through these modes of heat transfer are of the order of 45%, 30% and 25% respectively.④ Relative to the surface conditions of the body:

-convection heat loss (or gain) depends on air dry-bulb temperature and air velocity;
-radiation heat loss/gain depends on the temperatures of the surrounding room surfaces, including the surfaces of heat-producing equipment within the room. The average temperature of all these surfaces is usually expressed as the mean radiant temperature;
-evaporation heat loss through insensible perspiration depends on the air vapour pressure and the air velocity.

The four variables of the physical environment that affect the heat loss from the body are therefore:

-air dry-bulb temperature;
-air vapour pressure (or relatively humidity);
-air velocity;
-mean radiant temperature.

For any individual, the sensation of thermal comfort is a complex subjective reaction to an environment, depending on a number of personal factors, such as age, sex and state of health. However, for a group of people there are only two personal factors which have a

significant correlation with comfort, these being:
   -amount of physical activity (rate of work);
   -amount of clothing.

Notes

①但是，空气条件保持不变的情况是很少的，一般常常允许在最佳条件上下变动。
②偏离正常体温几度一般是病态和甚至于生命危险的症状；中暑和体温过低是体温高和低的例子，即使这些情况相对来说少见。
③正是人体的生理机能起着调节产热量和耗热量的作用从而达到使体温不变的平衡。
④be of the order of… 大约是…

Reading material B

Effect of Shifting Sun Load on Different Zones of Building

As the sun swings around from east to west during the day, this shifting sun load has a dramatic effect on the exterior area cooling required.①

The east, south and west perimeter exposures of the building, the different zones are most greatly effected. The maximum loads can be double or triple the minimum loads.

The interior and north perimeter zones directly under roofs are effected to some degree also by the shifting sun. The interior and north perimeter zones of in between floors in multi-story buildings are not effected by the sun's radiation.

The VAV system varies its air volume to these areas from minimum to maximum settings proportional to the loads.②

1. The sun load and the outside air ventilation load with its rising temperature and humidity during the day are the most volatile cooling load factors.
2. The wall, window and roof conduction loads are second in intensity of variation.
3. Lighting, people and internal equipment loads reach a peak at the start of the occupied day and remain rather constant during the day, then drop off sharply at the day's end.
4. Cafeteria, kitchen, laboratory exhaust loads have their own peak times.

Also since the cooling loads from various load factors vary during the day, and since occupant conditions vary also, there are a number of different cooling load profiles as follows:

1. Actual occupied maximum simultaneous load, 220 tons, 88,000 cfm.
2. The actual average occupied load, 130 tons, 53,000 cfm.

3. The actual minimum occupied load, 78 tons, 31,000 cfm.
4. The night time unoccupied load, 20 tons, 4000 cfm.
5. The weekend daytime unoccupied load.

If the size of the cooling, heating and air distribution equipment is selected based on a lower actual maximum occupied simultaneous load, rather than on a higher design, there is a diversity factor.

This diversity factor can be 20 or 30% in many cases. This means that since all the areas will never peak at the same time, this sum of all the peaks will really never be needed and hence the equipment need not be sized that large.[3]

ZONE LOADS FOR DIFFERENT TIMES OF DAY

	Zone	Peaks			
	9AM	Noon	3PM	6PM	Total Loads
Z1 North	4	8	10Max	8	10
Z2 East	14Max	10	7	4	14
Z3 South	7	22Max	20	10	22
Z4 West	4	6	14Max	11	14
Z5 Interior	3	6	8Max	6	8
Total Load	32Min	52	59Max	39	68

The above loads were calculated for four different times of the day and then summarized to determine:

1. When the maximum and minimum simultaneous occupied loads occur for all the areas as a lump as well as for each area individually.
2. What the total zone peak loads are.

Notes

①shifting sun load 变换的日照负荷，shifting 变换，改变。
②VAV system 变风量系统，VAV：Variable Air Volume。
③这就是说，因为各区域不会在同时达到峰值，所以实际上就不会需要各峰值之和的负荷，这样设备就没有必要设计到那么大的规格。

UNIT FOUR

Text   Fluid Bed Technology is in Transition

[1]   Fluidized bed technology is currently in a commercial transition period, says EPRI's Kurt Yeager, and he calls that "a dangerous stage for a new technology.[①]"
      Calling on developers and users not to be "mesmerized" by the commercial success of fluidized bed combustion, Yeager said that much technical development is still required. He mentions issues such as operability, maintenance procedures, erosion, and detrition. Operating problems have already cropped up at many new units. While most supplies and owners appear to be confident that debugging will succeed, these problems have been serious in some cases.

[2]   One supplier representative says there is as much heartache with fluidized bed combustion right now as there was with boilers burning western coal in the early '70s.[②] He recalls that it took several years to solve those operational problems, and he predicts that fluidized bed combustion will have the same kind of experience.

[3]   There are still fundamental open questions about fluid bed boiler design. While the circulating bed technology appears to be dominating, there are still advocates of the bubbling bed design. The conventional wisdom seems to be that the bubbling bed is suitable for small new units or boiler retrofits while the circulating bed is best for most new units.

[4]   Gilbert/Commonwealth's Nick Gaglia provided an interesting overview of the circulating vs bubbling bed controversy. The bubbling bed has heat transfer tubes in the bed of limestone and fuel. The velocity of fluidizing air is in the range of 4 to 12 ft/sec. Very little material leaves the bubbling bed—about 2 to 4 pounds of solids are recycled per pound of fuel burned.

[5]   The circulating bed is designed to move a lot more solids out of the furnace area and to achieve most of the heat transfer outside of the combustion zone. Some circulating bed units even have external heat exchangers. The fluidizing velocity in circulating beds ranges from 12 to 30 ft/sec and solids recycle is 50 to 100 pounds per pound of fuel burned.

[6]   Furnace temperature is roughly the same in both types, but the circulating bed is said to achieve better calcium-to-sulfur utilization—1.5 to 1 vs 3.2 to 1 for the bubbling bed.

[7]   The catch in the circulating bed design is the requirement for huge mechanical cyclones to capture and recycle the large amounts of bed material and the requirement for a tall boiler.[③] At a fluidizing velocity of 20 ft/sec and fuel residence requirement of three to five seconds, the combustor must be approximately 100 ft high regardless of unit capacity. The circulating bed design lends itself to larger unit sizes. Gaglia puts the break point at 50,000 lb/hr to 100,000 lb/hr of steam.

[8]　　The next step in FBC design may be a hybrid CFB/BFB. B&W's Bob Johns says he expects that Babcock & Wilcox will be offering a hybrid design in the future. What's needed, he said, is a concession: a lower recycle rate than CFBs now have, but elimination of the in-bed tubes required for BFB.

[9]　　Foster-Wheeler described a combined BFB/CFB design under development at the ASME conference. The design features two cells that are straight bubbling bed design and a third recycle cell that brings some of the advantages of circulating bed design to the plant. At present NSP has not committed to build such a unit. There is no site, no permits, and no design fuel, NSP's Jensen says. ④However, if load growth justifies it, the utility will be ready to go out for bids at the end of 1987 and the plant could be on line in four and a half years, he added. The executive said that the governors of the two states in which NSP operates have said they would smooth the way—a far different reception from that given the last nuclear plant the utility planned to build. ⑤

[10]　　One of those demos is currently starting up at Colorado Ute's Nuclear station. In that project, a new circulating-bed, non-reheat AFBC boiler supplied by Pyropower and a new 75-MW steam turbine were installed at an existing power plant site. Three existing 12-MW steam turbines will be driven by extraction steam from the new turbine. The total capacity is 110MW. The boiler is designed to produce 925,000 lb/hr of steam at 1005 F and 1510 psig. It will burn local bituminous coal with a sulfur content of 0.7%, 26% ash, and a heating value of 9700 But/lb.

Now Words and Expressions

transition [træn'siʒən]	n.	过渡，转变
mesmerize ['mezməraiz]	vt.	催眠，使入迷
fluidize * ['fluːidaiz]	vt.	使流化
operability * [ˌɔpərə'biliti]	n.	操作
erosion [i'rəuʒən]	n.	侵蚀
crop up	vt.	暴露
detrition * [di'triʃən]	n.	耗损
debug * [diː'bʌg]	vt.	排除
heartache ['hɑːteik]	n.	痛心，伤心
advocate * ['ædvəkeit]	vt.	提倡
dominate ['dɔmineit]	vt.	支配
controversy ['kɔntrəvəːsi]	n.	争论
limestone ['laim'stəun]	n.	石灰石
catch	n.	难题
cyclone * ['saikləun]	n.	旋风分离器
combustor [kəm'bʌstə]	n.	燃烧室（器）

hybrid ['haibrid]		n.	混合物
		a.	混合式的
concession * [kən'seʃən]		n.	让步，妥协
reheat ['ri:'hi:t]		vt.	再（加）热
executive * [ig'zekjutiv]		n.	主管企业的人
demo * =demonstration		n.	示范
pyropower * ['paiərəu'pauə]			火（热）力
psig=pounds per square inch gauge			表压（磅/英寸^2）
bituminous * [bi'tju:minəs]		a.	沥青的

Notes

①句中 EPRI＝Electric Power Research Institute。
②One supplier representative …early，70s. 句中 as…as 是比较结构，as there was with boilers …比较状语从句中省略主语 heartache。
③The catch in the circulating bed design …循环流化床设计中的难题…
④NSP＝Northern State Power。
⑤The executive said … to build. 句中 that … to build 是 said 的宾语从句；in which …引出定语从句，which 的先行词是 the two states；a far diffifferent reception from that …中，that 代替 reception；given …to build 过去分词短语作定语修饰 that；the utility planned to build 定语从句修饰 the last nuclear plant。

Exercises

Reading Comprehension

Ⅰ. Say whether the following statements are true (T) or false (F) according to the text.
1. Generally speaking users and developers feel satisfied with the fluidized bed combustion. ( )
2. Operating problems have already been solved at many new units. ( )
3. Conventionally it seems that the bubbling bed is suitable for small new units while the circulating bed is best for most new units. ( )
4. The furnace temperature is completely different in both types. ( )
5. The requirement for huge mechanical cyclones to capture and recycle the large amounts of bed materials is easy to meet. ( )

Ⅱ. Fill in the chart with the information you have got from the text.

Items	Bubbling bed	Circulating bed
velocity of the fluidizing air	1) _____ ft/sec	2) _____ ft/sec
weight of solids recycled per pound of fuel burned	3) _____ pounds	4) _____ pounds
proportion of calcium to sulfur use	5) _____	6) _____

III. Fill in the chart with the information you have got from para. 10.

capacity	1) _____ lb/hr of 2) _____	at 3) _____ °F and 1510 psig
coal burned with	4) _____ % sulfur and 5) _____ % ash	and having a heating value of 6) _____ % Btu/lb

IV. Fill in the blanks with the information given in the text.

There are some developments of the fluidized technology that need to be improved, such as   1) , maintenance procedures,   2)   and   3) . There are two kinds of design of fluid bed boiler: One is the   4)   bed which is suitable for   5)   new units. The other is the   6)   bed which is best for new units. The circulating bed technology appears to be   7) , but the next step in FBC design may be a   8)   CFB/BFB. What's needed is a concession, a lower   9)   rate than CFBs have, but   10)   of the in-bed tubes required for BFB. The design features two   11)   that are straight   12)   bed design and a third cell that brings some of the advantages of   13)   bed design to the plant.

Vocabulary

I. Fill in the blanks with the words given below. Change the form if necessary.

| fluidize, operability, detrition, advocate, cyclone, concession, pyropower, executive |

1. Nowadays people use the gas which is _____ to cook in the kitchens.
2. Do you _____ keeping all children at school till the age of 16?
3. The _____ is so strong that sailing is forbidden at sea.
4. As a _____ to the public outcry, the Government reduced the tax on petrol.
5. Whether an enterprise is successful or not usually deponds on the _____ authorities.

II. Find words in the text which mean almost the same as the following.
1. para. 1: a change or passage from one place, action to another.
2. para. 3: control, exert authority over
3. para. 4: prolonged argument over sth.
4. para. 7: the combustion chamber and its ancillary equipment.
5. para. 10: an off spring resulting from crossbreeding; a word composed of elements

from two or more languages.

Ⅲ. Now use the words you have found to complete the following sentences. Change the form if necessary.

1. The frequent _____ from cold to warm weather this spring has caused much illness.
2. A great man can _____ over others by force of character.
3. Students of group 1 held a _____ against students of Group 2 on some moral views last week.
4. The _____ of the boiler is 150 ft high and can holds 500 Kg coal burning in it.
5. 'Cablegram' is a _____ word; half the word is Latin and half is Greek.

Writing   Outline Writing (2)

Directions: Read the text of Unit Four again and write a topic outline of the text.

Reading Material A

Draft of Boiler

The principle of draft and air regulation is explained by reference to the handfired boiler, using a natural draft. The stack produces a draft of 1.0 in of water, which is regulated by the stack damper to give the required furnace draft. As the rating increases, more air is required to burn the additional fuel, and the stack damper must be opened to compensate for the draft loss caused by the increased flow of gases. Draft loss occurs across the fuel bed, the boiler, the damper, and the breeching (flue). Finally, at 152 percent of rating, the stack damper is wide open and no more air can be supplied, thus limiting the ability of the furnace to burn additional coal efficiently.

The type of fuel determines the amount of draft differential required to produce a given airflow through the fuel bed. ①This is one of the reasons that more load can be carried with some fuels than with others.

Early boilers met their total draft requirement with natural draft which was supplied by the height of the stack. ②As units became larger and included additional heat traps, such as superheaters, economizers, and air heaters (and thereby having a higher draft loss), it was not practical to draft the entire unit from the stack. These units required fans in addition to the stack, using a forced-draft (FD) fan alone or in combination with an induced-draft (ID) fan. ③

Most combustion equipment use forceddraft fans for supplying air to the furnace either through the burners or through the grates. The fan supplies the air at a pressure

33

above that of the atmosphere and forces it into the furnace. The forceddraft fan produces a pressure under the stoker and causes the necessary air to flow up through the fuel bed. An increase in rating requires an increase in pressure under the stoker to cause the additional air to flow through the fuel bed. The stack produces the draft necessary to circulate the gases through the boiler and breeching(fuel). By automatic regulation of the stack damper, the furnace draft is maintained constant at 0.05 in of water. Operating a furnace at a constant draft slightly below atmospheric pressure is referred to as balanced draft.④ When the combustion rate increases, more air is added to the furnace and a corresponding increased amount of gases is removed.

This results in a greater flow but maintains a constant pressure in the furnace. Since the total effect of the stack is now available in overcoming the resistance through the boiler, a higher rating can be obtained than with the same unit operating without a forced-draft fan and with hand-fired grates.⑤

The stack provided an adequate means of circulating the air and gases through hand-fired grates or burners and boilers. The application of stokers necessitated the use of forced-draft fans. Induced-draft fans are required when economizers, air heaters, or flue-gas cleaning equipment is applied to balanced-draft boilers.

Notes

① 燃料种类的不同决定了通过燃料床产生一定气流所需送风量的不同。
② Natural draft 自然通风。
③ Forced-draft 机械通风。
④ 在通风量一定的条件下，以略低于大气压的压力使炉膛运行，这种通风方式称为平衡通风。
⑤ 由于已经有了烟囱效应来克服穿过锅炉的阻力，锅炉出力就能比没有机械通风风机而用手工操作炉栅的锅炉高。

Reading Material B

Safety Valves

Boilers are designed for a certain maximum operating pressure. If this pressure is exceeded, there is danger of an explosion unless this pressure is relieved. This danger is so great that it necessitates equipping all boilers with safety valves to maintain the boiler pressure within design limits. Rules governing safety valves, design, and installation are as follows:

Each boiler shall have at least one safety valve, and if it has more than 500 ft^2 of water-heating surface, it shall have two or more safety valves. The safety-valve capacity for each boiler shall be such that the safety valve or valves will discharge all the steam that can be generated by the boiler without allowing the pressure to rise by more than 6 percent above the highest pressure at which any valve is set and in no case by more than 6 percent above the maximum allowable working pressure. ①

One or more safety valves on the boiler proper shall be set at or below the maximum allowable working pressure. If additional valves are used, the highest pressure setting shall not exceed the maximum allowable working pressure by more than 3 percent. The complete range of pressure setting of all the saturated-steam safety valves on a boiler shall not exceed 10 percent of the highest pressure to which any valve is set. The ASME code should be carefully reviewed for the required number and size of valves as well as their proper setting.

When two or more safety valves are used on a boiler, they may be mounted separately or as twin valves made by placing individual valves on Y bases or duplex valves having two valves in the same body casing. ② Twin valves made by placing individual valves on Y bases or duplex valves having two valves in the same body shall be of equal size. When not more than two valves of different sizes are mounted singly, the relieving capacity of the smaller valve shall not be less than 50 percent of that of the larger valve.

The safety valve or valves shall be connected to the boiler independently of any other steam connection and attached as closely as possible to the boiler, without any unnecessary intervening pipe or fitting. Every safety valve shall be connected so that it stands in an upright position. The opening or connection between the boiler and the safety valve shall have at least the area of the valve inlet. The vents from the safety valves must be securely fastened to the building structure and not rigidly connected to the valves, so that the safety valves and piping will not be subjected to mechanical strains resulting from expansion and contraction and the force due to the velocity of the steam.

No valve of any type shall be placed between the required safety valve or valves and the boiler or on the discharge pipe between the safety valve and the atmosphere. When a discharge pipe is used , the cross-sectional area shall not be less than the full area of the valve outlet or the total of the areas of the valve outlets which are being discharged into the pipe. ③ The pipe shall be as short and straight as possible and shall be arranged to avoid undue stresses on the valve or valves.

All safety-valve discharges shall have proper clearances from areas such as platforms. Ample provision for gravity drain shall be made in the discharge pipe at or near each safety valve and at locations where water or condensation may collect. Each valve shall have an open gravity drain through the casing below the level of the valve seat.

Notes

①每台锅炉安全阀的总容量应该是安全阀或阀门组能排出锅炉所产生的全部蒸汽,不允许压力上升超过阀门设定最高压力的6%;在任何情况下,不能超过最大允许工作压力的6%。

②如果锅炉上使用两个或两个以上的安全阀,阀门可以单独安装或者作为孪生阀安装(阀门装在Y型管上)或者作为双联阀安装(两个阀装在同一壳体里)。

③使用排气管时,排气管截面积不得小于阀门出口总面积或向所连排气管排气的阀门出口部分的总面积。

UNIT FIVE

Text   Compressor Failure

[1]   Many compressors fail because of one or more of the following conditions: (1) slugging, (2) liquid flooding, (3) loss of lubricating oil, (4) contamination, (5) bad piping practices, (6) improper thermostatic expansion valve superheat setting, and (7) flooded starts.

[2]   (1) **Slugging.** Slugging usually occurs on compressor startup and lasts for only a short time. However, it can occur while the compressor is running during a rapid change in the system operating conditions. It is associated with a clattering noise much like an automobile engine under a heavy strain. This noise is created by the compressing of the liquid refrigerant and/or oil.① Compressors are designed to compress vapor only and not liquid. When liquid is compressed by the compressor a hydraulic pressure that may exceed 1000 psig (6890 kPa) is created in the cylinder.

[3]   Slugging can result in blown head and/or valve plate gaskets, broken valve reeds, broken pistons, and damaged piston wrist pins. If any of these conditions are found, the conditions that cause slugging should be checked and if found corrected.②

[4]   (2) **Liquid Flooding.** Liquid flooding is the constant flow of liquid refrigerant droplets to the compressor. When liquid refrigerant enters the compressor, it goes into the crankcase, where the oil is diluted. Liquid refrigerant is an excellent cleaning agent and will wash oil from the compressor surfaces. In most cases the oil will foam, reducing its lubricating value and resulting in overheating of the bearing surfaces. This condition is more likely on air-cooled compressors than on refrigerant-cooled compressors.

[5]   In cases of severe liquid floodback, damage to the pistons, valves, and rings is probably due to the lack of lubrication. Also, there may be broken parts which show very little wear. Usually, liquid flooding is indicated by more wear on the parts farthest from the oil pump.③

[6]   (3) **Loss of Lubricating Oil.** The loss of lubricating oil will result in damage to the compressor. The wearing surfaces will be galled, overheated, and as a result, ruined. The compressor motor will be overheated and will possibly burn out. As the quantity of oil drops in the crankcase, the temperature of the remaining oil increases. Compressor oil starts vaporizing at 310 to 320°F (136.66 to 142.22°F), which reduces the amount of lubrication the cylinders receive, resulting in excessive ring and cylinder wear. The oil breaks down completely at 350°F (158.89°F), causing contaminants and a complete loss of lubricating qualities.

[7]   (4) **Contamination.** The contaminants in a system include air, moisture, dirt, and other foreign matter.④ These contaminants cause several system malfunctions, such as

high discharge pressure, poor system performance, moisture freezing in the flow control device, oil contamination, and acid.

[8]　(5) **Bad Piping Practices.** Bad piping practices can also contribute to oil leaving the compressor. When unnecessary traps are allowed to remain in the system, oil will settle in them and cause the compressor to operate short of oil. Sizing of the suction line is extremely important for proper oil return. If an accumulator is used, it must be of the proper size for the system. Accumulators should be capable of holding approximately one-half of the total refrigerant charge on smaller systems. It is generally desirable to check with the accumulator and equipment manufacturers for their recommendations. Also, an accumulator will not protect the compressor from refrigerant floodback during the off cycle.

[9]　(6) **Improper Thermostatic Expansion Valve Superheat Setting.** When checking and adjusting thermostatic expansion valve superheat settings, the procedure should be to start at the evaporator coil. If there is more than one expansion valve, they must all be set to maintain the same superheat setting. If they are set to maintain different superheat settings, oil logging is quite possible, especially on low-temperature applications.

[10]　(7) **Flooded Starts.** A flooded start generally is caused by refrigerant migration to the compressor during the off cycle. The refrigerant moves into the compressor crankcase and mixes with the oil when the compressor is colder than the remainder of the system.⑤ When the compressor starts, the liquid refrigerant quickly boils off, causing the oil to foam.

[11]　The amount of refrigerant absorbed by the oil is determined by the oil temperature and the pressure in the crankcase. The lower the temperature and the higher the pressure, the more refrigerant will be absorbed by the oil.⑥ Under certain conditions the refrigerant-oil mixture will separate and stratify, with the liquid refrigerant settling to the bottom of the crankcase where the oil pump will pick it up first. When the compressor starts, the oil pump forces the liquid refrigerant into the bearings and any oil that is there will be washed away.⑦

New Words and Expressions

slugging ['slʌgiŋ]	n.	缓动
lubricating ['lju:brikeitiŋ]	a.	润滑的
clatter ['klætə]	n.; v.	（机械转动等）（发出）卡搭声
gasket ['gæskit]	n.	衬圈，衬垫
reed [ri:d]	n.	簧片
bearing ['bεəriŋ]	n.	轴承
wrist pin	n.	[活塞，曲柄] 销
droplet ['drɔplit]	n.	微滴
crankcase ['kræŋkeiz]	n.	曲轴箱

foam [fəum]	n.	泡沫
	v.	起泡沫
gall [gɔːl]	v.	咬住，卡死
break down		分解
contaminant [kənˈtæminənt]	n.	污染物
lubrication [lʌbriˈkeiʃən]	n.	润滑
malfunction [mælˈfʌnkʃən]	n.	机能失常，发生故障
accumulator [əˈkjuːmjuleitə]	n.	贮液器；收集器
check with		与……联系，与……接洽
charge [tʃɑːdʒ]	v.	注入，装填
setting [setiŋ]	n.	定位，调整
coverage [ˈkʌvəridʒ]	n.	有效范围
procedure [prəˈsiːdʒə]	n.	程序，工序
coil [kɔil]	n.	蛇［盘，旋，螺］管
logging [lɔgiŋ]	n.	阻塞
migration [maigˈreiʃən]	n.	流动
boil off		汽化，蒸发
stratify [ˈstrætifai]	v.	分层
pick up		吸收

Notes

①… the liquid refrigerant and/or oil 释义是 the liquid refrigerant 或者 oil 或者二者。

②… and if found corrected ＝ …and if the condition that cause slugging are found, they should be corrected.

③Usually … farthest from the oil lamp 句中 farthest from the oil lamp 短语作定语修饰 the part；farthest 是 far 的最高级。

④foreign matter：异物，杂质。

⑤…when the compressor is colder than the remainder of the system… ……当压缩机比系统其余部分温度低时，remainder：其（剩）余部分。

⑥The lower… and the higher …, the more … by the oil 句中是越……就越……句型，the lower … and the higher …表示条件，the more refrigerant …表示结果。

⑦…and any oil that is there will be washed away. 句中 that is there 是定语从句,修饰 any oil。

Exercises

Reading Comprehension

Ⅰ. Say whether the following statements are True (T) or False (F) according to the text.
  1. Only when the compressor is operating smoothly will slugging occur and last for a short time. ( )
  2. Usually, more wear on the parts which are farthest from the oil pump indicates liquid flooding. ( )
  3. As lubricating oil is lost, the wearing surfaces will be put closely together, overheated and as a result, ruined. ( )
  4. Accumulators should have the capacity to contain approximately one and half of the total refrigerant charge on smaller systems. ( )
  5. The higher the oil temperature and the lower the pressure in the crankcase, the more refrigerant will be absorbed by the oil. ( )

Ⅱ. Skim through Conditions (1) — (7) and complete the following table.

Conditions	Causes	Results
slugging	usually on compressor startup or during a rapid change in the system operating conditions	blown head and/or valve plate gaskets, broken valve reeds, broken pistons and damaged piston wrist pins
(1)	the constant flow of liquid refrigerant droplets to the compressor	(2)
loss of lubricating oil	———	(3)
contamination	———	several system malfunctions
bad piping practices	———	(4)
Improper thermostatic expansion valve superheat setting	(5)	(6)
(7)	refrigerant migration to the compressor during the off cycle	(8)

Ⅲ. Fill in the blanks with the information given in the text.
  1. Slugging _____ much like an automobile engine under a heavy strain.
  2. Liquid flooding is _____ than on refrigerant-cooled compressors.
  3. Compressor oil starts vaporizing at 310 to 320 ℉ (136.66 to 142.22 ℃), which _____, resulting in excessive ring and cylinder wear.

4. These contaminants cause several system malfunctions, such as _____, _____ in the flow control device, oil contamination, and acid.
5. It is generally desirable _____ manufacturers for their recommendations.

Vocabulary

I. Fill in the blanks with the words and expressions given below. Change the forms if necessary.

> droplet, break down, malfunction, gall, coverage, check with, pick up, stratify

1. The oil _____ completely at 350°F, causing contaminants and a complete loss of lubricating qualities.
2. When the liquid refrigerant settles to the bottom of the crankcase, the oil pump will _____ it _____ and when the compressor starts, the oil pump will force the liquid refrigerant into the bearings.
3. The translation of the science paper _____ the original, sentence for sentence.
4. Oil contamination can cause system _____ .
5. Liquid flooding is caused by the constant flow of liquid refrigerant _____ to the compressor.

II. Find the words in the text which almost mean the same as the following.
1. para. 2: moving slowly
2. para. 2: make a long, continuous, resounding noise
3. para. 6: put oil or grease into (machine parts) to make (them) work easily
4. para. 10: moving from one place to another
5. para. 11: form into strata

III. Now use the words you have found to complete the following sentences. Change the form if necessary.
1. The foamed oil reduced its _____ value and resulted in overheating of the bearing surfaces.
2. Scientists have studied the _____ of fish from one part of the ocean to another over long distances.
3. The geologists have obtained _____ soil samples from the area.
4. Slugging with a _____ noise can also occur while the compressor is running during a rapid change in the system operating conditions.
5. During a rapid change in the system operating conditions, _____ can occur while the compressor is running.

Writing   Outline Writing (3)

Directions: Read the text of Unit Five and match the paragraph numbers in Column A with proper sentence in Column B to form a sentence outline.

Column A	Column B
1. para. 1	A. Many compressors fail because of one or more of the conditions.
2. para. 2—3	B. The loss of lubricating oil will result in damage to the compressor.
3. para. 4—5	C. Contaminants cause several system malfunctions.
4. para. 6	D. If there is a clattering noise, or blown parts, or broken parts or damaged parts, the conditions that cause slugging should be checked.
5. para. 7	E. When a flooded start occurs, the liquid refrigerant quickly boils off, causing the oil to foam and the oil pump forces the liquid refrigerant into the bearings and any oil that is there will be washed away.
6. para. 8	F. Usually, liquid flood, which is the constant flow of liquid refrigerant droplets to the compressor, is indicated by more wear on the parts farthest from the oil pump and also there may be brother parts or damaged parts.
7. para. 9	G. Bad piping practices can also contribute to oil leaving the compressor.
8. para. 10—11	H. When checking and adjusting there on static expansion valve superheat settings correct procedures should be followed.

Reading Material A

Compressor Overheating Due to Electrical Problems

Overheating in single-phase motors could be the result of problems in the starting circuit. Generally, these problems are due to the use of wrong starting capacitors, wrong run capacitors, and/or a wrong starting relay.

Another cause of motor winding overheating is short cycling. When the compressor is allowed to cycle rapidly on refrigerant controls, temperature controls, and safety devices, the motor windings will become overheated, causing damage to the motor winding insulation and early failure of the motor.①

In operation, every time the motor starts it draws locked rotor (LR) amperage for a brief period of time. Each start of the compressor requires several minutes of normal operating time for the refrigerant and oil to remove the heat generated in the winding by the locked rotor current draw. Therefore, short cycling of the compressor causes the motor to become overheated because all the heat generated during the previous locked rotor condition (startup) was not completely removed.

Three-phase motor overheating can be caused by unbalanced voltage, unbalanced current, and single phasing. Either/or both an unbalanced voltage condition and an unbalanced current condition can go undetected for a long period of time and can cause many problems due to overheating. The maximum amount of current or voltage unbalance from winding to winding is 2%. This is significant because the temperature rise of the winding, in percentage, is equal to an amount double to the square of the voltage unbalance. For example, a 2% voltage unbalance will cause an 8% increase in the temperature of the motor winding; a 3% voltage unbalance will cause an 18% increase in winding temperature; and a 5% increase in voltage unbalance will cause a 50% increase in winding temperature. A motor cannot withstand this kind of temperature for very long before being ruined.

An unbalanced voltage can cause an unbalanced current, but an unbalanced current does not always indicate an unbalanced voltage. For instance, in a threephase system a dirty or pitted starter contact or a loose connection could cause a current unbalance by causing a higher resistance in that one leg. Because electricity follows the path of least resistance, more current will flow down the other two legs. Therefore, the problem is actually in the leg that has the least amount of current flowing through it. The current increase in the other two legs causes more than normal heat to be generated in those two windings. The percent of current unbalance is determined in the same manner as a voltage unbalance.

Single phasing of a three-phase motor occurs when one leg of the three-phase is lost. This will cause a higher-than-normal current draw and overheating in the other two windings. This condition is a more advanced condition of the one described above with the high resistance in one leg. However, the motor will fail more quickly when single phasing exists. The two windings will overheat and burn while the winding on the lost leg will not be affected.

If a motor is running when the single phase occurs, it may continue running. The problem is that the other two legs will try to carry the total load and their current draw will increase to about $1\frac{1}{2}$ times their normal running current.② On the other hand, if the compressor is fully loaded and one phase is lost, the overcurrent draw of the motor will cause the overload protection to trip and stop the motor. Should the motor be operating with a partial load, the current draw may not reach the cutout point of the overload protectors and the motor will continue to run. ③ When this situation occurs, the windings in use will become overheated.

In most cases, if the motor stops when a single-phase condition is present, it cannot restart and will repeatedly trip the overload protectors if they are of the automatic reset type. In this case the motor will usually fail because of the heat generated in trying to start.

Voltage that is either too high or too low will also cause the motor to overheat. For a compressor that is rated for 230V only, the normal operating voltage limits are 10%, or 207V for a minimum and 253V for a maximum. For a compressor rated for 208/230V, the limits are 10% below the 208V and 10% above the 230V, or 187V minimum and 253V maximum.

Notes

①如果允许压缩机在制冷剂控制器、温度控制器和安全装置间迅速循环，那么电机线圈就会过热，从而引起电机线圈的损伤和使电机过早损坏。

②问题是其他两相将设法承受总负荷，其电流负荷将增加到正常运行电流的约3/2倍左右。
leg，（三相系统的）相（位）。

③要是电机部分负荷运行，电流负荷达不到超负荷保护器的断流点，电机就会继续运转。

Reading Material B

District Heating and Cooling Systems

District heating and cooling systems are thermal energy networks that distribute hot water, chilled water, or steam through insulated pipes to serve commercial, residential, institutional, and industrial energy needs for space heating, space cooling, and industrial purposes. District heating and cooling systems permit energy, as distinguished from fuel, to be bought and sold as a commodity.

While district heating has been used for more than a century and is a wellunderstood technology, it remains relatively unknown to the general public. Many people live or work in buildings served by district heating and cooling systems without knowing it. In part, this stems from the variety of names the technology is known by. ①

In the United States, district heating and cooling systems have been known as central plant heating, cooling, and steam; municipal heat, power, and steam; campus or areawide heating; total energy systems; municipal integrated utility systems; integrated central energy systems; and total integrated or community energy systems. In Europe, the terms for such systems generally translate as distance heating or urban heating. In some cases,

European district heating is called block central systems, referring to systems that supply heat to more than one building from a central heating source.

In part, the different U.S. and European terms reflect differing energy needs. For example, district cooling is found mainly in the United States; most European systems supply hot water or steam for heating and domestic hot water only. Most major U.S. cities are located farther south than their European counterparts with district heating, and many high-rise buildings require air conditioning on their southern and western sides most of the year. In addition, Americans have become accustomed to air conditioning.

Further, European district heating systems are defined as only those that sell heat to many different customers. In the Netherlands, systems are further limited to those that use waste heat or municipal solid wastes as a fuel source. For these reasons, many Europeans view district heating's contribution to the U.S. energy supply as minimal (IEA, 1983).

In the United States, however, most district heating and cooling systems now serve high-density unitary developments such as college and university campuses, industrial and commercial complexes, military bases, and similar institutions. These applications are not like European systems in that they do not strictly involve the buying and selling of energy. Nevertheless, they are characterized by the same increased energy efficiency (compared with multiple smaller heating plants) and low-cost energy services achieved by supplying thermal energy from a central source.

This report will not address the issue of buying and selling energy in determining the extent of district heating and cooling in the United States, nor in discussing the technological features, prospects, and impediments of various systems.②

District heating and cooling have had two basic development patterns in the United States. In the first, steam systems were developed to serve a variety of users and types of buildings located in an urban area, typically in the central business district. Such urban systems are typically run by private, for-profit corporations subject to regulation and taxes. Most have been operated by investor-owned electric utilities.③

The second type of system was developed to serve institutional needs. these systems serve a single user, a single or a few related buildings, or a complex of buildings. They are typically found on college and university campuses, military installations, industrial parks, multifamily housing developments, and office, commercial, and medical complexes. These systems are frequently referred to simply as "central heating".

Institutional systems are generally run by nonprofit groups, such as governments, hospitals, and universities, which are generally not regulated or subject to taxes. Nevertheless, there are some institutional systems that are owned by private enterprises to serve their industrial, commercial, or residential uses.

Notes

①部分原因是因为这是由于人们藉以知道这种技术的各种名称而引起的。
②这份报告没有谈到在决定美国区域供暖和制冷程度方面能量的买卖问题，也没有谈到在讨论各种系统的技术特征、前途和障碍方面能量的买卖问题。
③for-profit 利润性的。

UNIT SIX

Text　　　Injection Odorization System Design

[1]　　Over the years, several methods have been developed, and used to place odorant in natural gas. One commonly utilized style of odorization system is the injection style odorizer, which systematically injects small volumes of odorant into the natural gas flow. This type of system has undergone developments which have led to improvements in the injection process.

[2]　　There are basic considerations of system operation, which when included in design, make the system valuable.① These should include:
- Odorant selection.
- Flow proportional operation.
- Flowrate and injection rate capabilities.
- Basic system design.
- Verification of operation.
- System monitoring.
- Determination of malfunction and alarm.
- Fail-safe operation.

[3]　　Matching the odorant recipe to the natural gas in the stream involves knowledge of the chemical composition, the physical layout of the pipeline system, and the desired odorant level.② Consultation with an odorant manufacturer is suggested.

[4]　　Chose a system that will operate in proportion-to-flow.③ All odorant systems should use a ratio relating injection rate to measured flowrate as the principal method of operation. Usually, this ratio is referenced in pounds of injected odorant per million cubic feet of gas measured. The odorizer is not the determining device in evaluating whether the proper amount of smell is in the gas. This is measured using the human nose. Instruments are frequently used which deliver a small amount of gas for the technician to sniff. When the gas is detectable by the technician, the odorant level is identified using the instrument. This device is commonly referred to as an odorometer. The injection system allows a proportional rate of odorant, which achieves a level of smell, is recognizable, and exceeds regulatory requirements, to be injected.④

[5]　　The system must have the ability to perform a prescribed injection rate over a wide range of possible flowrates, usually depending on ambient temperatures, or industrial load. These flowrates may be as low as 100 MCF/day, or as high as 300MMCF/day.⑤ Additionally, the system must be operational over a broad range of injection rates. These injection rates may be as low as 0.3 lbs./MMCF to sometimes as high as 3 to 4 lbs./MMCF, depending on what rate is required to achieve the proper smell throughout the sys-

tem. Insure that the system will operate at a desired injection rate throughout the entire range of anticipated flowrates.

[6] Systems should have a means of injecting a known, variable, and consistent amount of odorant with each injection. This volume should be accounted for, within the system, in order to verify the successful performance of the system.

[7] Because all systems are mechanical and endure wear, a primary concern has to be malfunction. New pump designs have significantly reduced required maintenance. However, no part within a system may be guaranteed for life. Therefore, new designs incorporate important, innovative concepts such as on-board system monitoring, and alarm outputs upon malfunction, as a standard problem alert. These two new capabilities allow reduction in the critical time period between malfunction, notification of company personnel, and repair, and reduce the likelihood for gas with improper levels of odorant.

[8] The components of a typical injection type odorizer are:

- Injection pump.
- Injection rate controller.
- Injection rate verification system.
- Monitoring and alarm system.

[9] The injection pump is one of the most important components and is usually a positive displacement pump. New pump designs take into consideration the compatibility of internal seals and working parts with the chemical characteristics found in odorants, and reflect a segregated design approach. In this approach, the moving parts and critical seals in the pump operate in an environment containing hydraulic fluid. Compression of this fluid allows for displacement of odorant residing in a sealed separate chamber. The pump may be adjusted to displace a variable volume per injection (0.1 to 1.0 cc/injection). Virtually all injection pumps are pneumatically actuated, plunger style. This pneumatic supply is communicated to the pump when it is determined by the system controller that an injection is required.

[10] The injection rate controller receives flowrate information from an electronic measurement device and, using a microprocessor, automatically actuates the pump at a frequency to match a preprogrammed injection rate (lb./MMCF). This ability to track a flowrate, and match an injection frequency with it, is termed proportional-to-flow injection. The controller allows for simple programming of critical information:

1. Injection rate desired (lb./MMCF).
2. Chemical density of the odorant.
3. Pump displacement/stroke desired.
4. Fail-safe injection rate (min./injection).

[11] The verification system meters fluid consumed by the pump. Calculations are performed and displayed on the LCD.[6] Actual pump displacement is not only shown but compensated for to maintain a steady injection rate. Temperature effects upon the odorant den-

sity are also taken into account.

[12] Odorant consumption may be monitored both locally and remotely. Every time 0.01 lbs. are consumed, an internal totalizer is updated as is switch closure. This closure is available for SCADA.⑦ If any part of the system fails, an alarm contact is made.

[13] Downloading provides verification that proper odoration was taking place.

[14] The requirement for a safe, clean, and inexpensive fuel supply has given rise to various techniques of odorizing natural gas. With the developments of new injection systems, the confidence level for the safety of the public using natural gas can be raised. Contributing to that raised confidence level are improvements in odorization technology which allow for 24-hr. verification, monitoring, and alarm capability, while decreasing the response and repair time necessary when maintenance is required.

New Words and Expressions

odorization * [ˌɔdəraizeiʃən]	n.	加臭，加臭剂
odorant * ['əudərənt]	n.	加臭
odorizer * ['ɔdəraizə]	n.	加臭器
verification [verifi'keiʃən]	n.	验证
malfunction [mæl'fʌnkʃən]	n.	发生故障，机能失灵
recipe * ['resipi]	n.	配方
flowrate * ['fləurit]	n.	流量
sniff * [snif]	vi.	以鼻吸气，嗅
odorometer * [ˌəudərə'mi:tə]	n.	臭味计
regulatory ['regiuleitəri]	a.	调节的，调整的
ambient * ['æmbiənt]	a.	周围的
verify * ['verifai]	vt.	证实，检验
incorporate [in'kɔ:pəreit]	v.	合并，纳入
notification * [nəutifi'keiʃən]	n.	通知
innovative ['inəuveitiv]	a.	变改的，革新的
likelihood ['laiklihud]	n.	可能性
displacement [dis'pleismənt]	n.	排水量，移置
positive displacement pump		容积式泵
compatibility [kəm'pætə'biliti]	n.	兼容器
segregate * ['segrigeit]	vt.	使分离，使隔离
pneumatically * [nju:mætikəli]	ad.	靠压缩空气，由空气
actuate	vt.	开动，驱使
plunger * ['plʌndʒə]	n.	活塞
microprocessor *	n.	微处理器
preprogram (me) *	vt.	预先规定，预先安排

compensate ['kɔmpenseit]	vt.	补偿
totalizer * ['təutəlaizə]	n.	累加器

Notes

①There are basic considerations … the system valuable. 句中 which 引出非限制定语从句，which 的先行词是 basic considerations；which 在定语从句中是主语，make 是谓语，中间被 when included in design，分割；when included 是省略句，中间省略了 basic considerations …are。

②Matching … involves …level. 句中 matching … the stream 动名词短语作主语；involves 后面有三个并列的宾语 knowledge of …，the physical layout …，以及 the desired odorant level。

③proportion-to-flow 按比例调节流量。

④The injection system … to be injected. which 引出的定语从句有三个并列的动词：achieves …，is …以及 exceeds…。

⑤MCF/day 千立方英尺/天；MMCF/day 百万立方英尺/天。

⑥LCD 液晶显示器。

⑦SCADA＝Supervisory Control and Data Acquisition 监控和数据测取装置。

Exercises

Reading Comprehension

Ⅰ. Say whether the following statements are True (T) or False (F) according to the text.

1. The injection style odorizer systematically injects small volumes of odorant into the natural gas flow, which is one commonly used style of odorization system. (Para. 1)   (   )

2. All odorant systems should choose a ratio relating injection rate to proportion-to-flow as the principle method of operation. (Para. 4)   (   )

3. The system must have the ability to perform a prescribed injection rate over a wide range of possible flowrates, usually depending on what rate is required to achieve the proper smell throughout the system. (Para. 5)   (   )

4. In fact all injection pumps are pneumatically actuated plunger style. This pneumatic supply is passed on to the pump when the system controller deter mines that an injection is required. (Para. 9)   (   )

5. The requirement for a safe, clean, and inexpensive fuel supply has caused various techniques of odorizing natural gas to be developed. (Para. 14)   (   )

Ⅱ. Skim through Para 2, 8, and 10, and complete the following table.

1.

Basic considerations of system operation	
①odorant selection	②
③	④Basic system design
⑤verification of operation	⑥
⑦	⑧Fail-safe operation

2.

The components of a typical injection type odorizer
①Injection pump
②
③Injection rate verification system
④

3.

Simple programming of critical information
①Injection rate desired (Ib./MMCF)
②
③
④Fail-safe injection rate (min./injection)

Ⅲ. Fill in the blanks with the information given in the text.

1. Matching the odorant recipe to the natural gas in the stream involves _____.

2. If the gas is detected by the technician, the odorant level is identified using the instrument which _____.

3. Insure that the injection system will operate _____ throughout the entire range of expected flowrates.

4. New designs adopt important innovative concepts such as _____, as a standard problem alert.

5. The injection rate controller receives flowrate information from an electronic measurement device and, using a microprocessor, automatically causes the pump to act _____.

Vocabulary

Ⅰ. Fill in the blanks with the words and expressions given below. Change the forms if necessary.

> verification, malfunction, ambient, innovative, compatibility, segregate, incorporate, actuate

1. The _____ system meters fluid consumed by the pump and then calculations are performed and displayed on the LCD.
2. Many new safety features _____ in the new version of this popular car.
3. The library _____ oversized books and puts them on a separate shelf.
4. In designing the new pumps they took account of the _____ of internal seals and working parts with the chemical characteristics found in odorants.
5. There followed a wave of selling on the stock market, _____ by the rumour that the currency was to be devalued.

II. Find the words in the text which almost mean the same as the following.
1. para. 2: fail to function in a normal or satisfactory manner
2. para. 5: on all sides
3. para. 6: show the truth of
4. para. 7: probability
5. para. 11: give something to make up (for loss, injury, etc.)

III. Now use the words you have found to complete the following sentences. Change the form if necessary:
1. We should take this boy away from the bad _____ influences in which he lives.
2. In all _____, we shall be away from our institute for a week to on-the-spot investigation.
3. The government _____ the families of the men who were killed in the accident.
4. Everything he said then _____ by what happened later.
5. The two new capabilities of on-board system monitoring and alarm outputs allow reduction in the critical time period between _____, notification of company personnel and repair.

Writing   Outline writing (4)

Directions: Read the text of Unit Six and write a sentence outline of the text.

Reading Material A

Safer Repair of Plastic Pipe

Gas distribution piping is most often made from plastic—specifically, polyethylene. Although PE has many advantages, special care has to be taken during its repair to discharge any static electricity. ① Charges could be very high—enough to pose potential danger to repair crews.

The electrostatic charge is created when minute particles that may be carried by natural gas impinge against the pipe wall. ② The process is much the same as scuffing one's shoe on a nylon carpet. A static charge first builds up on the inside of the pipe; a charge may also be induced on the outside due to several factors, including humidity conditions or surface contamination. Treatment of the exterior of the pipe does not affect the internal charge whatsoever. Until now, there had not been a way of removing electrostatic charges from the inside of pipe. And the conventional methods used to discharge static electricity from the exterior of the pipe have operational disadvantages.

GRI solution③

Working under a GRI contract, with cofunding from The Brooklyn Union Gas Company, Southwest Research Institute has developed an electrostatic discharger system that eliminates static electricity from both the inside and outside of PE pipe. ④

The result is that safety is greatly enhanced for work crews who must handle or repair PE gas pipe. The system consists of three components: (1) a split tapping tee or tapping saddle with a built-in pipe cutter and nozzle; (2) an antistatic fluid; and (3) antistatic polyethylene film. The system is very simple to use. It takes only a single person with appropriate training to discharge the inner and outer surfaces of the pipe.

Until the new technology was developed for GRI, no effective method existed for neutralizing charges inside plastic pipe. The interior charge problem is evident after gas flow has been cut off, and a defective section of pipe is cut with a saw or circular cutter. When a metal object penetrates the inner wall of a charged pipe, a spark discharge is inevitable. Repairing PE gas pipe will now be much safer with the elimination of electrostatic charges both inside and outside the pipe.

The concept

A common procedure used to reduce the electrostatic hazard is to wet the outsidesurface of the pipe. The gas industry currently uses a wet soapy burlap wrap or tape to make the pipe slightly conductive to neutralize excess exterior static electricity. This procedure has distinct disadvantages: when frozen, the wrap no longer acts as a conductor; keeping the wrap properly wet makes the ditch messy; and some soap solutions may damage PE materials. ⑤

With the new system, the repair crew wraps the antistatic film around the pipe to neutralize the exterior charge. It is a dry process that replaces the wet soapy burlap wrap and avoids the problems of proper wetting and use in cold weather. The split tapping tee, which is reusable, is mounted on the pipe. The built-in cutter in the tapping tee is then used to penetrate the pipe wall so that the antistatic fluid can be sprayed through a built-in nozzle in the cutter to neutralize the inside charge.⑥ The fluid has been specially formulated for this application and will not freeze, evaporate, or adversely affect the properties of the PE pipe. The antistatic fluid is safe to handle and is environmentally benign.

Southwest Research Institute has developed a simple step-by-step procedure to teach the use of the discharger system effectively under typical field conditions.

The antistatic film wrap and the antistatic fluid are inexpensive disposables. The split tapping tee, which will be manufactured for different pipe sizes, is both economical and reusable for several years.

The prototype discharger system was fabricated and successfully tested in the laboratory by Southwest Research Institute. Subsequently, pilot field evaluations were held at Minnegasco, Mountain Fuel Supply Company, and Lone Star Gas Company. Several manufacturers have expressed interest in the system.

Notes

①这里 PE 为 polyethylene 的缩写。
②天然气可能携带的微小粒子撞击管壁时,就产生了静电荷。
③GRI=govenment rubber-isobutylene：丁基橡胶。
④利用布鲁克林联合燃气公司的合作基金,西南研究院在使用丁基橡胶过程中已改进了静电放电器系统,从聚乙烯管管壁内外两侧消除静电。
⑤这种做法有明显的不利因素：在上冻的时侯缠绕材料不起导体作用。缠绕物适度潮湿使管沟变脏,而且一些肥皂溶液可能损伤聚乙烯材料。
⑥在开通三通管儿的过程中,使用管体内刀具穿透管壁,以便防静电液体能从刀具内喷嘴喷出,抵消内侧电荷。

Reading Material B

Computers Analyze Odorant Concentration①

Brooklyn Union Gas purchases odorized natural gas from many pipeline suppliers and distributes it to more than a million active meters within a 187-sq. mi. service area.②

Using customized gas standards and special computer software integrated to our chromatography data acquisition system, we have mechanized a procedure to determine the total concentration of odorant in natural gas samples.③ This unique computer analysis system has reduced our paperwork and enhanced laboratory productivity—ensuring levels are adequate, but not so excessive as to cause false warnings. [4]

To comply with state and federal regulations, Brooklyn Union Gas odorizes natural gas at a quantitative concentration of 0.3 to 1.0 lbs./MMcf of odorant.

The computer analysis used separates odorant compounds by gas chromatography, using direct data acquisition and custom software prepared by Analytical Solution Inc. The concentrations of dimethyl sulfide, isopropyl mercaptan, normal propyl mercaptan, and tertiary butyl mercaptan are automatically calculated in units of lbs./MMcf. [5]

By providing automated computations of odorant concentration, our custom software program produces accurate and timely quantitative reports without any tedious manual calculations. It also accepts information directly from our chromatography data acquisition system.

Software use

Brooklyn Union Gas began using special software for sulfur odorant analysis last year. It incorporates calculations provided by the Institute of Gas Technology to convert the results of gas chromatography odorant assays from ppmv to lbs./MMcf. [6]

Records are kept of sample locations, time of sampling, olfactory impressions at the time of sampling, concentration of components, time of analysis, and any notes about unusual observations. All samples are analyzed promptly because there could be a significant loss of sulfur components due to adsorption or absorption if samples are retained for more than 24 hrs.

In recent years, a number of odorant monitoring systems have evolved in the gas industry. Most include daily collection of gas samples from various locations in glass bottles or Tedlar bags. These samples are analyzed for odorant concentration by gas chromatography with flame photometric detection (GC/FPD), using a sulfur filter. [7]

Liquid standards problems

Another major urban gas utility has developed and publicized a GC/FPD analysis technique for the sulfur odorants dimethyl sulfide and tertiary butyl mercaptan. Because that method employs liquid calibration standards, new calibration factors must be determined experimentally for every analysis.

The solvent used for liquid standards interferes with the detection and analysis of gas samples. It must be eluted from the GC column after each standard injection. Brooklyn Union Gas has eliminated that time-consuming procedure by using gas standards prepared by Scott Specialty Gases. Both the samples and the standards are injected into the GC through a special inert gas valve assembly.

Our odorant monitoring equipment includes a Tracor 550 GC/FPD with sulfur filter, a

PE Nelson 2600 Chromatography Data Acquisition System, and the custom data interface and computation program written by Analytical Solutions. This custom software accepts data directly from the result files of the PE Nelson 2600 GC and processes that data in a batch mode.⑧

With accurate analysis of odorant compounds in useful quantitative figures, we have established a prompt and uniform reporting procedure for odorization from all test points. And our custom software program is saving many hours of time for chemists and technicians, thus enabling Brooklyn Union Gas to provide more efficient and improved service throughout its 187 sq. mi. service area.⑨

Notes

①计算机分析加臭浓度。
②布鲁克林联合燃气公司从多家管道输送供应商获得加臭的天然气,并将其分配到187平方英里服务区域内上百万个运行的流量表。
③…chromatography data acquisition system ……色谱法数据获取系统。
④这种独特的计算机分析系统减少了我们的书面工作,从而提高了实验室效率——确保浓度满足要求,但不过量以免引起错误的警报。
⑤二甲硫、异丙硫醇、正丙硫醇和特丁硫醇的浓度自动地以磅/百万立方英尺为单位计算出来。
⑥该软件结合了燃气技术学院提出的计算成果,用气相色谱法分析气味,验定结果从百万分之几伏特改为磅/百万立方英尺。
⑦GC/FPD=gigacycle/fission-product detection 吉周/裂变产物探测;借助火焰光度探测手段(吉周/裂变产物探测),通过气相色谱法(要使用硫滤波装置)对这些样本的气味浓度进行分析。
⑧这个专门编制的软件接收直接来自PE Nelson 2600 GC 结果文件的数据并以批量的模式处理该数据(或并对该数据进行批处理)。
⑨我们专门编制的软件程序正在为化学家和技术人员节省很多时间,这样就能供Brooklyn Union Gas 为其整个187平方英里的服务区域提供更有效和改进的服务。

UNIT SEVEN

Text Floor Heating: Achieving Thermal Comfort in Artificial Environments

[1]   Modern man demands high levels of thermal comfort in artificial environments. Linked to this international pressure grows to reduce demand on the earth's energy reserves. ① Modern technology has made great strides forward in developing new innovative heat sources but probably the greatest advance in combined thermal comfort and energy conservation is the modern wet floor heating system. The advent of high quality plastics pipes has made possible the utilisation of low temperature water in floor heating systems perfectly compatible with the new heat source technology. ② Fully developed for all types of floor construction, U. F. H. combines all types of heat, conduction, radiation and convection, matching the ideal temperature gradient throughout an entire building . ③ The safe, invisible, space saving, vandal and tamper proof system is both responsive and energy conscious offering passive self regulation.

[2]   Thermal comfort can be defined as the state of mind where satisfaction is felt with the thermal environment. Research shows that people feel most comfortable when their feet are a little warmer than their heads. Independent tests reveal that the most acceptable indoor climate is one in which the floor temperature ranges between 19~29℃ and the air temperature at head level ranges between 20 and 24℃.

[3]   However, since individuality is integral to all human activity it is not possible to specify one set of environmental conditions which will meet all cases. The best results we are likely to achieve depend on a 5% dissatisfaction factor. There is no temperature that will please everyone, but we can aim to establish a comfort zone that will satisfy the highest possible percentage of those using the area.

[4]   With radiator or convector heating systems a vertical temperature gradient is produced; colder at foot level than at the head. A modern indoor climate surely demands a heating system which will match the required conditions for human thermal comfort with the principal heating effect being evenly distributed at ground level and not above head level. We have seen that warm feet create good sensations, so let us examine the effect upon the indoor climate if we warm the whole floor to just the right temperature.

[5]   We have touched on improvements in building standards but no amount of insulation can change the laws of physics—heat still rises. ④ Efficient insulation will, however, serve to trap heat above head level in an area where it can make no contribution to human comfort. Solving this problem involves a close study of the three types of heat available to us. ⑤ Radiant heat provides the most pleasurable sensation of comfort. It contributes to the exhilaration of a walk in the spring sunshine even though the ambient air temperature may

be only a few degrees above freezing. We humans also respond well to conducted heat—the cat-like pleasure that comes from the warmth of a hot water bottle or just cuddling up to another person. ⑥ Lastly, there is convected heat caused by the effects of the radiation and conduction warming the air and causing it to rise. By using all three types of heat in association we can achieve very high levels of thermal comfort. The normal criterion for heating design is to achieve a specified air temperature against the given heat loss of the building at a specified outside ambient temperature. When designing a floor heating system, however, lower air temperatures may be acceptable because of the higher level of overall radiation and the added benefit of conduction from warm, friendly floors. ⑦

[6] In modern, well insulated buildings the temperature of the floor surface need be only just above air temperature in order to achieve the required comfort factor. These low temperature differentials result in gentle, low velocity convection throughout the entire building. Low velocity convection reduces the amount of dust in the air in comparison with other types of heating. There are no inaccessible areas behind radiators or convectors where dust or dirt can collect. It is also cost efficient to operate. Eliminating high velocity convection means there will be no stack of high temperature air above head level.

[7] A heated floor is a radiant plane: subjects standing on it will therefore receive the benefit of all round radiation.

[8] A high level of radiant comfort means that air temperatures can actually be slightly lower with an infloor heating system than those usually required for other methods of heating. Radiation, conduction and convection combine to create the ideal thermal environment for health and comfort.

New Words and Expressions

stride * [straid]	v.	跨过
	n.	大步
advent ['ædvənt]	n.	出现
utilisation [juːtilaiˈzeiʃən]	n.	利用
compatible [kəmˈpætəbl]	a.	配伍的，适合的，
vandal * [ˈvædəl]	n.	破坏者
	a.	破坏性的
tamper * [ˈtæmpə]	vi.	损害
integral [ˈintigrəl]	a.	整体的，一切的
convector [kənˈvektə]	n.	对流散热器
gradient * [ˈgreidiənt]	n.	梯度
sensation * [senˈseiʃən]	n.	感觉（知）
exhilaration * [igzilə'reiʃən]	n.	高兴
criterion [kraiˈtiəriən]	n.	标准，准则

cat-like	[ˈkætlaik]	a.	像猫一样的
cuddle *	[ˈkʌdl]	v.	蜷缩着身子躺（睡）
differential	[difəˈrenʃəl]	n.	差别
		a.	分异的
inaccessible	[ˌinækˈsesəbl]	a.	不可达到的

Notes

①linked to this 过去分词短语做状语，this 指前面的一句话。
②The advent … the new heat source technology. 句中 advent 是主语；possible 是宾语补足语；the utilisation of low … technology 是宾语，因为宾语长而移到宾语补足语后面；compatible with … 形容词短语修饰 floor heating systems。
③U. F. H. ＝Under Floor Heating。
④heat still rises 是对 the laws of physics 的补充。
⑤Solving … to us. 句中 solving this problem 动名词短语作主语。
⑥We humans … another person 句中破折号后面 the cat-like pleasure … 补充说明前面整个句子；a hot water bottle 名词短语和 just cuddling up to another person 动名词短语是介词 of 的宾语。
⑦… to achieve … a floor heating system 动词不定式短语作表语；against（抵消）引出的介词短语作状语；at a specified air temperature 介词短语作定语修饰 the building。

Exercises

Reading Comprehension

Ⅰ. Say whether the following statements are true (T) or false (F) according to the text.
  1. A modern indoor climate surely demands a heating system for thermal comfort with more heating effect above head level than at ground level.   (   )
  2. If you walk in the spring sunshine you feel very comfortable with radiant heat.   (   )
  3. There are no accessible areas behind radiators or convectors where dust or dirt can collect.   (   )
  4. High velocity convection reduces the amount of dust in the air in comparison with other types of heating.   (   )
  5. Radiation, conduction and convection are together to create the ideal thermal environment for both health and comfort.   (   )

Ⅱ. Find out the definition of the thermal comfort.
   Thermal comfort: _____ .

Ⅲ. Fill in the gap with the information you have got from the text.

1. The most acceptable indoor climate is one in which the floor temperature ranges between _____ .
2. The air temperature at head level ranges between _____ .

IV. What are the functions of the three types of heat:
   1. Radiant heat _____ .
   2. Conducted heat _____ .
   3. Convected heat _____ .

V. Fill in the blanks with the information according to the text.

   A modern indoor climate surely demands a heating system which will __(1)__ the __(2)__ condition for human thermal comfort with the __(3)__ heating effect being evenly distributed at __(4)__ level and not above __(5)__ level. Low velocity convection reduces the amount of __(6)__ in the air in __(7)__ with three types of heating.

Vocabulary

I. Fill in the blanks with the words given below. Change the forms if necessary:

   vandal, sensation, exhilaration, convector, stride, stack, tamper

   1. When winter comes, people have a cold _____ .
   2. The climbers had a great _____ when they climbed the summit of the highest mountain of the world.
   3. In the room a _____ is used to exchange hot and cold air.
   4. Chinese people are making great _____ forward both in science and technology now.
   5. Earthquake is _____ to buildings as well as to people.

II. Find words in the text which almost mean approximately the same as the following.
   1. para. 1 able to exist together with ; in accord with
   2. para. 1 rise or fall of temperature; pressure in passing one region to another
   3. para. 1 coming or arrival
   4. para. 3 necessary to the completeness of a whole
   5. para. 5 lie close and comfortable

III. Now use the words you have found to complete the following sentences. Change the forms if necessary.
   1. The children _____ up under the blankets.
   2. The old method of the operation is not _____ with the innovation of the technology.
   3. They opposed a flat increase for all workers because that would upset the wage _____ .
   4. Since the _____ of jet aircraft, travel has been speeded up.
   5. Steel is _____ part of a modern skyscraper.

Writing   Summary Writing (1)

Summarizing means writing a short version of an article. To write a summary you skim the article so as to have a general idea of the material, underline the main points, make a list of all the points to be used and then with this list write the summary in an Introduction-Body-Conclusions structure, with transition words like "but",   "and", "however", "also". etc.

Directions: The following is a summary of the text of Unit Seven and there are several words missing. Now fill in the blanks with some of the words given below: (10 words given, 8 blanks to be filled)

insulated, radiant, subjects, thermal, convectors, sensation, reduction, gradient, infloor, comfort

The modern wet floor heating system probably is the greatest advence in combined ___ 1. _____ comfort and energy conservation. The advent of high quality plastics pipes has made possible the utilization of low temperature water in floor heating systems perfectly compatible with the new heat source technology. A modern indoor climate surely demands a heating system which will match the required conditions for human thermal ___ 2. _____ with principle heating effect being evenly distributed at ground level and not above head level. Warm feet create good sensations. By using all three types of heat in association ___ 3. _____ heat, convection heat and conduction heat very high levels of thermal comfort can be achieved. Fully developed for all types of floor construction, U. F. H. combines all types of heat, conduction, radiation and convection, matching the ideal temperature ___ 4. _____ throughout an entire building. A heated floor is a radiant plane: ___ 5. _____ standing on it will therefore receive the benefit of all round radiation. A high level of radiant comfort means that air temperatures can actually be slightly lower with an ___ 6. _____ heating system than those usually require for other methods of heating. And in modern well insulated buildings the temperature of the floor surface need be only just above air temperature in order to achieve the required comfort factor. These low temperature differentials result in gentle, low velocity convection through the entire building, the ___ 7. _____ of the amount of dust in the air comparison with other types of heating, no inaccessible areas behind radiators or ___ 8. _____ where dust or dirt can collect and no stack of high temperature are above head level.

Reading Material A

Floor Heating Design Criteria

The project has developed, modelled, and optimised several floor heating systems for residential, recreational, and light commercial applications. The developed systems have an overall thickness of around 30 mm (depending on insulation specification) and can be retrofitted into existing buildings. These are high performance heating systems with flow temperatures in the range 35 ℃ to 45 ℃ at maximum heat output and have a very low thermal resistance.

Floor heating systems are by no means new. Several designs and concepts including electric elements, hot air circulation, and embedded pipes have been installed with varying degrees of success. It is widely accepted that floor heating, with its predominantly radiant heating component, provides a much higher level of comfort than traditional convective systems (so called 'radiators' actually supply heat largely by convection).① Despite this, floor heating in the UK has often met with a relatively bad press due to several compromising features:②

(1) High Thermal Mass. This particularly applies to heating pipes or elements embedded in a concrete screed floor. These systems have long response times and poor controllability.

(2) High thermal Resistance. Traditional floor heating systems with screed or chipboard floor surfaces require moderate to high flow temperatures at maximum heat output.

(3) High Surface Temperatures. Installations in poorly insulated buildings (e.g., electric floor heating in the 1950s) led to uncomfortably hot floors.

The traditional problems of floor heating are effectively overcome when low thermal mass, low thermal resistance systems are installed in today's relatively well insulated buildings. The new-found success of floor heating in the more energy conscious European countries, especially the Federal Republic of Germany, supports this reasoning.

Modern building techniques including improved levels of insulation, double glazing etc., have improved the heat loss characteristics-the U-value-of our buildings greatly. Heat source technology has also taken a lead forward with the introduction of heat pumps, condensing boilers, solar panels, night storage systems, etc. It is worth noting that all these innovations operate at higher levels of efficiency when linked to a low temperature water distribution system. The greatest advance in creating thermal comfort in indoor climates however, has been the development of the modern wet floor heating system. The coming of the plastics age has made it possible to reduce energy consumption by utilising low water temperatures. These systems, based on the development of special, high quality plastic pipes, now account for over 40% of some European heating markets.

Extensive thermal performance testing has taken place in the laboratory and on a local full-scale installation (100m² floor area). The results of these tests have verified that demonstrable reductions in flow temperature, and energy consumption are achieved.

Thermal performance was measured using surface mounted thermocouples together with infra red thermography techniques with thermal image enhancement.

When considering the floor surface temperature the required heat output must be balanced against the limits of comfort. International Standards Organisation (I.S.O.) 7730 states that the most comfortable range is between 19~26℃, which falls ideally within the scope of a well designed U.F.H. system.

Whilst I.S.O. 7730 states that floor surfaces up to 29℃ are acceptable, with U.F.H. it would be unusual for such a high surface temperature to be necessary to meet the heat demand in a building that complies with modern standards of insulation.③

Floor heating normally requires water temperatures ranging between 35~50℃. The system and thus make the best use of low grade heat sources such as heat pumps or solar panels, but high temperature water from boilers can be equally well used by mixing down to the low temperature flow required with the aid of a simple by-pass arrangements and three port valve.

Individual zones within the project can be controlled by motorised valves connected to the loop flows at the manifold and operated via room thermostats.④ Each loop should also be balanced with a Lockshield valve installed at the manifold on the return loop.

Notes

①由于辐射供热成分占绝对主要部分，地板供热提供了比传统的对流供热系统高得多的舒适性，（所谓"散热器"实际上通过对流来供热）这一点已被人们所接受。
②虽然有这方面的有利条件，但是由于地板供热在英国的一些不利因素，常常是声誉不佳。
③虽然 I.S.O. 7730 指出，对于地板供热系统，地面温度达 29℃是可以接受的，但是需要这么高的地面温度来满足符合现代隔热标准建筑物的采暖要求是不寻常的。
④本项目内的个别区域是可通过与支管环流相连接并通过房间恒温器来操作的电动阀门控制的。

Reading Material B

System Economics and Design
Optimisation of Floor Heating System

It has been demonstrated that floor heating reduces energy consumption by 11%~23%. This is achieved primarily by virtue of the distributed nature of the heat emission and the avoidance of temperature stratification which typically accompanies traditional heating systems. ① This, together with the ability to reduce air temperatures while maintaining acceptable comfort conditions means that floor heating has a large energy saving potential.

The floor heating systems outlined above were developed specifically for low grade heating systems. ② The market penetration of a number of relatively new heating source technologies is being hindered by the fact that they are often interfaced with unsuitable heating distribution systems. ③ All heat transfer devices benefit from being able to transfer heat to the lowest possible temperature, but the following relatively new devices have flow temperature dependent efficiencies:

(1): Heat Pumps: COPs can be almost doubled (depending on source temperatures) by reducing flow temperatures from 55~60℃ to 30~35℃.

(2): Condensing Boilers: Efficiencies improve from 80%~85% to 90%~95% by reducing return temperatures from 55~60℃ to 30~35℃, and if the change is from a non-condensing boiler the improvement is from 65%~70% to 90%~95%.

(3): Water Thermal Storage: Storage capacity can be increased by 25%~30% by reducing the low temperature limit from 55~60℃ to 30~35℃.

Both systems, by virtue of their surface-mounted aluminium fin, offer little thermal resistance and low thermal mass. System 2, with its aluminum extrusion, reduces the thermal resistance even more by doing away with the insulative plastic pipe and its associated contact resistance. Flow temperature reductions of up to 8℃, over System 1 have been demonstrated. System 2, though of very high performance, has potential problems in the areas of jointing and electrolytic corrosion of the extrusion. A double O-ring fitting has been developed which has excellent integrity if care is taken on assembly. Current commercial aluminum radiators are protected chemically against electrolytic corrosion. and the same techniques can be used with System 2.

Installation for both systems is a simple process of laying pre-laminated panels and lengths of extrusion or plastic pipe consecutively and can be considered a potential DIY exercise.

The designs have the respective merits of the jointless continuousplastic pipe of System 1 and the very low thermal resistance of System 2. At the time of writing a hybrid is being developed with the additional aims of lightweight, cheaper construction, and extremely simple and fast installation.

The system water temperature is determined by the thermal resistance between the water circuit and the heated environment. The system's thermal resistance decreases with increasing aluminum thickness and decreasing pipe spacing. Conversely, the capital and installation costs increase. ④ If appropriate limiting performance criteria are applied, the system design can be optimised for minimum overall costs.

A micro-computer based mathematical model was developed to aid the optimisation process. It uses a twodimensional finite element technique to solve for the heat transfer and

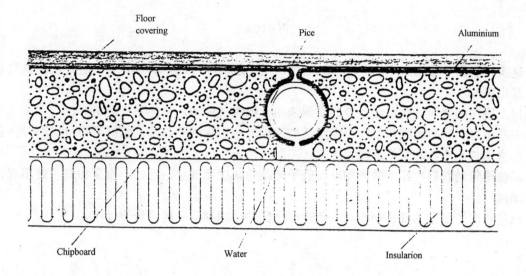

SYSTEM1

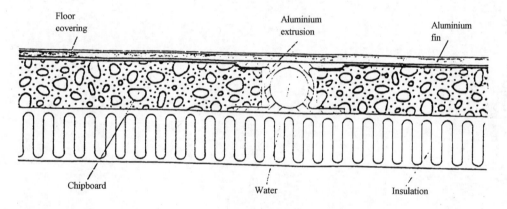

SYSTEM2

Fig. 7-1 The two systems design developed

temperature distribution within any simply specified floor heating system design. Good correlation between the predicted and experimentally measured results was found.

The model was used to predict the thermal and economic performance for various combinations of pipe spacing and fin thickness. An optimum pipe spacing /fin thickness ratio was found and applied to a number of system designs. [5]

Other applications where the introduction of a low flow temperature can transform the system's overall economic viability are solar heating, district heating, combined heat and power or waste heat utilisation.

Notes

①这实质上主要是由放热的分配性和避免产生温层而实现的,温层是伴随着传统的供热系统出现的。

②以上概述的地板供热系统是专门发展来用于低级(能源)供热系统的。

③一些相对新的热源技术在向市场渗透的过程当中正在受到这样的情况阻碍,也就是说,它们常常与不恰当的配热系统相连接。

④系统热阻随着铝片厚度的增加以及管子间距的减少而减小。反之,投资和安装费用就会增加。

⑤已经找出了最佳的管子间距与散热片厚之比并已用到了一些系统设计中。

UNIT EIGHT

Text   Fabric Filters

[1]   Fabric filters are by far the most common type of filter encountered in the industrial environment and the one most likely to be used in a local exhaust ventilation system. The filter itself consists of pieces of fabric sewn into cylinders or envelopes and mounted in a housing. During operation, exhaust air is drawn through the fabric by the fan; particles either collect in the fabric itself or in a dust cake on the fabric surface and are thus removed from the exiting exhaust stream.①

[2]   As with other filters, fabric filters must eventually be cleaned. In fact, cleaning is so important that fabric filters are classified by the cleaning method used. The three most common cleaning methods are shaking, reverse air flow, and pulse jet air. Each of the three cleaning methods has different applications, which will be described briefly.

[3]   Shaking is the oldest and simplest method to clean a fabric filter. The tops of the bags are oscillated in either the horizontal or vertical direction; this motion flexes the fabric and causes the collected dust cake to be dislodged and fall into the hopper. Shaker-cleaned bags are generally constructed of woven fabrics, which collect the dust as a surface cake which is easily dislodged by the fabric flexion.

[4]   The shaking mechanism is usually motor driven and can be initiated either automatically (e.g., by sensing excess pressure drop) or manually whenever the operator decides cleaning is necessary. Small units may not employ a motor and are cleaned instead by moving an external lever that oscillates the bags. Exhaust airflow must be shut down before a bag is shaken, to allow the dislodged dust to fall into the hopper. This means that either the process has to be shut down while the baghouse is cleaned, or the baghouse has to be divided into compartments so that one compartment can be isolated and shut down with dampers while the remaining compartments continue filtering the exhaust air.②The first alternative is possible for intermittent operations or operations which produce so little dust that the baghouse can be cleaned once at the end of the work shift; most applications, however, will require a compartmentalized baghouse.

[5]   In some instances bag shaking is supplemented by a gentle reverse airflow through the fabric; this reverse flow helps to carry the dislodged dust away from the fabric and into the hopper. Reverse flow cleaning requires a system of dampers to shut off the main flow and open the reverse flow; this tends to complicate the baghouse design and operation and increases capital and operating costs. Consequently, reverse air cleaning is usually found only in rather large baghouses filtering a dust that is difficult to remove with shaking alone.

[6]   High-temperature filtration requires the use of specialized fabrics, such as fiber-

glass, which can withstand this severe environment. Woven fiberglass cannot tolerate shaking, so baghouse using these fabrics employ gentle reverse air cleaning without shaking. Such systems usually require bags with special surface treatment to enhance the release of dust.

[7]   The last major fabric filter cleaning technique employs blasts of high-pressure air to remove collected dust. This methods is called pulse-jet cleaning. A short pulse of high-pressure compressed air is introduced into the top of the bag. This pulse travels down the bag, temporarily reversing flow through the fabric and flexing the bag outward. This sudden flexing dislodges dust from the outer surface of the fabric in the form of agglomerates, which fall toward the hopper. Cleaning pulses can either be applied at regular intervals by incorporating a timer or can be initiated by sensing excess pressure drop across the fabric.

[8]   Pulse-jet cleaning requires the use of felted fabrics rather than woven ones, to withstand the violent motion induced by the pulses. Felted fabrics tend to collect dust throughout the depth of the felt rather than at the surface as a cake; this porous dust deposit is more difficult to remove than a surface deposit, so pulse-jet cleaning is less efficient than the other methods and typically must be applied more often.③

[9]   Pulse can be applied to a bag either on-line, where normal airflow is maintained through the system during cleaning, or off-line, where a compartment is isolated from the exhaust flow during cleaning.④ Most pulse-jet systems use on-line cleaning; such systems constitute the simplest type of fabric filter since they require no moving parts, such as isolation dampers or shaking mechanisms. This is a big advantage from the point of view of maintenance, but naturally there are tradeoffs involved. On-line cleaning is not as effective at removing dust as off-line cleaning, since the exhaust airflow tends to redeposit dust onto the fabric after the pulse is over. Off-line cleaning allows the removed dust to fall into the hopper before filtration resumes, but requires the additional complication and expense of isolation dampers.

New Words and Expressions

filter * ['filtə]	n.	过滤器
oscillate ['ɔsileit]	v.	振荡,震动
flex * [fleks]	v.	(使)挠曲,
dislodge * [dis'lɔdʒ]	vt.	移去,除去
hopper * ['hɔpə]	n.	料斗
weave * (wove, woven)	v.	编织
flexion ['flekʃən]	n.	挠曲
initiate [i'niʃieit]	vt.	起动,开始
baghouse * ['bæghaus]	n.	集尘室
compartment * [kəm'partmənt]	n.	间隔;隔室

damper *	[ˈdæmpə]	n.	风门，风挡
intermittent	[intəˈmitənt]	a.	间歇的，断断续续的
compartmentalize *	[kəmpɑːtˈmentlaiz]	vt.	把……分成区，隔开
supplement *	[ˈsʌpliment]	vt.	增补，增添
		n.	补充，增刊
enhance	[inˈhɑːns]	vt.	提高，增强
agglomerate *	[əˈglɔmərit]	n.	附聚物，大块
		v.	聚结，结块
felt	[felt]	v.	把……制成毡
		n.	毡
induce	[inˈdjuːs]	vt.	引起，导致
porous	[ˈpɔːrəs]	a.	疏松的，多孔的
typically	[ˈtipikəli]	ad.	一般，有代表性地
on-line			联机
off-line			脱机
trade-off		n.	权衡，折衷（办法，方案）选择

Notes

①…particles either collect…or…. 句子中的意思是 either in the fabric itself or on the fabric surface；in a dust 短语中的 in 是以……的形式。

②This means that …the exhaust air. 句中 this 指前面整句话；that either…or…引出两个并列的宾语从句；either 后的宾语从句中有 while 引出的时间状语从句；or 后的宾语从句中有 so that 结果状语从句；而这个结果状语从句中又含有一个 while 引出的时间状语从句。

③depth 在这里是指厚度。

④Pulse … either on-line，where …, or off-line，where … cleaning. 句中 either on-line，or off-line，是主句状语；on-line 和 off-line 后各自有 where 引出的非限制性定语从句作修饰。

Exercises

Reading Comprehension

Ⅰ. Say whether the following statements are True (T) or False (F) according to the text, making use of the given paragraph reference number.

1. Cleaning is so important that fabric filters are classified by the cleaning method used. (para. 2) 　　　　　　　　　　　　　　　　　　　　　　　　　　　　(　)

2. The shaking mechanism is generally motor-driven and can be set working automatically whenever the operator decides cleaning is necessary. (para. 4)   ( )
3. Reverse air flow is usually used in all kinds of baghouses, easily filtering a dust that is difficult to remove with other cleaning methods. (para. 5)   ( )
4. Pulse-jet cleaning requires the use of specialized fabrics, such as fiberglass to resist the violent motion induced by the pulses. (para. 8)   ( )
5. Off-line cleaning is more effective than on-line cleaning at removing dust because off-line cleaning allows the removed dust to fall into the hopper before filtration resumes. (para. 9)   ( )

II. Choose the best answer.
1. Fabric filters are the most common type of filters found in the industrial environment and the one most likely to be used
   A. in HVAC systems
   B. for a particular application
   C. in a local exhaust ventilation system
   D. for housecleaning.
2. Shaker-cleaned bags are usually made of woven fabrics to collect the dust as a surface cake which is easily removed
   A. by the fabric flexion   B. by the operator
   C. by airflow   D. by a motor
3. Reverse flow cleaning needs a system of dampers to close off the main flow and open the reverse flow,
   A. which tends to complicate the baghouse design
   B. which tends to complicate the operation
   C. which increases capital and operating costs
   D. which tends to complicate the baghouse design and operation and increases capital and operating costs.
4. In pulse-jet cleaning, a short pulse of high-pressure compressed air is introduced
   A. toward the hopper   B. into the top of the bag
   C. across the fabric   D. into the bottom of the bag
5. Most pulse-jet systems use on-line cleaning because
   A. on-line cleaning is the oldest and simplest method
   B. on-line cleaning is more effective
   C. such systems require no filtration resumptions
   D. such systems require no moving parts and constitute the simplest type of fabric filter.

III. Fill in the blanks with the information given in the text.
1. The filter itself consists of _____ and mounted in a housing.

2. Fabric filters are classified by the cleaning method used. The three most common cleaning methods are _____ , _____ , and _____ .

3. Shaking is _____ to clean a fabric filter.

4. Reverse air flow helps to carry the dislodged dust away _____ .

5. Pulse can be applied to a bag either on-line or off-line.

   1) on-line, where _____ through the system during cleaning.

   2) off-line, where _____ from the exhaust flow during cleaning.

Vocabulary

I. Fill in the blanks with the words and expressions given below. Change the form if necessary.

| cylinder | dislodge | oscillate | hopper |
| compartment | initiate | incorporate | supplement |

1. The gas spins around the _____ and particles are thrown toward the walls by centrifugal force.

2. Since airborne (空中的) particles settle at a constant velocity (速率) due to the force of gravity, the gravity settling device is designed to allow particles sufficient time to fall into the _____ .

3. Cyclones (旋风除尘器) can be made out of almost any material and can thus be used to _____ dusts from hot or corrosive gas streams.

4. They briefly described the most common types of equipment _____ the methods, concentrating on the important characteristics.

5. In some instances bag shaking is _____ by a gentle reverse air flow through the fabric to help remove the dust from the fabric and into the hopper.

II. Find words in the text which mean almost the same as the following.

1. para. 3: shake or swing
2. para. 4: start or set (a scheme, etc.) working
3. para. 6: add to (the value, attraction, powers, price, etc.)
4. para. 8: bring about
5. para. 8: representatively or characteristicly

III. Now use the words you have found to complete the following sentences. Change the form if necessary.

1. The growth of a city often _____ the value of land close to it.
2. The technical innovation of the young workers _____ its desired effect.
3. They were large vessels made of clay, _____ having long curved necks.
4. Exhaust airflow must be shut down before a bag _____ , to allow the dislodged

dust to fall into the hopper.

5. The museum _____ the fund-raising drive with a special exhibition.

Writing   Summary Writing (2)

Directions The following is a summary of the text of Unit Eight. There are several words and/or phrases missing. Please fill in the blanks with words or phrases found from the text.

Summary:

Fabric filters are by far the most common type of filter. The filter itself consists of pieces of fabric sewn into ___(1)___ and mounted in a housing. ___(2)___ are classified by the ___(3)___ used. The three most common cleaning methods are shaking, reverse airflow, and pulse jet air and each of them has ___(4)___. (para. 1-2). ___(5)___ is the oldest and simplest method to clean a fabric filter. By shaking the bags the fabric ___(6)___ and the collected dust cake ___(7)___ and falls into the hopper. The shaking mechanism is usually motor driven and can ___(8)___ either automatically or manually. (para. 3-4) ___(9)___ requires a system of ___(10)___ to shut off the main flow and open the reverse flow and is usually found only in rather large baghouses. ___(11)___ requires the use of ___(12)___ to with-stand the severe environment. (para. 5-6) ___(13)___ can either be applied at ___(14)___ by incorporating a timer or can be initiated by ___(15)___ across the fabric. Pulse-jet cleaning requires the use of ___(16)___ to withstand the violent motion induced by the pulse. Pulses can be applied to a bag either ___(17)___ or ___(18)___. Most pulse-jet systems use on-line cleaning. (para. 7-9)

Reading Material A

Particle Removers

The principal particle collection methods are gravity settling, centrifugation, filtration, electrostatic precipitation, and scrubbing. In this section we briefly describe the most common types of equipment incorporating some of these methods, con-centrating on the characteristics that are important in selecting an air cleaner for a particular application.①

Gravity Settling Devices. This type of device is the simplest available and has the most limited application.② the simple horizontal flow gravity settling chamber operates by increasing the cross-sectional area of the duct, thereby reducing the gas velocity and increasing the particle residence time inside the settling chamber. Since airborne particles settle at a constant velocity due to the force of gravity, the device is designed to allow particles sufficient time to fall into the hoppers.

In theory, any particle size could be collected in a settling chamber by making the device sufficiently large to give the smallest particles time to fall out of the gas stream. In practical applications, such devices are limited to the collection of very large particles because of the low settling velocities of small particles. This limitation is illustrated in Table 8-1, which lists theoretical gravitational settling velocities for a range of particle sizes.

It should be apparent that only particles with an aerodynamic diameter larger than about 50μm will be collected efficiently in such a device. ③ Inhalable and respirable particles are difficult to collect; gravity settlers are thus limited to applications where high concentrations of large particles are generated and present a housecleaning problem which is solved by collecting the particles in a local exhaust ventilation system. ④

Table 8-1   Terminal Settling Velocities of Particles with Selected Aerodynamic Diameters

Particle Diameter (μm)	Settling Velocity (cm/s)
0.01	0.000007
0.1	0.00008
1	0.004
5	0.08
10	0.3
20	1.2
50	7.5
100	25

Centrifugal Collectors. These devices, commonly called cyclones, are probably the most common air-cleaning device found in industry. This popularity is due to their simple construction, with no moving parts, which makes them inexpensive to buy and easy to maintain. An offsetting limitation, however, is the large amount of energy required to collect small particles.

Cyclones are similar to gravity collectors in concept, except that they use centrifugal force rather than gravity to separate particles from the airstream. ⑤ In a conventional cyclone the air is introduced tangentially into a cylindrical body section and above a conical section leading to a hopper. The gas spins around the cylinder and particles are thrown toward the walls by centrifugal force. Particles that strike the walls fall into the hopper, while those too small to be influenced by the centrifugal force travel with the gas stream into the cone and back up through the outlet. ⑥

Since centrifugal forces can be achieved that are many times larger than that due to gravity, these devices can better collect small particles than can gravity settlers. ⑦ As with gravity settlers, it is theoretically possible to collect particles of any size in cyclones; in practice, excessive energy requirements usually limit their use to particles with an aerodynamic diameter greater than 10μm.

Cyclones are relatively compact devices and can be integrated into an exhaust system rather easily. Because of the particle-size limitations, they should be used primarily for the collection of nuisance dusts and as preseparators for other more efficient particle removal devices. They can collect both solid and liquid particles, but should not be used for sticky dusts or other materials that would not easily fall down the walls and be collected in the hopper. Cyclones can be made out of almost any material and can thus be used to remove dusts from hot and/or corrosive gas streams.

Notes

①本节中，我们将简单叙述应用这些方法的最常见设备，集中讨论其特性，对于为某一特定用途选择空气净化器来说是主要的。

②重力沉降室：这种装置是最简单有效的，但却也是使用范围局限性最大的。

③Aerodynamic diameter 空气动力学直径。其定义是在相同沉降速度下，单位密度球体的直径。

④被吸入的和能够呼吸的微粒是难以捕集的；因此重力沉降室局限用于产尘颗粒大而且密度高的场合，从而产生了房屋清洁的问题，这个问题要通过局部排气通风系统收集尘粒来解决。

⑤从概念上讲，旋风除尘器与重力集尘器相似，只是前者使用离心力而不是重力把颗粒从气流中分离出来。

⑥撞击管壁的颗粒掉入料斗，而那些太小而不受离心力影响的颗粒则随着气流进入锥顶，而从出口流出。

⑦由于能够得到大于重力很多倍的离心力，这些装置能够比重力沉降器更好地收集小颗粒。

Reading Material B

Dust Classification

The classification of dust by size is achieved by sieving it through a series of gauze sieves ranging from 42μ upwards.① The weight percentage of the various fractions is determined by weighing the residues on the sieves. Finer dust fractions smaller than 42μ are treated in air elutriators, which enable the weight percentage of individual fractions to be determined and also allow these fractions to be classified according to their settling velocities.② The nickel-plated inner surface of each separator tube is very smooth, so that very little of the dust that is blown through the separator sticks to the walls and this small amount is easily dislodged by lightly tapping the outside of the tube. To the lower part of the separator, by means of a rubber union, a small glass fitting or dust holder is attached in which a weighed sample of the dust on test is placed. This fitting has a glass tube sealed into it, not extending to the bottom; the outside end of this tube is connected by a rubber tube to the air blower. A good fitting of this kind should produce a symmetrical flow of air into the separator without swirl and with uniform dispersion of the dust sample.

Microscopic analysis of the size of dust particles, with subsequent conversion to their weight, does not give accurate results; but it is useful for appraising the size and shape of particles which are captured on slides treated, for instance, with Canada balsam.

The results of a dust analysis are plotted graphically as a distribution curve in which the abscissae represent particle size and the ordinates the percentage by weight within given ranges of size. [3]

Table 8-2 Properties of Cement Dust (Density 3.36g/cm³, moisture content 1.9 percent)

Fractions by setting velocity (cm/sec)	0-0.125	0.125-0.5	0.5-2	2-8	8-16	16-32	32-128	Residue >128
Fractions by size (μ)	0-3.33	3.33-6.65	6.65-13.3	13.3-26.6	26.6-37.6	37.6-53.4	53.4-106.3	>106.3
Average size in (μ)	1.66	5	10	20	32	45	80	>80
Percentage of total eight within frac-tion	4.4	13.8	13.8	22.6	7.1	19.5	17.0	1.8
Percentage by weight of particles larger than lower limit of this fraction	100	95.6	81.8	68.0	45.4	38.3	18.8	0

A cumulative curve can then be plotted by adding in succession the percentages within fractions ranging from the largest size to any specified smaller size. The ordinate of this curve at any particular particle size indicates the percentage by weight of particles larger than that size in the whole sample. [4]

Table 8-2 shows the size distribution of cement dust, split into fractions, as determined in an air elutriator according to the settling velocity and subsequently converted to particle size.

The distribution curve and cumulative curve are both plotted using the average particle size for each fraction (Fig. 8-1)

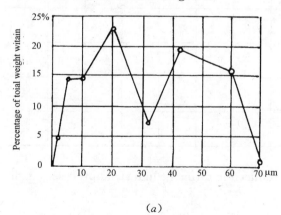 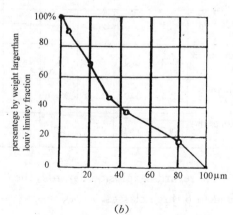

(a) (b)

Fig. 8-1 size analysis for cement dust (a) distribution curve (b) cumulative curve[5]

Table 8-3 shows typical compositions of industrial dust according to the number of particles within given size limits, as percentages of the total number. [6]

Table 8-4 shows the distribution of the sizes in μ for various industrial dusts. It will be seen from Table 8-3 that most particles of mineral, vegetable, and animal dust are 6-25μ in size, and metallic dust particles are up to 2μ.

Table 8-3 Particle Size Distributions (percentage by number)

Type of dust	Percentage (by number) of particles within size range (μ)							Maximum size
	<2	3-5	6-10	11-25	26-50	51-100	>100	
sand (screening)	11.7	22.7	28.0	29.3	7.1	1.2	—	104
Emery (dry dressing of wheel)	52.2	16.0	9.8	15.4	5.0	1.4	0.2	—
Hemp (manual sorting)	2.9	15.1	29.2	35.8	11.3	3.9	1.8	202
Anthracite (pulverization in labo-ratory)	28.5	22.1	19.3	23.6	5.3	1.2	—	76
Cast iron (turning)	73.0	8.8	6.6	8.1	2.3	1.0	0.2	124
Copper (turning)	59.6	18.1	10.5	10.1	1.3	0.4	—	104
Lead (machining)	59.7	14.0	14.4	9.9	1.8	—	0.2	120
Zinc oxide (at galva-nizing furnace)	6.0	16.6	27.5	30.8	13.4	4.7	1.0	146

Table 8-4 Particle Size Distributions (percentage by number)

Source or type of dust	Average particle size (μ)	0-0.49	0.5-0.99	1-1.49	1.5-1.99	2-2.49	2.5-2.99	3-3.49	3.5-3.99	4-4.99	4.5-4.99	5-5.49	5.5-5.99
Sandblasting apparatus	1.4	1.4	19.7	34.7	20.3	12.6	5.2	2.8	1.6	1.1	0.2	0.2	0.2
Crushing	1.4	—	13.0	39.0	33.0	10.5	2.5	2.0	—	—	—	—	—
Riddling	1.3	2.0	31.5	33.0	16.0	10.0	4.5	2.5	0.5	—	—	—	—
Foundry air	1.2	—	26.0	48.0	17.0	8.0	1.0	—	—	—	—	—	—
Aluminium dust	2.2	3.0	8.0	25.0	14.0	11.5	9.0	6.5	3.0	3.5	4.0	7.0	10.0
Bronze dust	1.5	1.0	12.0	33.0	25.0	21.0	6.0	1.5	—	—	—	—	—
Atmospheric dust	0.5	56.0	41.0	2.5	0.5	—	—	—	—	—	—	—	—

As regards explosion hazards, the dust produced in different industrial processes is divided into three classes.

Class I covers the dusts that are most highly inflammable. A very slight heat source, such as that from striking a match, is enough to ignite them. This class includes the dust of sugar, dextrin, cork, starch, cocoa and rice flour.

Table 8-5　　　　　　　　Explosive Concentration As Function of Mode of Ignition

Dust	Concentration (milligrams per litre air)		
	Incandescent body	Electric arc	Spark from induction coil
Sulphur	7.0	13.7	13.7
Sugar	10.3	17.2	34.4
Aluminium	7.0	7.0	13.7
Coal	17.2	24.1	no flash

The next class covers dusts which can be ignited only by a more powerful heat source (electric arc, Bunsen burner). This applies to the dust of hides, sawdust, oil-cake, bran (siftings), silk (floss) and so on.

The third class of dusts do not ordinarily explode in industrial conditions owing to their larger particle size and because they contain large percentages of incombustible matter. They include tobacco, foundry coal, charcoal, foundry soot, coke, graphite and so on.

Table 8-5 shows the explosive concentrations of some types of dust for three methods of heating: (a) incandescent body, e.g. a red-hot platinum wire, (b) electric arc, and (c) spark from an induction coil.

Notes

①按粒径大小对尘粒的分类是用一组 42μm 以上的金属网筛分而实现的。
②粒径小于 42μm 的细粉尘部分在空气淘析器中处理，这种装置能确定各粒径级别的重量百分比，而且能根据沉降速度进行粒径分类。
③尘粒分析结果是以分布曲线的形式标绘在坐标纸上，其中横坐标表示粒径；纵坐标表示一定粒径范围内的重量百分比。
④对任何特定颗粒粒径，其曲线纵坐标表示大于所有样本中那个粒径的重量百分比。
⑤累积曲线。
⑥表 8-3 表示根据在给定粒径范围内的颗粒数量而得出的典型的工业粉尘的组成，以相对于尘粒总数量的百分比给出。

UNIT NINE

Text   Introduction to VAV Systems

[1] Variable air volume systems are the most promising and versatile type of HVAC systems available today. It is an exciting approach that knows no limit in its application and is restricted only by lack of knowledge and past habits.

[2] Variable air volume systems, in addition to helping to solve energy problems, can save 20 to 30% in building energy costs over conventional constant air volume systems. VAV systems can also reduce first costs by using smaller equipment such as fans, pumps, boilers, chillers and less costly ductwork and piping distribution systems.

[3] Furthermore, VAV systems can provide beautiful comfort when designed, maintained and operated properly. VAV systems provide excellent flexibility in zoning and can easily be expanded or contracted, rearranged, or partially shut down without affecting the central equipment to any degree.

[4] In the bad news department there have been problems over the past years since the conception and inception of VAV systems, not all of which have been 100% resolved or are very easy to control.①

[5] For an example of the kinds of problems the HVAC industry has been involved with over the past decade, just imagine for a moment you have some business to transact in a new multi-story building in your city or town. Let's see what it's like as you walk through the building.②

[6] You tug on the door at the entrance and it doesn't budge. You yank on it with both hands and it suddenly swings open. As you enter a gale of air rushes in with you.

[7] The air noise from the ceiling diffuser overhead disturbs you and the jet or air blasts the toupee off your head. You scramble to set it back in place. Under another diffuser the air is stagnant and still, and further down under a third diffuser a glob of cold air sinks down and chills you.

[8] In the first office you visit, where the heat is stifling, you take off your suit jacket and loosen your tie. In the next office, you turn your collar up and shudder. It feels as frigid as an early winter day.

[9] The air in the building feels generally stale-as if there is no ventilation.

[10] A sheet metal man standing on a ladder with his head thrust up into the ceiling space tells you that he sure is busy with a lot of testing and adjusting on a system that is, theoretically, selfbalancing. He relates other problems to your sympathetic ears, "Not enough pressure at this box to operate it, too much at that box, and over yonder the terminal regulator isn't holding the maximum cfm."

[11] You ride the elevator up to the mechanical room to investigate the situation there

and you hear air gushing up the shaft.

[12]   In the equipment room you see cardboard covering the combustion air louver. The building engineer complains of not enough heat in the mornings upon startup. Ductwork rumbles and throbs. He worries about changing the hot, humming motor on a vaneaxial fan.

[13]   We could continue the story, but the point's been made; as versatile and powerful as VAV systems might be, they haven't always operated altogether cor-rectly in the past.③

[14]   PROBLEMS RESOLVED IN LAST DECADE

1. Fan volume modulation improved.
2. DDC controls allow for more precise controls of fans.
3. Separate microprocessor controls of individual terminals.
4. Lower intake pressures required on VAV terminals to operate them.
5. Inverters used to maximize VAV energy savings.
6. Computerized static regain design of ductwork which lessens fluctuating duct pressure and noise.
7. Proper startup of VAV systems.
8. Proper testing and balancing.
9. More effective locations and settings of ductwork static pressure sensors for fan volume control.
10. More effective settings of and actual control of VAV terminal units.

New Words and Expressions

versatile	['və:sətail]	a.	通用的，万能的
ductwork *	['dʌkt,wə:k]	n.	风道
flexibility	[fleksə'biliti]	n.	适应性，机动性，灵活性
conception	[kən'sepʃən]	n.	构思，设想
inception	[in'sepʃən]	n.	开始，开端
transact *	[træn'zækt]	v.	处理，办理，进行（交易等）
tug	[tʌg]	v.	吃力的拉
budge	[bʌdʒ]	v.	动（一动），挪动
yank	[jæŋk]	v.	猛拉，使劲拉
pull on			（用力）拉，拽
diffuser *	[di'fju:zə]	n.	散流器
gale	[geil]	n.	（一）股，（一）阵
blast	[blɑ:st]	n.	（气）流，（气）浪 一阵突然的风
toupee *	['tu:pei]	n.	（尤指头顶上的）一缕

79

			头发；另用假发
scramble *	[skræmbl]	v.	（急忙）抢，夺
stagnant *	['stægnənt]	a.	停滞的，滞止的
stifle *	['staifl]	v.	（使）感到窒息，气闷
glob	[glɔb]	n.	团块
shudder *	['ʃʌdə]	v; n.	发抖，打颤
frigid *	['fridʒid]	a.	寒冷
stale	[steil]	a.	陈旧的；不新鲜的
ventilation	[ventilei∫ən]	n.	通风，通风装置
yonder *	['jɔndə]	a; ad.	（在）那边（的）
			（在）远处（的）
gush *	[gʌʃ]	v; n.	涌（喷）出
shaft *	[ʃɑ:ft]	n.	竖井
louver *	['lu:və]	n.	（通风用）气窗，天窗
startup	[s'tɑ:tʌp]	n.	开动，启动
rumble *	['rʌmbl]	v.	（发出）隆隆声
throb *	[θrɔb]	v; n.	震动，跳动
hum *	['hʌm]	v.	（发出）嗡嗡声
vaneaxial fan			翼式轴流风扇
modulation *	[mɔdju'leiʃən]	n.	调节器
static *	['stætik]	a.	静止的，静态的
fluctuate *	['flʌktjueit]	v.	波动，起伏

Notes

①In the bad news department …, not all of which … to control. 句中 bad news 是麻烦的事情；department 是领域；not all of which …是代词＋介词＋关系代词引出的非限制性定语从句，which 代的是 problems。

②Let's see … 句中 what it's like 是 see 的宾语；like 是介词：像…。

③as versatile and powerful as VAV systems might be＝although VAV systems might be versatile and powerful。

Exercises

Reading Comprehension

Ⅰ. Say whether the following statements are True (T) or False (F) according to the text.

1. In addition to helping to solve energy problems, variable air volume systems can save

20% to 30% in building energy costs, compared with conventional constant air volume systems. ( )

2. VAV systems are easily changeable to suit new conditions in zoning and can easily be expanded or contracted, rearranged, or partly stop working without affecting the central equipment. ( )

3. In the past years there have been many problems in the bad news department since conceiving and starting of VAV systems, all of which have been 100% resolved or are very easy to control. ( )

4. VAV systems have always operated entirely correctly over the past decade as versatile and powerful as they might be. ( )

5. VAV systems are the most promising, powerful and versatile type of HVAC systems available today. ( )

II. Skim through the last paragraph and complete the following table.

	Problems Resolved in Last Decade
1)	Fan volume modulation ( ).
2)	DDC controls allow for ( ).
3)	( ) of individual terminals.
4)	( ) required on VAV terminals.
5)	Inverters used to ( ).
6)	Computerized static regain design of ductwork to lessen ( ).
7)	( ) of VAV system.
8)	( ) and balancing.
9)	More effective locations and settings of ductwork static pressure sensors ( ).
10)	More effective settings of and actual control of ( ).

III. Fill in the blanks with the information given in the text.

1. It is an exciting research that knows no limit in the application of VAV systems and is limited _____.

2. VAV systems can also cut down first costs _____ such as fans, pumps, boilers, chillers and less costly ductwork and piping distribution systems.

3. For an example of the kinds of problems the HVAC industry _____, just imagine what it is a new multi-story building like as you walk through building in which you have some business to transact.

4. The air noise from the ceiling diffuser overhead disturbs you and the jet or air blasts the toupee off your head. You struggle _____.

5. Ductwork rumbles and throbs. The building engineer worries about _____ on a vaneaxial fan.

Vocabulary

I. Fill in the blanks with the words and expressions given below. Change the forms if necessary.

> versatile, inception, blast, stagnant, conception, pull on, stifle, throb

1. He is a very _____ performer; he can act, sing, and play the piano.
2. At the moment of its _____ , every detail of a great musical work would be come clear in Mozart's mind.
3. How to put some life back into our _____ industry is the most urgent problem of our city.
4. I can hardly breathe in the _____ atmosphere of this room.
5. The house _____ the traces when getting up the hill.

II. Find the words in the text which almost mean the same as the following.

1. para. 5 conduct, carry through
2. para. 11 burst, flow out suddenly
3. para. 12 (of the heart, pulse, etc.) beat, esp beat more rapidly than usual
4. para. 12 make a deep, heavy, continuous sound
5. para. 14 move up and down

III. Now use the words you have found to complete the following sentences, Change the form if necessary.

1. Today is her special birthday. Her heart _____ with excitement.
2. With prices _____ so much, it's hard to plan a budget.
3. He tried to put on an appearance of booming business. He said he had _____ business with stores all over the country.
4. He can hear ductwork _____ , like distant thunder.
5. Oil _____ from the new well runs along the oil piping to the crude fractionating tower.

Writing   Summary Writing (3)

Directions: Read the text again and complete the summary of the text. You need to add about 100 words. This following is a part of the summary.

Summary:

VAV systems are the most promising and versatile type of HVAC systems available today. VAV systems, in addition to helping to solve energy problems, can save building energy cost, reduce first cost by using smaller equipment and provide beautiful comfort and excellent flexibility.

Reading Material A

Test Method of the Air Conditioning Plant

Test method

In general, to devise a suitable test, it is necessary to identify the variables upon which the output of the piece of equipment depends to obtain a simple mathematical relationship. ① If possible a linear relationship should be used and a statistical linear regression line calculated from the results. ②

This will be of the form:

$$y = a + bx$$

where y = the dependent variable

x = the independent variable

b = the slope of the line

a = the intercept on the y axis

Calculation of the regression line will usually be necessary, due to the scatter of the test results. The standard error (SE) of the estimate of y can also be calculated to enable confidence limits to be placed on the results.

In analyzing the overall performance it is necessary to break down the system into component parts. Consider the conventional air-conditioning system. The preheater and zone heaters are supplied from a hot water boiler, the cooler by a refrigeration plant and to investigate the complete system the following sub-systems would be considered:

-boiler capacity to satisfy total humidifying and heating loads;

-zone heater capacity to meet room heating loads;

-plant cooling capacity to meet room cooling loads;

-preheat and cooling section humidifying efficiency and cooling capacity to meet relative humidity requirements;

-refrigeration capacity to satisfy the total air conditioning cooling load.

Before testing commences checks should be made that plant items function correctly; a faulty control valve or ghost circulation, for instance, could invalidate a test.③ Instruments must, likewise, be accurate and calibrated where necessary. The technique is illustrated by considering the boiler and reheater loads. Boiler capacity and total heating load

Reference to a typical psychrometric diagram shows that the main independent variable, x, on which the heating load depends, is the difference between the supply and the outdoor air enthalpies.④ As the supply condition is relatively close to the room condition, an approximation for x could be achieved by using the difference between the room air and the outdoor air enthalpies. If the room condition is con-sidered to be constant then the independent variable can be taken as the outdoor air enthalpy. The use of this approximation makes data collection relatively simple.

The dependent variable, y, is the fuel consumption per unit time. To obtain valid data it is necessary to obtain time-averaged values of the outdoor air enthalpy over daily periods for two or three weeks during winter and spring/autumn; these results are plotted.

The confidence limits represent the band within which the boiler load will lie on 95% of days of a given outdoor air enthalpy.⑤ The band is due to effects of miscellaneous heat gains and to experimental error.

To investigate maximum zone cooling requirements, lines are extended to cut the summer design condition line. Individual conditions are plotted for days with continuous sunshine, these test results based on, say, one-hour periods with an appropriate allowance made for the thermal lag of the building. The results lie within the 95% confidence limit line which intercepts the summer design condition above the design supply temperature. It can be inferred that the air cooling capacity is satisfactory.

It will be observed that the plot of supply temperatures is similar to those obtained from theoretical load calculation. Since load and temperature diagrams are used for design analysis then it should be possible to verify them from test measurements.

Notes

①一般说来，要设计一个合适的实验，必须鉴别该设备输出所基于的变量以获得一个简单的数学关系式。variables：变量，mathematical relationship：数学关系式。
②regression line：(统计学)回归线。
③测试开始以前，应该检查设备各部分的功能是否正常，例如有毛病的控制阀或不正常的循环都会使测试无效。
④查一张有代表性的空气湿度图可以看出，决定供热荷载的主要的独立变量(x)是供气和室外空气焓之差。
⑤confidence limits：置信界限。

Reading Material B

Air Conditioning Water System Characteristics

System Characteristics

Closed water systems, including hot, chilled, and dualtemperature systems, can be categorized as follows:

CONSTANT-FLOW OR VARIABLE-FLOW. A constant-flow water system is a system for which the volume flow at any cross-sectional plane in the supply or return mains remains constant during the operating period.① Three-way mixing valves are used to modulate the water flow rates to the coils. In a variable-flow system, all or part of the volume flow varies when the system load changes during the operating period. Two-way valves are used to modulate the water flow rates to the coils or terminals.

DIRECT-RETURN OR REVERSE-RETURN. in a direct-return water system, the various branch piping circuits are not equal in length. Careful balance by means of throttling valves is often required to establish the design flow rates for a building loop when a direct-return distribution loop is used. In a reverse-return system, the piping lengths for each branch circuit, including the main and branch pipes are almost equal.

TWO-PIPE OR FOUR-PIPE.② In a dual-temperature water system, the water piping from the boiler or chiller to the coils and the terminals, or to various zones in a building, can be either a two-pipe system, with a supply main and a return main, or a four-pipe system, with a hot water supply main, a hot water return main, a chilled water supply main, and a chilled water return main.③ For a two-pipe system, it is impossible to heat and cool two different coils or terminals in the same zone simultaneously. Changeover from summer cooling-mode operation to winter heating-mode operation is required. A four-pipe system doesn't need changeover operation. Chilled and hot water can be supplied to the coils or terminals simultaneously. However, a four-pipe system requires a greater installation cost.

Changeover④

In a dual-temperature two-pipe system, changeover refers to when the operation of one zone or the entire water system in a building changes from heating mode to cooling mode, or vice versa.⑤ During changeover, the water supplied to the ter-minals changes from hot water to chilled water, or vice versa. The changeover temperature T_{co}, in ℉, is the outdoor temperature at which the space sensible cooling load can be absorbed and removed by the combined effects of the conditioned outdoor air, the primary air, and the space transmission and infiltration loss. Such a relationship can be expressed as

$$T_{co} = T_r - \frac{\Sigma Q_{ris} + \Sigma Q_{res} - KV_{so}(T_r - T_{so})}{q_{ti}}$$

$$K = 60 p_{so} c_{pa}$$

where T_r = space temperature, ℉

ΣQ_{ris} = sum of internal sensible loads from electric lights, occupants, appliances, and solar loads, Btu/h

ΣQ_{res} = sum of solar loads through building shell, Btu/h

V_{so}, ρ_{so} = volume flow rate and density of conditioned outdoor air, cfm

c_{pa} = specific heat of air, Btu/lb • ℉

T_{so} = supply temperature of outdoor air or primary air, ℉

q_{tl} = transmission and infiltration losses per 1℉ of outdoor-indoor temperature difference, Btu/h • ℉

Changeover usually takes from three to eight hours to complete. The greater the size of the water system, the longer the changeover period. In order to prevent more than one changeover per day, the changeover temperature T_{co} may have a tolerance of ±2℉.

Changeover may cause a sudden flow of a large amount of hot water into the chiller or of chilled water into the boiler. Such a rapid change of temperature imposes a thermal shock on the chiller or boiler and may damage the equipment. For chillers, the temperature of water entering the chiller should be no higher than 80℉ to prevent excessive refrigerant pressure in the evaporator. For boilers, a temperature control system bypasses most of the low-temperature water until the water temperature can gradually be increased.

Changeover may be performed either manually or automatically. Manual changeover is simple but may be inconvenient during periods when daily changeover is required. With sufficient safety controls, automatic changeover reduces the operating duties significantly. A compromise is a semiautomatic changeover system in which the changeover temperature is set by a manual switch.

Outdoor reset control is often used to vary the supply water temperature T_{ws}, in ℉, in response to the outdoor temperature T_0 for a hot water system. Typically, T_{ws} is 130℉ at the winter design temperature and drops linearly to 80℉ at the changeover temperature.

Notes

①恒定水流系统是在运行时供水管或回水管的任意截面上容积流量保持不变的系统。

②TWO-PIPE OR FOUR-PIPE：两管制或四管制。

③在双温水系统中，从锅炉或冷却器到盘管和末端装置或到建筑物的各个区的水管路可能是两管制系统（有一个供水干管和一个回水干管），也可能是四管制（有一个热水供水干管，一个热水回水干管，一个冷水供水干管和一个冷水回水干管）。

④Changeover：转换。

⑤在双温两管制系统中，转换是指建筑物的一个区域整个水系统的运行从加热方式向冷却方式改变，或者从冷却变成加热。mode：方式、工况。

UNIT TEN

Text   Horizontal-Return-Tubular Boilers

[1]   The HRT boiler consists of a cylindrical shell, today usually fusion-welded, with tubes of identical diameter running the length of the shell throughout the water space.① The space above the water level serves for steam separation and storage. A baffle plate (or dry pipe) is ordinarily provided near the steam outlet to obtain greater steam dryness.

[2]   The HRT boiler is simple in construction, has a fairly low first cost, and is a good steamer. It is more economical than the vertical tubular or locomotive types, but the scotch marine boiler is replacing it.② One disadvantage is that hard deposits of scale are difficult to remove from water surfaces of inner rows of tubes. Another disadvantage is the danger of burning the shell plates above the fire if thick scale or deposits of mud form on the waterside on these plates. But difficulty of cleaning scale from the tubes holds true for all other types of fire-tube boilers.

[3]   Blowdown connection: The blowdown pipe cannot be merely screwed into the shell, for there would not be a sufficient number of threads in contact to give proper support. Instead, a pad is riveted or welded to the bottom of the shell, and the blowdown pipe is screwed into this pad.

[4]   The minimum size of blowdown pipe for boilers over 10 horsepower (hp) (100 ft^2 of heating surface) should be 1 in. A minimum size of 3/4 in. is permitted by most states for boilers of less than this size. The maximum-size blowdown pipe in any case should be 5/2 in.

[5]   Feedwater inlet: The feedwater should enter through the upper part of the shell or front head, and it should discharge clear of any riveted seam or part of the boiler exposed to radiant heat or high temperatures.③

[6]   If the boiler is over 40-in. diameter, a manhole is provided above the tubes. Then the feed piping should enter through a boiler bushing. An internal feed pipe should discharge the water approximately three-fifths the length of the boiler from the hottest end—usually from the front—so that solids in the feedwater will not be precipitated onto the hot shell plate at the front, where overheating and damage might result.④

[7]   Circulation: The circulation of water in the HRT boiler at operating temperatures is as follows: The radiant heat of the fire on the shell causes the water to rise around each side of the shell; since the tube temperature is somewhat less, the water then returns downward between the tubes. Also, there is some difference in circulation at different longitudinal locations. The hot gases enter the rear ends of the tubes, and as the gases progress toward the front, some of the heat is absorbed by the boiler water. Although the temperature of the gases at the rear ends may be over 1000°F, the exit temperature at the

front end may be 500℉. Thus, the circulation in a longitudinal axis will tend to rise between the tubes at the rear of the boiler and to be downward at the front end.

[8] Rating: The conventional means of rating an HRT boiler is according to its heating surface. Most authorities accept the standard of 10 ft² of water heating surface per boiler horsepower. The water heating surface of this type of boiler is taken as one-half the area of the shell plus the total area of all tubes, based on their inside diameter, plus two-thirds the area of the rear tube sheet minus the aggregate area of the tube holes.

[9] Inspection: Because the shell is exposed to fire, an HRT boiler requires careful internal inspection for scale, bulging and blisters.

[10] During an inspection, some of the areas to check carefully on an HRT boiler are the following: Internally, on the section above the tubes, check for corrosion and pitting. Look for grooving on the knuckles of heads, shells, welds, rivets, and tubes. Check the seams for cracks, broken rivet heads, porosity, and any thinning near the water-line of the shell plate. Check all stays for soundness and proper tension. Examine the internal feed pipe for soundness and support, and see that it is not partially plugged. Check the openings to the water-column connections, safety valve, and pressure gauge for scale obstruction. Also check shell and tube surfaces for scale buildup. Follow the same procedure internally below the tubes. Then check the opening to the blowdown connections and make sure that the bottom of the shell is pitched toward blowdown and that it has no blisters or bulges.

[11] Externally, remove the plugs from the crosses of water-column connections and make sure they are free of scale. Examine the blowoff piping pad and the blowoff pipe to make sure it is protected from the fire, that the pipe is sound, and that the blowoff valves are in good order. ⑤ Examine tube ends and rivets or welds for cracks and weakening of the tube to the tube-sheet connection. Check for fire cracks around the circumferential seam and for leakage at the caulked edge. Then examine the setting and supports for soundness.

New Words and Expressions

horizontal [hɔri'zɔntl]	a.	卧式的
fusion ['fju:ʒən]	n.	熔化
baffle-plate ['bæflpleit]	n.	缓冲板,挡板
scale [skeil]	n.	水锈,锅垢
tubular ['tju:bjulə]	a.	管(状、型)的
blowdown ['bləu'daun]	n.	排污
screw * [skru:]	n.	螺旋
	vt.	拧(紧),旋
feed-water ['fi:dwɔ:tə]	n.	给(供)水
	a.	给(供)水的

manhole ['mænhəul]	n.	检查孔，入孔
bushing ['buʃiŋ]	n.	加固垫
rivet ['rivit]	v.	铆接
seam [siːm]	n.	缝
precipitate [pri'sipitit]	n.	沉淀
	v.	沉淀
longitudinal [lɔndʒi'tjuːdinl]	a.	纵向的
aggregate ['ægrigeit]	a.	集合的，合计的
bulging ['bʌldʒiŋ]	n.	膨胀，凸部
blister * ['blistə]	v.	鼓泡
corrosion [kə'rəuʒən]	n.	腐蚀
pit [pit]	n.	凹点
	vt.	使凹下，挖坑于
groove [gruːv]	vt.	开槽
knuckle * ['nʌkl]	n.	万向接头
porosity [pɔː'rɔsiti]	n.	气孔
blowoff ['bləu'ɔf]		排污
circumferential [sə'kʌmfə'renʃəl]	a.	圆周的
caulk [kɔːk]	vt.	填隙

Notes

①running the length of the shell：沿外壳的纵向长度。
②scotch marine boiler：苏格兰式船用锅炉。
③clear of any riveted seam：避开任何铆接的缝隙。
④An internal feed pipe …damage might result. 句中 three-fifths the length of the boiler from the hottest end—usually from the front 是地点状语修饰 discharge the water；so that 引出结果状语从句；where 引出非限制性定语从句修饰 at the front。
⑤… make sure … in good order 句中 make sure 后面跟了三个并列的宾语从句：it is protected from the fire，that the pipe is sound，and that the blowoff valves are in good order。

Exercises

Reading Comprehension

Ⅰ. Match Column A with Column B to see the circulation of the water and gas in the boiler.

A	B
1. The radiant heat of the fire on the shell causes	a. 1000 °F
2. The water then returns downward between the tubes	b. 500 °F
3. The temperature of the gasses at the rear ends may be over	c. water to rise around each side of the shell.
4. the exit temperature at the front end	d. since the tube temperature is somewhat less

Ⅱ. Fill in the chart with the information given in the text.

Advantages of the HRT boiler	
construction	1.
first cost	2.
a…steamer	3.

Ⅲ. Fill in the blanks with the information given in the text:

1. One of the two disadvantages of the HRT boiler is _____ .
2. The other is _____ .
3. The maximum-size of blowdown pipe should be _____ in.
4. The minimum size of blowdown pipe for boilers over 10 horsepower should be _____ in.
5. The result of the circulation in the longitudinal axis at the rear will tend to _____ .
6. The circulation in the longitudinal axis at the front will tend to be _____ .

Vocabulary

Ⅰ. Fill in the blanks with the words given below. Change the forms if necessary.

| blister porosity bulge knuckle caulk seam screw feed-water |

1. After brushing the house, Mr. James found some parts of the surface of the wall _____ .
2. The metal pin of the machine was loose, so the old worker _____ it with a screwdriver.
3. The sailor _____ the crack of the ship during the sail.
4. There is a small _____ in this type, so the air leaks out from it.
5. The best design of _____ and draining off water is essential in each construction of buildings.

Ⅱ. Find words in the text which mean almost the same as the following:

1. Para 1. mixing or being mixed as the result of melting

2. Para 3. fasten with a metal tin
3. Para 6. cause to be deposited in solid form from a solution
4. Para 7. running lengthwise
5. Para 8. total; amount to

Writing   Summary Writing (4)

Directions: Read the text of Unit Ten and write a summary of the text in about 200 words.

Reading Material A

Blueprints in the Fire

Selling coal-fired plant has never been more competitive. Customers demand innovative designs with the latest clean-burning techniques. The problem is they also want reliable, proven technology.

There are three major problems for designers of coal-fired boiler plant. Firstly they must resolve the conflict between repeating tried and tested ideas while at the same time introducing new concepts, improved materials and innovative technology. Their customers, the utility operators, want a boiler plant that is reliable, easily maintained and has a proven efficiency, with many working examples available for them to inspect. However, they do not want yesterday's designs.

It is a conflict which goes some way in explaining the slow but gradual devel-opment of coal-fired boiler design.

The second problem is the growing concern for the environment. This has become the principal issue of the Nineties and will continue to dominate design concepts.① Operators of coal-fired plant have been wrong-footed by the speed and depth of concern for environmental issues. The rush to retrofit pollution and emission control equipment to coal-fired stations only a few years old is proof of their unreadiness to meet today's environmental standards.

Designers can be forgiven for being cynical of their environmental concerns when they are asked to build in million-dollar pollution control equipment to satisfy the public's 'greenness' while power station managers will instruct staff to 'sootblow' at night so that local residents will not see the black mass squirted from the chimney stacks as the steam lances clean the deposits off the boiler tubes.

The third problem is of supply. With a glut of oil and a turn to gas on a scale never previously contemplated, it is difficult to see large scale coal-fired boilers being built even if there is a decline in nuclear power and cheap, open-cast coal available.② India and China are continuing to develop their coal-based industries and could keep the large-boiler manufacturers busy.

On going debates on the advantages of supercritical once through corner-fired or double reheat types of boilers all have there champions.③

Europe has seen a number of once-through supercritical boilers, in the 600 to 660MW range. built in the past few years. The inefficiencies of the obligatory fluegas desulphurisation plant need to be won back and improved steam conditions is one way of doing it.④

New materials are the key to improved steam conditions. It was less than 40 years ago when the largest turbine/boiler units being built were in the 60MW, 62bars at 482℃ range. Today, reheat boilers working at 250bars at 540/540℃ are installed and have been improved to double reheat versions with steam conditions going up to over 300bars as 580/580/580℃. Coal-fired plant efficiencies up to 46 per cent are now possible.

Steels used to construct boiler and high-pressure steam pipework comprise principally of carbon and low alloy steel for steam conditions up to 180bar/568℃. As the steam conditions increase the demands of the boiler and pipework material change. At 180bars/589℃ feritic steels are used. Steels with chemical compositions such as 9CrMoVnb and 12CrMoV continue to be developed and operating temperature increases of 650℃ will be possible. A boiler for a 660MW unit takes around 1035 tonnes of steel to put together but its expected life of 20 years can be drastically reduced merely operating it a few degrees over its designed temperature conditions.⑤

Notes

①Nineties: 90年代。
②随着石油的供过于求和以从未预料的规模转向使用燃气，即使在核能下降和可得到廉价的露天开采的煤的情况下，人们也往往难以看到生产大型燃煤锅炉。
③对于超临界，强制循环，角布置燃烧器或双再热型锅炉优点的辩论大有支持者。
④强制性的烟气脱硫装置的低效率必须得到弥补，而改善蒸汽条件则是弥补的一种方法。
⑤660MW的锅炉需要大约1035吨钢装到一起，但是运行时只要超过设计温度条件几度，20年的预计工作寿命就会下降。

Reading Material B

Coil Watertube Boilers

Coil boilers were developed to satisfy industry's need for a compact, fast-steaming, factory-assembled packaged boiler. They find special application where a process requires high-pressure steam in one part of the process flow and the capacities required are moderate. ① A packaged unit is placed where the load need exists, and this makes it unnecessary to operate large, centralized boilers at reduced capacity during periods of operation when other parts of the plant may have low demand. Several packaged boilers can be placed close to the steam loads of a plant at widely separate locations, thus avoiding long steam-line losses that may exist with a centralized steam plant. Coil-type boilers are used over packaged firetube types when high pressures and capacities may be required. Pressures up to 900 psi are possible with coil-type watertube boilers. Capacities generally are below 10000 lb/hr, but units of greater size are available.

The generating tubes of coil-type boilers consist of small-diameter helical, spiral, or horizontal coils of tubing. ② Some large units consist of a series of bundles connected to make a continuous coil. In case of a coil failure, the affected coil section need only be removed and connected to the remaining coil sections. Note the boiler uses forced circulation and forced recirculation, which permits smaller tubes to be used with high steam velocities and high heat-transfer rates.

The flow of water and steam in the system starts with water entering the feed-water section of the water pump with the water pumped directly to the steam accumulator. The feedwater rate is controlled by the water-level control, which in turn responds to the liquid-level control in the accumulator. The circulating liquid from the accumulator is then pumped to the heating coils of the boiler. Flow of liquid in the coils is downward through the coils spiral-wound in a counterflow direction to the combustion gases. When leaving the spiral generating section, the fluids pass through the ring thermostat and the helically wound waterwall section and then to the separating nozzle in the accumulator. The centrifugal action of the nozzle separates dry steam from the liquid and allows excess liquid to return to the lower section. The dry steam from the accumulator is discharged on top through the discharge valve.

Another design has three nests of coils and inlet and outlet headers. It is widely used in small sizes up to 300 hp and pressures to 250 psig.

Malfunctions in the loop may cause a coil failure from overheating. ③ This could come about from pump failure, partial blockage of inlet and outlet lines, blocked tubes (scale), fireside soot accumulation in concentrated heat zones, malfunction of controls, etc. Thus it is essential to keep both the waterside and fireside of the coils clean; proper feedwater treatment is vital. A pressure-differential chart is often used to show whether the difference between suction and discharge pressure on the recirculation pump exceeds a certain pressure differential. In a conventional boiler of multitube design, a leaky tube can be plugged, then the boiler operated until it is convenient to replace the affected tube. With a coil-type boiler, the entire coil must usually be replaced. All coil-type packaged boiler manufacturers supply excellent instruction manuals with their units which include maintenance and feedwater treatment sections as well as a description of the controls used. ④

Notes

① 盘管型锅炉发展起来是为了满足工业上对结构紧凑,产气快,工厂组装快装锅炉的需求。在生产过程的某一部分需要高压蒸汽和需出力适中的生产过程中有特殊用途。

② 盘管型锅炉的产汽管由小管径螺旋形的、螺旋上升的、或水平盘管组成。

③ 环路中的故障可能会引起盘管过热损坏。

④ 盘管型快装锅炉生产厂家常常为他们的产品提供很好的产品说明书,包括维护和锅炉用水处理以及对控制器的叙述。

UNIT ELEVEN

Text   Absorption Heat Pumps

1. Functions of Absorption Heat Pump

[1]   An absorption heat pump extracts heat from a low-temperature heat source, such as waste heat or surface water, and delivers its heat output at a higher temperature for winter heating or other applications at a coefficient of performance greater than 1.

[2]   In Japan and Sweden, absorption heat pumps have been installed in industrial and district heating plants using industrial waste heat to provide hot water, typically at 165 ℉, for winter heating or other purposes at a COP between 1.4 and 1.7.[1]

[3]   Absorption heat pumps can be used either for winter heating or for cooling in summer and heating in winter.

[4]   The coefficient of performance for cooling COPc for an absorption heat pump can be calculated. The coefficient of performance for heating for a two-stage absorption heat pump COP_{hp} can be calculated as

$$COP_{hp} = \frac{Q_{ab} + Q_{con}}{Q_{lg}}$$

where Q_{ab} = heat removed from the absorber, Btu/h

Q_{con} = heat removed from the condenser, Btu/h

Q_{lg} = heat input to first-stage generator, Btu/h

[5]   Several absorbants, or working fluids, other than aqueous LiBr solution are being developed, such as $LiBr/ZnCl_2$ and $LiBr/ZnBr_2/CH_3OH$.[2] $LiBr/H_2O$ is still the most widely used solution in absorption heat pumps.

2. Comparison Between Absorption and Vapor Compression Heat Pumps

[6]   Although the coefficient of performance for heating COP_{hp} for a centrifugal heat pump has a value between 4 and 4.5 and for an absorption heat pump it is only 1.3 to 1.7, electric energy used by a centrifugal machine is far more expensive than heat energy used by an absorption machine.

[7]   A life-cycle cost analysis should be performed during selection. When the ratio of cost per unit of electricity to natural gas is considered especially when demand charge, and higher electricity rates during peak hours are taken into account, absorption heat pumps may be more cost-effective in many locations.

3. Series-Connected Absorption Heat Pump

[8]   The series-connected absorption heat pump consists of two single-stage absorption heat pumps, each with an evaporator, absorber, generator, condenser, heat exchanger, and solution pump.

[9]   Liquid water refrigerant evaporates in the evaporator. Water vapor is extracted by

the concentrated solution in the absorber. The heat of absorption transferred to the hot water in the absorber is then used for district heating. The diluted solution is pumped from the absorber to the generator through the heat exchanger. In the generator, steam from the plant boils off the water vapor from the diluted solution. The boiled-off water vapor is extracted to the condenser and condensed into liquid form. Latent heat of condensation is again transferred to the district heating hot water.

[10]　　Concentrated solution from the generator flows to the absorber through the heat exchanger. Condensed liquid water enters the evaporator via a throttling orifice and is sprayed over the tube bundle in which flue gas cooling water flows from the plant.③ After absorbing the latent heat of vaporization from the flue gas cooling water, liquid water evaporates into water vapor in the evaporator.

[11]　　In the series-connected absorption heat pump, the first-stage absorption heat pump is operated at higher temperatures and the second-stage heat pump is operated at lower temperatures.

[12]　　During operation, the return hot water from district heating is heated from 144℉ to 152℉ in the absorber and condenser of the second-stage absorption heat pump, and from 152℉ to 160.5℉ in the absorber and condenser of the first-stage absorption heat pump. In the evaporator, heat is extracted from the lowtemperature heat source, the flue gas cooling water which enters the absorption heat pump at a temperature of 97.7℉ and leaves at a temperature of 75.2℉. The high-temperature heat source, steam, is supplied at 320℉ at a flow rate of 66,000 lb/h from the incineration plant. The average COP_{hp} for the series-connected absorption heat pump is about 1.6.

4. Operating Characteristics

[13]　　The absorption heat transformer operates at two pressure levels: high pressure, including the evaporator and absorber, and low pressure, including the generator and condenser.

[14]　　There are three temperature levels of input and output fluid streams:

• The fluid stream carrying the heat output from the absorber is at the highest temperature level.④

• The heat source (the waste heat input to the evaporator and generator) is at the intermediate temperature level.

• The condenser cooling water in the condenser is at the lowest temperature level.

[15]　　The purpose of an absorption heat transformer is to boost the temperature of the input waste heat fluid stream, and the function of an absorption heat pump is to attain a higher COP from the lower temperature heat source.

New Words and Expressions

absorption [əb'sɔːpʃən]　　　　　　　　*n.*　吸收

extract [iks'trækt]		vt.	提取
coefficient [kəui'fiʃənt]		n.	系数
absorbant * [əb'sɔːbənt]		n.	吸收剂
aqueous ['eikiəs]		a.	水的，水状的
centrifugal [sen'trifjugəl]		a.	离心的
		n.	离心机，离心
life-cycle		n.	整个使用周期
cost-effective		a.	划算的，经济的
series-connected		a.	串联的
refrigerant * [ri'fridʒərənt]		n.	制冷剂
concentrated * [kən'sentreitid]		a.	浓缩的
diluted [dai'ljuːtid]		a.	稀释的
boil off			汽化
latent ['leitənt]		a.	潜在的
latent heat			潜热
via [vai]		prep.	经过，通过
throttle ['θrɔtl]		vt.	节流
orifice ['ɔrifis]		n.	（管子等的）孔
spray * [sprei]		v.	喷射
tube bundle			管束
flue [fluː]		a.	烟道
flue gas		a.	烟气，废气
boost * [buːst]		vt.	升高，增加

Notes

①COP＝coefficient of performance：效能系数。
②other than＝besides：除了……，还……。
③…is sprayed over the tube bundle in which … 句中 in which 引出定语从句，which 的先行词是 the tube bundle。
④carrying the heat output …现在分词短语修饰 the fluid stream。

Exercises

Reading Comprehension

Ⅰ. Say whether the following statements are True (T) or False (F) according to the text, making use of the given paragraph reference number.

1. An absorption heat pump gets heat out from a high temperature heat source and delivers its heat output at a low-temperature for winter heating or other applications. (Para. 1)   (   )
2. A few absorbants except aqueous LiBr solution are being developed. (Para. 5) (   )
3. Heat energy used by an absorption machine is much cheaper than electric energy used by a centrifugal machine. (Para. 6)   (   )
4. A series-connected absorption heat pump is composed of an evaporator, ab-sorber, generator, condenser, heat exchanger, and solution pump. (Para. 8)   (   )
5. The absorption heat transformer operates at two pressure levels and at three temperature levels. (Para. 13, 14)   (   )

II. Skim through Series-Connected Absorption Heat Pump and complete the following table:

1	Liquid water refrigerant	evaporates	in the evaporator
2		is extracted	
3	The heat of absorption		
4			from the absorber to the generator
5			to the condenser

III. Fill in the blanks with the information given in operating characteristics:
1. The fluid stream carries the heat output from the absorber at _____ .
2. The condenser cools water in the condenser at _____ .
3. The waste heat is carried into the evaporator and generator at _____ .
4. The evaporator and the absorber operate at _____ .
5. The generator and the condenser operate at _____ .

Vocabulary

I. Fill in the blanks with the words and expressions given below. Change the forms if necessary.

extract, dilute, concentrated, boost, cost-effective, spray, boil-off, throttle

1. The temperature of the _____ solution in the heat exchanger starts to drop and may fall below the crystallization line.
2. The skin should _____ with insect repellent to discourage mosquitoes.
3. If the temperature of the cooling water is too low, the _____ solution temperature may fall low enough to reduce the temperature of the concentrated solution to the point of crystallization.
4. The vapor pressure of the concentrated solution during absorption should be slightly less than the evaporating pressure so that water vaporized in the evaporator can

_____ to the absorber.
5. Condensing pressure should be slightly lower than the _____ vapor pressure in the second-stage generator in order to extract the vapor and be condensed in the condenser.

II. Find the words in the text which almost mean the same as the following.
1. para 7: economical compared with money spent
2. para 10: by way of.
3. para 10: a number of articles fastened, tied, or wrapped together
4. para 10: present but not yet fully developed or visible
5. para 15: increase.

III. Now use the words you have found to complete the following sentences. Change the form if necessary
1. He is going from New York to California _____ the Panama Canal.
2. Taking into account higher electricity rates during peak hours, absorption heat pumps may be more _____.
3. The company has taken measures to _____ production by 15%.
4. _____ heat of vaporization is the primary factor that affects the heat input in an absorption chiller.
5. We collected a _____ of old clothes to be given to poor people.

Writing   Abstract Writing (1)

An abstract is a greatly condensed version of a writing. An abstract is different from a summary in that it is much shorter than a summary and so is called "summary of a summary". An abstract only lists the topics without supplying detailed information. Be sure to include the following items if there are any.
   a) The problems/processes/phenomena/mechanism involved or described;
   b) The scope of work;
   c) The significant findings or results;
   d) Major conclusions/recommendation.
Directions: The following is an abstract of Unit Eleven (No more than 100 words) and there are eight words missing. Please fill in the blanks with some of the words given. (12 words given. 8 blanks to be filled.)

economy, source, two-stage, districting functions, series-connected, vapour, pump, coefficient, characteristics, absorption, condenser

In the article, a brief introduction to _____ and applications of _____ heat pumps is made and the definition of the _____ of performance for a _____ absorption heat _____ is given. And a comparison between absorption and vapor compression heat pumps is also made in terms of _____. Moreover, the average coefficient of performance for the _____ absorption heat pump is obtained, according to the composition and actual operating principles of the absorption heat pumps. And the operating _____ for the absorption heat pump is introduced.

Reading Material A

Operating Characteristics and Design Considerations of the Refrigeration System

Difference Between Absorption and Centrifugal Chillers

In a vapor compression refrigeration system, compressor power input is primarilyaffected by head $(p_{con}-p_{ev})$ or temperature lift $(T_{con}-T_{ev})$ of the refrigeration cycle. In an absorption chiller, $(T_{con}-T_{ev})$ is also a factor that influences the heat input to the first-stage generator, but its influence is significantly smaller than that of centrifugal chillers.

For the two-stage direct-fired parallel-flow absorption chiller described in the text of Absorption Heat Pumps, the heat input to first-stage generator q_{lg} is distributed as follows:

heat input q_{lg}	9108Btu/h. ton	100 percent
Latent heat of vaporization h_{fg}	5422Btu/h. ton	60 percent
Heating of diluted solution	3686Btu/h. ton	40 percent

Latent heat of vaporization is the primary factor that affects the heat input in an absorption chiller and temperature difference $(T_{con}-T_{ev})$ has only a minor effect on h_{fg}. This is the primary difference between an absorption chiller and centrifugal chiller.

Evaporating Temperature

As in the centrifugal chiller, the evaporating temperature T_{ev} and pressure p_{ev} in an absorption chiller depend mainly on the chilled water temperature leaving the evaporator T_{el}. The difference $(T_{el}-T_{ev})$ in current absorption chiller design is about 5 °F. A smaller $(T_{el}-T_{ev})$ means a higher COP and a large heat transfer surface area in the evaporator. It is actually a compromise between energy cost and investment.

For a $T_{el}=44$ °F and a $(T_{el}-T_{ev})=5$ °F, the evaporating pressure is around 6 mm Hg abs (0.238 in. Hg abs).

The vapor pressure of the concentrated solution during absorption should be slightly less than the evaporating pressure p_{ev} so that water vaporized in the evaporator can be extracted to the absorber.

Both T_{ev} and T_{el} affect the refrigeration or cooling capacity of the absorption chiller as well as the heat input to the firststage generator.

Cooling Water Entering Temperature.

The temperature of cooling water entering the absorber T_{ca}, in °F, has the following effects on the performance of an absorption chiller:

- Lower T_{ca} means a higher cooling capacity.
- Lower T_{ca} results in a lower T_{con}.
- Lower T_{ca} means a lower heat input to the first-stage generator per ton of refrigeration produced and, therefore, a high COPc.
- At high load ratios, a too low T_{ca} may cause crystallization.

Manufacturer recommendations should be followed. For example, one manufacturer recommends that at design load, T_{ca} can be lowered to 75 $\mathrm{°F}$. At a load ratio $0.6 \leqslant LR < 0.85$, $T_{ca} \geqslant 65\,\mathrm{°F}$. When $0.1 < LR < 0.6$, $T_{ca} \geqslant 55\,\mathrm{°F}$.

Heat Removed from Absorber and Condenser

The total amount of heat to be removed from the absorber and condenser in a typical two-stage direct-fired parallel-flow absorption chiller is about 1.5 times the heat released from the condenser in a centrifugal chiller.[1] The heat to be removed in the absorber is about 70 percent of the total heat to be removed. Heat removed from the condenser is about 30 percent of total heat removal.

Usually, a cooling water temperature increase of 10 to 15 $\mathrm{°F}$ is used. For a cooling water temperature increase of 10 $\mathrm{°F}$ when the temperature entering the absorber is 85 $\mathrm{°F}$, the temperature of cooling water is about 92 $\mathrm{°F}$ entering the condenser and 95 $\mathrm{°F}$ leaving the condenser.

Condensing Temperature

Condensing temperature T_{con} depends mainly on the temperature of cooling water available and the heat transfer surface area. If cooling water is at 85 $\mathrm{°F}$, allowing for a temperature increase of 7 $\mathrm{°F}$ in the absorber and 3 $\mathrm{°F}$ in the condenser and a difference between the condensing temperature and cooling water temperature leaving the condenser $(T_{con} - T_{el}) = 5\,\mathrm{°F}$, condensing temperature T_{con} can then be calculated as[2]

$$T_{con} = 85 + 7 + 3 + 5 = 100\,\mathrm{°F}$$

Condensing pressure p_{con} should be slightly lower than the boiled-off vapor pressure in the second-stage generator in order to extract the vapor and be condensed in the condenser.

Corrosion Control

Lithium bromide is very corrosive. It attacks steel, copper, and copper alloys in the presence of air at temperatures above 300 $\mathrm{°F}$. Corrosion inhibitors should be used to protect the internal components against corrosive attacks, as specified by the manufacturer.

Selection of Absorption Chiller

When selecting a two-stage direct-fired parallel-flow absorption chiller, the chiller's refrigeration capacity must meet the required system refrigeration load.

Absorption chillers are rated under the following conditions:

Leaving chilled water temperature	44 $\mathrm{°F}$
Chilled water temperature increase	10 $\mathrm{°F}$
Entering cooling water temperature	85 $\mathrm{°F}$

Fouling factor $\qquad$ 0.00025h·ft²·℉/Btu

At design load, under operating conditions other than the standard rating conditions, both the refrigeration capacity and the heat input should be modified.③

Notes

① 从典型的双级直燃并联吸收式冷却器的吸收器和冷凝器中释放出的总热量大约是从离心式冷却器的冷凝器中释放出的热量的 1.5 倍。
② 如果冷却水在 85℉，吸收器内温度增加 7℉，冷凝器内温度增加 3℉，冷凝温度与离开冷凝器的冷却水的温度之差 $(T_{con}-T_{el})=5℉$，那么冷凝温度 T_{con} 可以计算为：$T_{con}=85+7+5+3=100℉$。
③ 在设计负荷，在非标准的额定工况下运行时，制冷量和热输入都应加以调整。

Reading Material B

Absorption Chiller Controls

Crystallization and Controls

In an absorption chiller using aqueous LiBr as the absorbant, the LiBr in a solution of constant concentration starts to crystallize when the solution temperature drops below the crystallization line on the equilibrium chart.① The crystals formed are pure LiBr salt. Crystallization does not harm the absorption chiller, but it eventually decreases the concentration of the remaining solution. It is also a symptom of malfunction, and the cause of crystallization must be determined before normal operation can resume.

Absorption chillers are now designed to operate in the region away from the crystallization line. There are also devices available that prevent crystallization and dissolve crystals if crystallization occurs. Crystallization is no longer a serious problem for currently designed absorption chillers, as it was before the energy crisis.

Causes of crystallization include the following:
• Air leaks into the system raise the evaporating temperature and the chilled water leaving temperature T_{el}. A higher T_{el} increases the heat input and the solution concentration to the point of crystallization.
• When the system is operated at full-load, if the temperature of the cooling water is too low, the diluted solution temperature may fall low enough to reduce the temperature of the concentrated solution to the point of crystallization.
• If the electric power is interrupted, the system ceases to operate. The temperature of the concentrated solution in the heat exchanger starts to drop, and may fall below the crystallization line.

Manufacturers have developed several devices to minimize the possibility of crystallization. One such device uses a bypass valve to permit refrigerant to flow to the concentrated solution line when conditions that can cause crystallization are detected by the sensor.② A newly developed microprocessor-based DDC panel uses measured temperatures and pressures at key points to calculate the concentration of the solution to prevent crystallization.

An overflow pipe is often used to carry the concentrated solution from the generator to the absorber in case of crystallization or other failures.

Cooling Water Temperature Control

Earlier absorption chiller designs required close control of the cooling water temperature to prevent crystallization. Current absorption chiller designs include control devices to prevent crystallization, so many manufacturers now allow the temperature of the cooling water to fall to 60°F at part-load, as when the load ratio is reduced to 0.6. A three-way mixing bypass valve should be installed to mix bypass recirculating water from the condenser and maintain the temperature of cooling water entering the absorber at or above a predetermined value at a certain load ratio.③ At high load ratios, lower cooling water entering temperatures may cause crystallization. Cooling tower fans can be cycled to supplement the bypass control.

Safety and Interlocking Controls

LOW TEMPERATURE CUT-OUT. If the temperature of refrigerant in the evaporator falls bellow a preset value, the DDC panel shuts down the absorption chiller to protect the evaporator from freezing. As soon as the refrigerant temperature rises above the limit the DDC panel starts the chiller again.

CHILLED-WATER FLOW SWITCH. When the mass flow rate of chilled water falls below a limit, a pressure-sensitive or flow-sensitive sensor alerts the DDC panel, which stops the absorption chiller.

COOLING-WATER FLOW SWITCH. When a drop in cooling water supply is detected by the pressure or flow-sensitive sensor, the DDC panel shuts down the absorption chiller. The chiller is started again only when the cooling water supply is reestablished.

HIGH-PRESSURE RELIEF. A high-pressure relief valve or similar device is often installed on the shell of the first-stage generator to prevent the maximum pressure in the system from exceeding a preset value.

DIRECT-FIRED SAFETY CONTROLS. A direct-fired absorption chiller needs controls of high-pressure and low-pressure switches, flame ignition, and monitoring for its burner and generator.

INTERLOCKED CONTROLS. Absorption chillers should be interlocked with chilled-water pumps, cooling-water pumps, and cooling-tower fans so that the absorption chiller starts only when these devices are in normal operation.

OPTIMIZING ON-OFF CONTROL. If multiple absorption chillers are installed in a chiller plant, as in a plant with multiple centrifugal chillers, optimizing controls can be used to turn the absorption chillers on and off.

Notes

①在使用液态溴化锂作为制冷剂的吸收式冷却器中，在等浓度溶液里的溴化锂在溶液温度下降到平衡图中结晶线以下时开始结晶。
②一个这样的装置是使用旁通阀，让制冷剂流到由传感器检测的能引起结晶条件的浓缩溶液位置。
③应当安装一个三通混合旁通阀以混合来自冷凝器的旁通再循环水，并且以某一负荷比率维持进入吸收器的冷却水温度为预定值或在预定值之上。

UNIT TWELVE

Text New Emphasis on Natural Gas Storage

[1]　The ability to store natural gas has always provided additional flexibility for customers and gas companies alike. But now, with federally mandated restructuring of the industry under Order 636, the availability of storage services has assumed greater importance, and demand by local utilities and other customers for contract storage services is rising.

[2]　As a result, interstate pipeline companies like ANR and CIG are storing larger volumes of gas under contract agreements to accommodate customers that want storage availability for spot-market gas purchases.

[3]　Moreover, storage performance has become increasingly important in recent years, according to Dave Dowhan , one of ANR's marketing directors. That's because local utilities, who make up the bulk of ANR's 29 firm-storage-service customers, experience fewer—but more severe—peak-demand days since their markets are now dominated by temperature-sensitive residential and commercial "core" customers. Most large industrial customers, who operate at a relatively flat demand-level throughout the year, are taking advantage of new industry rules by making their own gas supply arrangements, Dowhan notes.

[4]　The net effect is that ANR'S traditional storage withdrawal season, from Nov. 1 to March 31, has been compressed into a narrower time frame of about 70 days.

[5]　Against this backdrop, ANR in 1989 began examining ways the company could reap the maximum benefit from its extensive storage operations.① "Because of the changes taking place in the industry, we felt there was an emerging opportunity for us to become a profit center," Gentges recalls.

[6]　Gentges and his staff, including Nowaczewski and Mark Miron, another project geologist, began to scrutinize the performance of ANR's 15 Mchigan underground storage reservoirs, where up to 193 billion cubic feet of gas is stashed away in porous rock formations for withdrawal during peak demand periods.

[7]　As they reviewed years of well and storage-field performance data, they discovered that over their 40-plus years of service, some of ANR's older storage fields had lost a considerable amount of their withdrawal capability—the volume of gas that can be extracted from the reservoir during a 24-hour period. Gentges says the loss of withdrawal capability was caused by formation damage as a result of normal operation over the years.

[8]　To reverse the trend and restore storage capability, Gentges, Nowaczewski, Miron and Bob Scheid, manager of well maintenance and drilling, considered several options, including drilling more wells. One alternative was to expand the existing well-reconditioning

maintenance program.

[9] Storage gas is injected and withdrawn via hundreds of storage wells. Like others in the industry, ANY usually reconditions a certain number of these wells each year as a part of its regular maintenance program. Without reconditioning, over time, accumulated debris restricts gas flow and reduces the rate at which gas can be withdrawn from storage.

[10] "When we compared the cost and logistics of expanding our well-maintenance program with drilling additional gas well, we felt an infill drilling program—drilling between existing wells producing from the same reservoir—was the most economical way to go," explains Rick Gengtes.②

[11] Meanwhile, the Gas Research Institute (GRI) had published results of a gas storage-industry survey showing that 85 percent of the U.S. storage operators surveyed were losing an average of five percent of their deliverability each year. Restoring this lost deliverability was costing the industry a hefty price— $100 million annually.

[12] GRI recommended that storage operators consider horizontal drilling because, under the right conditions, it could be far more productive than conventional vertical wells.

[13] In July 1990, inspired in part by the GRI study, Gengtes and his staff hit the books, reading all they could find on horizontal drilling.

[14] "The technology has evolved a great deal in the past eight to 10 years—it's gone from an art to a science,"Gengtes says. "The biggest advance has been in the inertial guidance system that controls the drilling process. In essence, today's horizontal drilling contractors use military-grade technology similar to that used for guided missiles."

[15] A key part of the high-tech guidance system is located 38 feet behind the drill bit. As drilling progresses, this device sends electrical signals to a computer on the rig so the operator can adjust the angle and direction of the drill bit to stay on course. A "downhole" motor and stabilizers attached to the drill pipe provide power to the drill bit as it slides along a horizontal path 1,200 to 1,500 feet below the surface.③

[16] After meeting with horizontal-drilling consultants and contractors. Gengtes staff began preliminary studies, using a special computer model to help identify locations where horizontal drilling would provide the most benefit.

[17] Follow field inspections and further analysis, they decided to drill up to three experimental horizontal wells in ANR's Reed City and Lincoln storage fields in Michigan as part of a 25-well infill drilling program to restore lost deliverability in those fields.

[18] Gengtes and his staff spent the next several months climbing a steep learning curve. One of the many important details involved testing and selecting the correct drill bit for horizontal duty. After extensive testing, they at first settled on a natural diamond drill bit. A year later they found a man-made diamond bit more successful.

[19] On July 5.1991, after nearly two years of preparation, drilling began on the first horizontal well at Reed City. The first two wells were completed in 40 days and both tested successfully. The first had 840 feet of "open hole"; the second had 920—compared with

only 15 feet in a conventional vertical well.

New Worlds and Expressions

flexibility	[ˌfleksəˈbiliti]	n.	机动性，
mandated	[ˈmændeitid]	a.	命令的，下令的
restructuring	[ˈriːˈstrʌktʃəiŋ]	n.	调整
availability	[əˌveiləˈbiliti]	n.	存在，可得到，可获得
interstate *	[ˈintəsteit]	a.	州际的，州（与州之）间的
spot-market	[ˈspɔtmɑːkit]	n.	销售点
peak-demand		n.	需求高峰期
flat	[flæt]	a.	平坦的，平缓的
withdrawal	[wiðˈdrɔːəl]	n.	提取，回采
back-drop *	[ˈbækdrɔp]	n.	背景
reap *	[riːp]	v.	从……获得
scrutinize *	[ˈskruːtinaiz]	v.	仔细检查，核对
stash *	[stæʃ]	v.	储存；n. 储存处
option	[ˈɔpʃən]	n.	选择，任选项
inject	[inˈdʒekt]	v.	罐入
recondition	[rikənˈdiʃən]	v.	修理，检修
accumulate *	[əˈkjuːmjuleit]	v.	累积，存储
debris *	[ˈdebriː]	n.	岩屑
logistics *	[ləuˈdʒistiks]	n.	后勤工作，后勤学
infill	[inˈfil]	n.	补充
deliverability	[diˌlivəiˈbiliti]	n.	供应能力
hefty *	[ˈhefti]	a.	异常大的，很高的
hit	[hit]	v.	查到，偶然找到
inertial *	[iˈnəːʃiəl]	a.	惯性的，惯量的
contractor	[kənˈtræktə]	n.	承包商
in essence			本质上，大体上
military-grade	[ˈmilitərigreid]	n.	军事级别的
rig	[rig]	vt.	安装
preliminary *	[priˈliminəri]	a.	前期的，预备的

Notes

①the company…storage operations 是 ways 的定语从句，中间省略了关系词。
②这里 to go：动词不定式作定语修饰 way。

③ "down-hole" moter: 下行钻孔电机。

Exercises

Reading Comprehension

Ⅰ. Say whether the following statements are True (T) or False (F) according to the text, making use of the given paragraph reference number

1. It is only for customers that storing natural gas provides additional flexibility. (para. 1)   (   )
2. Most large industrial customers who run at a high demand-level are taking advantage of new industry rules by making their own gas supply arrangements. (para. 3)
                                                                                    (   )
3. Against this backdrop, ANR in 1989 began examining ways the company could not get the minimum benefit from its extensive storage operations. (para. 5)   (   )
4. Today's horizontal drilling contractors use the same military-grade technology as it is used or guided missiles. (para. 14)   (   )
5. A "down-hole" motor and stabilizers attached to the drill pipe make it possible to provide power to the drill bit as it slides along a horizontal path 1,200 to 1,500 feet below the surface. (para. 15)   (   )

Ⅱ. Match Column A with Column B according to the text.

A	B
1. Contract storage is rising	a. because of the contract agree-ment
2. The storage availability for spot-marked gas purchases are wanted	b. because of the changes taking place in the industry
3. The loss of with-drawal capability was caused	c. because it is demanded by local utilities and other customers
4. Horizontal drilling could be far more productive than conventional vertical wells	d. because of the formation damage of normal operation
5. The company felt there was an emerging opportunity for it to become a profit center	e. if it is under right conditions

Vocabulary

Ⅰ. Complete the following sentences with the words listed below.

inertial   interstate   reap   from   scrutinize   stash   logistics   debris   hefty

1. The company _____ a lot of profits _____ its extensive storage operations.
2. The quality inspector _____ the final products.
3. The corn _____ in the cornloft (谷仓) after the cropping.
4. The accumulated _____ restricts gas flow and reduces the rate at which gas can be withdrawn from storage.
5. It is in the _____ guidance system which controls the drilling process that the technology of drilling has evolved a great deal in the past eight to 10 years.

II. Find words in the text which mean approximate the same as the following.
 1. para. 1. easiness of changing to suit new condition
 2. para. 8. right or power of choosing
 3. para. 9. fill sth with gas or liquid by driving or forcing
 4. para. 9. put into good condition again
 5. para. 11. ability of delivering

III. Now use the words you have found to complete the following sentences. Change the form if necessary.
 1. Eighty-five percent of the U. S. storage operators surveyed were losing an average of five percent of their _____ each year.
 2. There are three _____ open to us in this situation.
 3. The car with a _____ engine runs as fast as usual.
 4. Storage gas _____ and withdrawn via hundreds of storage wells.
 5. The company has always provided additional _____ with storage of natural gas for customers.

Writing   Abstract Writing (2)

Directions: The following is an abstract of the text of Unit Twelve and there are 8 words missing. Please fill in the blanks with the words found from the text or with your own words.

 This paper, starting from analysing operations of ANR-an interstate __1.__ company, gives a description both of __2.__ and __3.__ of natural gas and the loss of withdrawal __4.__ existing for years, presents results in economy from the __5.__ between the two methods to solve the above mentioned problems (e. g. the __6.__ of new wells and the __7.__ of old wells). This paper emphatically proposes a new drilling method—to drill __8.__ —which is likely to raise the output and gives more detailed descriptions of (1) the progress of the method, (2) cruxes of technology (3) the way to carry out the scheme and (4) the process to success.

Reading Material A

SCADA Cuts Pipeline①

If your pipeline operations data communications cost more than you'd like, you may want to look at a new Supervisory Control and Data Acquisition system used at Big There Industries. ② Although the system is used for their industrial gases operations, the same cost-saving principles apply to our operations as well.

Big Three Industries decided on the system when they watched their annual data communica-tions phone bill hit $350,000. There had to be a better way to link people and processes together across their 1,500-mi.-long pipeline delivery system. ③ The expandability of satellite technology made it especially attractive, but start-up costs were too high until Big Three discovered innovative ways to use satellite communications to not only reduce their costs of operations, but also to increase efficiency, and, most importantly, to improve their ability to respond to their customers.

Big Three Industries is an American subsidiary of L'Air Liquide of France, the world's leading and largest supplier of industrial gases. At Big Three, air is put through a process that produces pure oxygen, nitrogen, and other gases. Many customers take deliveries via Big Three's Gulf Coast and Mississippi River Pipeline Systems which stretch from Corpus Christi, Texas, to Lake Charles, Louisiana, and from New Orleans to Baton Rouge. ④ Other customers take deliveries in tanks delivered by rail or truck, and several large isolated customers like NASA and the U. S. Air Force facilities at Cape Kennedy and Texas Eastman's Longview plant are served by stand-alone Big Three plants. Big Three wanted to be able to watch every production facility and the entire distribution system from their head-quarters. They also wanted to improve the monitoring and control of processes at each plant.

SCADA communications

As a result, Big Three designed, procured, and installed components for a new SCADA system. Big Three chose GTE's Spacenet system which uses the 7-yr.-old K-Band GSTAR Ⅱ satellite. At up to 56,000 baud the satellite directs data transmissions between VSAT earth stations installed at 12 Big Three processing plants and the dish at Big Three headquarters. ⑤

The satellite system features a standard X.25 network protocol to support fully-distributed operations. ⑥ The SCADA Master Station is located at Big Three's corporate headquarters in Houston. Supplied by Amocams/Modular, Inc., it consists of a pair of Model 4000 DEC VAX station computers running A/MI's ADACS software in a hot standby configuration. ⑦ The master station is networked to a number of A/MI's personal computer based winTerm operator stations located in offices throughout the headquarters. It is through these operator stations that employees access the SCADA database. Operator stations in the headquarters are used by management, marketers, engineers, and others, to view system data in real-time, historical, and simulation modes. ⑧ Because winTerm operator stations run under DOS and MS-Windows, raw and trended data from the master station database can be imported through the network by these personnel for use in standard desktop PC spreadsheets, word processors, and database software. ⑨

Control Room personnel use side-by-side winTerm operator stations to monitor nearly 15,000 system variables through morn than 500 screens of high resolution computer graphics representing remote sites, coastline maps, piping diagrams, and data tables. Around the clock, operators in the control room watch for system anomalies, direct inter-plant traffic, update delivery schedules, confer with customers on the telephone, dispatch maintenance crews, and perform many other tasks. The computer database includes a Current Customer file which helps operators ensure that flow rates and product quality conform to customer expectations. Ethernet cables provide an SNA link to Big Three's existing corporate computer, which automatically integrates custody transfer quality flow data from the SCADA system database into its billing applications. The business computer system has its own direct satellite link to other facilities' business computers, as well.

Sub-masters

To date, 12 Big Three processing plant sites have their own sub-master stations enabling plant operators to monitor and control as 2,000 local process variables. These sub-masters consist of Model 3100 DEC VAX station computers running ADACS software. ⑩ They have three basic purposes: 1) maintain constant satellite communications with headquarters in order to keep the master station database current; 2) support local PC-based winTerm operator stations from which plant operators can call up to 100 computer screens to monitor local processes; and 3) maintain continuous radio and wireline communications with a local group of flow measurement devices and remote terminal units that monitor local process variables, and the status of the control room and switch gear. The flow computers perform custody transfer flow measurements at customer locations along the pipeline. Pipeline control functions can be initiated by an operator locally via a plant sub-master or by an operator at the Houston master stations via the satellite link. ⑪

Notes

①SCADA＝Supervisory Control and Data Acquisition (System)；监控和数据探测（系统）消减了管道（操作数据通讯的成本）。
②Big Three Industries 是法国 Air Liquide 设在美国的一家公司。
③在跨越 1500 英里长的管道输送系统中必须有一种更好的办法把人和工艺过程联系起来。
④很多客户通过 Big Three 的海湾海岸和密西西比河的管道系统得到燃气，这个管道系统从得克萨斯州的 Corpus Christi 延伸到路易斯安那州的 Lake Charles，从新奥尔良到 Ba-

ton Ronge。

⑤这个卫星以56000波特安装在12 Big Three加工厂的VSAT地面站和Big Three总部的抛物面天线之间进行数据资料传输。

⑥X.25 network protocol：一种计算机通讯语言。

⑦Amocans/Modulor, Inc.：一家公司，简称A/MI；hot standby configuration：随时可用的备用装置。

⑧… in real-time, historical, and simulation modes…，用真实的、历史的和模型的模式…。

⑨因为win Term工作站在DOS和MS-Windows下运行，自主控站数据库由员工输入的原始数据和趋势数据能通过网络标准台式PC机的扩展芯片、文字处理程序和数据库软件处理。

⑩这些辅助控制站是由使用ADACS软件运行的3100型DEC VAX station计算机组成的。

⑪管道控制功能是由现场操作员通过分控站或在休斯顿主控站的操作员通过卫星通讯而实现的。

Reading Material B

Flow Measurement up Grade Enables Cost-effective Monitoring

By installing low-cost programmable logic controllers (PLCs) to provide communications for older flow computers, Peoples Gas System, Inc., Tampa, Fla, has upgraded numerous electronic flow measurement (EFM) sites throughout the state.①

The sites now can collect and store near real-time data for a company-wide supervisory control and acquisition (SCADA) system placed online in October.②

Peoples is Florida's largest natural gas distributor with 11 service divisions in most major metropolitan areas.

GOFR. The new SCADA system, called Gas Online Flow Reporting (GOFR), helps Peoples comply with FERC Order 636 by permitting large customers to purchase gas directly from pro-ducers and to transport it through transmission and local distribution lines to the user's site.③

GOFR enables Peoples to continuously monitor how much gas is entering service areas and how much is being consumed by the largest customers. Flow computers monitor 30 sites where gas enters service territories and several large customers' facilities.

Cost-effective. Cost of the PLC communications interfaces is about one-sixth that of replacing the flow computers with newer models having data storage and serial communications capabilities. Further, the PLCs constitutes an open-systems solution that can be configured by company personnel. In the event a communication link fails, the PLCs can store data onsite for future retrieval. Finally, the PLCs can provide control outputs should that capability be desired in the future.

As an additional benefit from the new PLCs, Peoples has begun upgrading pressure monitoring stations, installing electronic pressure transducers and low-cost PLCs to replace chart recorders. The PLCs collect and store data and provide serial communications.

Pressure data subsequently are gathered by GOFR from division SCADA systems or, in operating divisions without SCADA, from the meter stations themselves for retransmission back to personal computers in those divisions. Engineering consultant for interfacing the PLCs to the flow computers and pressure monitoring sites was Curry Controls, Inc., Lakeland, Fla.④

Single package. The PLC added to each flow computer and pressure point site is a Modicon Micro 612 that combines a central processing unit and 16 discrete inputs, 12 discrete outputs, 4 analog inputs, and 2 analog outputs in a self-contained package measuring 5.6 in. high by 10 in. long by 3 in. deep.⑤ The PLC has 2,000 words of logic space, 1,820 words of data space, a scan time of 2.5 milliseconds/thousand words of logic, two Modbus serial/ASC II ports, and time-of-day clock.⑥

Flow computer outputs fed to the PLC are corrected flow, 4 to 20 mA or 1 to 5 V signal; corrected totalized flow, usually 1,000 scf/pulse; and one or two pressure points, 4 to 20 mA or 0 to 5 V signal.⑦ Raw data are stored in registers. GOFR polls the PLC every two minutes and data are uploaded, employing Modicon Modbus RS-232C serial protocol.⑧

Should communications failure occur, the PLC will store hourly totalized flow values. Space is sufficient to hold seven day's data.

Fiber optic links. Communications between the PLCs and the GOFR host largely are over a fiber optic, digital frame relay packet switched telephone network. A digital data service unit (DSU) connects to the PLC for electrical transmission at 56,000 bytes/second to the nearest fiber optic hub. Hubs are in major Florida cities. Fiber optic communication was desired because of its added security.

The system communicates with company divisions that have SCADA networks through the same fiber optic network. The divisional SCADA systems are Intel 486 personal computers operating under the Open Desktop. UNIX system with Access Point software.⑨

GOFR host computer, in the gas control office at Peoples' Tampa head-quarters, is an IBM RISC/6000 UNIX workstation running CIM/21 application software.⑩ The host converts raw data to engineering units.

Notes

①通过安装成本低的程序逻辑控制器来为陈旧的流量计算器提供通讯，罗里达塔蒙帕民用燃气系统有限公司已经使全州范围内的许多电子流量计量系统更新换代。

②这里…online… 指联机。
③FERC Order 636：参考本单元课文 2-3 行。
④研究程序逻辑控制器与流量计算机以及压力监测点连结的工程顾问是 Curry Controls, Inc.,（公司名称）Lakeland, Fla。
⑤… self-contained package measuring 5.6 in. high by 10 in. long by 3 in. deep. 5.6 英寸高、10 英寸长、3 英尺厚的整装的外壳。
⑥two Modbus serial/ASC Ⅱ ports Modbus 两个 serial/ASC Ⅱ 孔口。
⑦输入到可编程序逻辑控制器的流量计算机的输出值都是校正流量，对应 4—20mA 或 1—5V 信号；校正的累计流量通常是 1000 标准立方英尺/脉冲；一个或两个测压点，输出范围 4—20mA 或 0—5V 信号。
⑧Modicon Modbus RS-232c serial protocol：一种计算机通讯语言。
⑨分区的 SCADA 系统是 Open Desktop Unix 系统下，以 Access Point 软件运行的 Intel486 个人计算机。
⑩在罗里达塔蒙帕民用公司总部的燃气控制室中，GOFR 主机是一台 IBM RISC/6000 U-NIX 型工作台，运行的是 CIM/21 应用软件。

UNIT THIRTEEN

Text   Design of District Heating Networks

[1]   In this article I describe three computer programs, which can be applied both for the design of district heating networks and for more basic applications in the domestic and industrial heating field.

These are:
NO. 1 PIPELINE;
NO. 2 BURIED; and
NO. 3 CONDUIT.

[2]   Program PIPELINE

Program PIPELINE is designed to determine heat losses from either hot water or steam lines when suspended vertically or horizontally. Heat passes from the medium to the outside through the following layers:

(a) From the medium to the wall of the pipe and through it.

(b) From the outside layer through the series of insulation layers and;

(c) By convection to the outside air.

[3]   This program can, of course, be used successfully for any general application in factories, public buildings, etc. wherever there is a need to insulate steam or hot water lines, or indeed any chimney, flue pipe, or whatever. The program is of particular use in district heating applications where pipelines are run through railway tunnels, cellars, etc.[①]. The results from program PIPELINE are also needed for input into programs BURIED and CONDUIT.

[4]   Program BURIED

The problem of buried heating pipes has been studied both at the Swedish Building Research Station and at the German Grafeling Research Institute for Heat Transfer. The mathematics which has been developed for this at these institutes is quite daunting, and the author must confess that he found extreme difficulty in using it, even though he has reasonable university qualifications in mathematics.

[5]   For example, even the simplest of all systems, i.e., where a bare pipe with external diameter of d meters is buried at a depth of h meters in soil with a thermal conductivity of k W/mK, has to be expressed by the equation:

$$R_{(soil)} = 1/(2\pi k)\mathrm{arcosh}(2/hd)$$

where:

$$\mathrm{arcosh}\, x = \ln[x + (1-x^2)^{1/2}]$$

[6]   When more complex systems are envisaged, i.e., when insulated pipes are used, or when twin pipes are buried, each at a different temperature (flow and return mains of

a district heating system) the equations become much more complicated, bristling with lots of Naperian logarithms, tanh, more arcosh, etc.

[7]　As far as the pipelines and their insulation layers are concerned, the answers obtained are 100% reliable,[②]as the mathematics used is able to make allowances for all the various relationships involved. There is only one source of uncertainty, namely the thermal conductivity value of the soil. If this can be measured accurately the calculated results would match the experimental results absolutely. However, in practice, the thermal conductivity of soils varies over the year, depending upon how moist it is.

[8]　I have tired to solve this problem by introducing a special sub-routine into my BURIED program to determine the k-value of the soil in which the pipelines are being buried.

[9]　The soil is sub-divided into four types:
　(a) Sand and sandy soil;
　(b) Light clay;
　(c) Heavy clay;
　(d) Solid or loose rock.

If the computer is now given the approximate wetness of the first three types of soil and the density of the last type, it provides an approximate k-value for the soil which can be used in the calculations. Obviously the k-value is by no means completely accurate as the moisture content of soil varies according to the depth at which it is measured, and there are also wide variations on different days.

[10]　The program is able to deal with both insulated and uninsulated lines.

[11]　Program CONDUIT

Program CONDUIT as the name implies, deals with heat losses from pipelines laid in conduits.

[12]　Five different systems are envisaged:

　(a) Twin pipelines, consisting of a flow main and a return main laid in the insulation so as to remain freely suspended in air, within a circular buried conduit;

　(b) Similar twin insulated pipelines supported freely within a rectangular section buried conduit;

　(c) Twin insulated pipelines buried inside an insulating substance inside a circular cross-section conduit;

　(d) Twin uninsulated pipes buried in insulating substance inside a circular cross-section conduit;

　(e) Twin uninsulated pipes buried in rectangular trench in soil without a solid conduit. The last type comprises pipelines laid in loose fill. For each selection of conduit type the program provides the correct sub-routine and is able to work out a reliable answer.

appendix:

Full list of computer programs developed by author

1: U-VALUE⑧ (For all walls and roof structures).
2: DAMPNESS (Interstitial and surface condensation prevention in buildings).
3: SOLAR (solar heat ingress through glazed areas).
4: LIVING (heat losses and gains due to occupation).
5: FLOOR (perimeter and area heat losses).
6: WINDOW (U-values for various types under varying conditions).
7: TOTAL (calculation of average annual heat load).
8: ECONOMY (optimum insulation thickness and economics of multiple glazing).
9: HEATTRANS (heat exchangers of varying types).
10: PIPELING (heat losses from uninsulated and insulated hot lines).
11: BURIED (district heating and group heating heat losses).
12: CONDUIT (district heating and group heating heat losses).
13: WATERPIPE (head losses and pump load requirements).
14: REGRESSION (mathematical analysis of data to replace graph plotting).
15: STEAM (heat calculations for superheated and saturated steam).
16: FREEVENT (air change rates and heat losses).
17: GASPIPE (dimensioning of all types of gas and steam lines).
18: RADSIZE (dimensioning of radiators in building).
19: OILPIPE (heat losses for all lines carrying non-aqueous fluids).
20: RHLIMIT (maximum internal relative humidity without condensation).
21: CONDCURE (extra ventilation needed to avoid condensation).
22: SUNHEAT (Solar heat entering through walls, windows and roofs).
23: HEATPUMP (To assess the viability of such an installation).
24: COAL (To determine numerous parameters for coal fired furnace design).
25: OIL (To determine the combustion parameters of various grades of oil).
26: GAS (Combustion parameters of 19 different gases are studied).
27: VENTAIR (The ventilation requirements of public areas are calculated).
28: AIRCOND (Cooling loads and chiller capacities are determined).
29: AIRDUCT (Pressure losses in complex ventilation system).
30: DUCTSIZE (Dimensioning of hot and cold air ducting systems).
31: PIPESIZE (Dimensioning of pipelines carrying fluids).
32: OFFICE (Combined program including 2 functions: (a): Envelope addressing (b): Bank account).
33: HEATBAL package for complete assessment of thermal properties of a building

New Word and Expressions

cellar *   ['selə]   *n.*   地道
conduit *   ['kɔndit]   *n.*   导管

daunt *	[dɔːnt]	v.	吓倒；使胆怯
conductivity *	[kɔndʌk'tiviti]	n.	传热系数
envisage	[in'viʒən]	v.	想象
bristle *	['brisl]	v.	充满；被充满
logarithm	[lɔgəriθəm]	n.	对数
tanh=hyperbolic tangent		n.	双曲正切
Naperian logarithms			（那皮尔）自然对数
sub-routine	['sʌb'ruːtin]	n.	子程序
main *	[mein]	n.	总管道
glaze *	[gleiz]	v.	装（配）玻璃于
regression *	[ri'greʃən]	n.	退回
plotting	['plɔtiŋ]	n.	绘制
saturate	['sætʃəreit]	vt.	使饱和
freevent	['friːvənt]	n.	通风
non-aqueous	['nɔn'eikwiəs]	a.	非水的
parameter	[pə'ræmitə]	n.	参数，系数

Notes

①The program is of particular use in district heating applications where pipelines are run through railway tunnels, cellars, etc. where 引导的限定性定语从句修饰前面的 applications 这个词。
②answers obtained are 100% reliable; answers 后面省略了 which are。
③程序名。

Exercises

Reading Comprehension

Ⅰ. Match column A with column B according to the text.

A	B
1. Program PIPELINE	a) dealing with both the insulated and uninsulated lines buried in different situations.
2. Program CONDUIT	b) dealing with the heat losses from either hot water or steam lines when suspended vertically or horizontally.
3. Program BURIED	c) dealing with the heat losses form pipelines laid in conduits.

II. Fill in the chart with the indication of the letters present in the calculation in para5.

letter	indication
d	1)
h	2)
k	3)

III. Find out the three layers that the heat passes form the medium to the outside in the text.
1. From the medium to _____.
2. Form the outside layer through _____.
3. By _____.

IV. Write out the four types of the soil which determine the k value in the program:
1. _____.
2. _____.
3. _____.
4. _____.

vocabulary

I. Fill in the following blanks with the words given bellow.

bristle conduit daunt glaze regression main flue cellar

1. Since the _____ area of it is very large, the hall is very bright.
2. The big forest _____ with so many wild flowers and bushes.
3. Usually a brave man can't be _____ by the difficulties he meets in front of him.
4. Something wrong with the flow of the gas in the _____, so it should be checked carefully.
5. Have you seen the buried _____ pipe in the soil?

II. Find words in the text which mean almost the same as the following:
1. para 6. picture in the mind esp. under a particular aspect.
2. para 6. a figure that shows how many times a number must be multiplied together to produce a given number.
3. para. 7. conducting power of specified material
4. para 12. cause one substance to absorb the greatest possible amount of another.
5. para. 12. the divided sections of the main computer program.

III. Now use the words you have found to complete the following sentences. Change the forms if necessary.
1. The _____ solution in the bottle doesn't precipitate after five hours.
2. The engineers _____ some targets in the program.

3. There are two _____ being used in this equation of mathematics.
4. The electrical _____ is so strong in this product that you can't touch it with your hand.
5. The main computer program has thirty-two _____ which can be used individually in this text.

Writing Abstract Writing (3)

Directions: Read the text of Unit Thirteen again and write an abstract of the text using the words and phrases given below. (list some key words and sentence pattern)
heat transmission, heat losses, district heating networks, package subroutines, program design thermal conductivity, effect

Reading Material A

Pipe Sizing for Steam Heating Systems

Pressure losses in steam piping for flows of dry or nearly dry steam are governed by the equations in the section General Principles.① This section incorporates these principles with other information specific to steam systems.

Pipe Sizes

Determining pipe sizes for a given load in steam heating depends on the following principal factors:

1. The initial pressure and the total pressure drop that can be allowed between the source of supply and at the end of the return system.
2. The maximum velocity of steam allowable for quiet and dependable operation of the system, taking into consideration the direction of condensate flow.
3. The equivalent length of the run from the boiler or source of steam supply to the farthest heating unit.

Initial Pressure and Pressure Drop

Table 13-1 list pressure drops commonly used with corresponding initial steam pressures for sizing steam piping.

Theoretically, there are several factors to be considered such as initial pressure and pressure required at the end of the line, but it is most important that: (1) the total pressure drop does not exceed the initial gauge pressure of the system, and in actual practice it should never exceed one-half of the initial gauge pressure, (2) the pressure drop is not great enough to cause excessive velocities, (3) there is a constant initial pressure, except on systems specially designed for varying initial pressures, such as the subatmospheric, which normally operate under controlled partial vacuums and (4) the rise in water from pressure drop does not exceed the difference in level, for gravity return systems, between the lowest point on the steam main, the heating units or the dry-return and the boiler water line.[2]

Table 13-1　　　　　　　**Pressure Drops in Common Use for Sizing Steam Pipe***
（For Corresponding Initial Steam Pressures）

initial steam pressure, kPa	Pressure Drop, Pa/m	Total Pressure Drop in Steam Supply Piping, kPa
Subatmos, or vacuum return	30-60	7-14
101	7	0.4
108	30	0.4-1.7
115	30	3.5
135	60	10
170	115	20
205	225	30
310	450	35-70
445	450-1100	70-105
790	450-1100	105-170
1140	450-2300	170-210

* Equipment, control valves, and so forth must be selected based on delivered pressures.

Maximum Velocity

For quiet operation, steam velocity should be 40 to 60m/s with a maximum of 75 m/s. The lower the velocity, the quieter the system. When the condensate must flow against the steam, even in limited quantity, the velocity of the steam must not exceed limits above which (1) the disturbance between the steam and the counter-flowing water may produce objectionable sound, such as water hammer or (2) result in the retention of water in certain parts of the system until the steam flow is reduced sufficiently to permit the water to pass.

Pipe Sizing

The velocity at which these disturbances take place is a function of: (1) pipe size, whether the pipe runs horizontally or vertically, (2) pitch of the pipe if it runs horizontally, (3) the quantity of condensate flowing against the steam and (4) free-dom of the piping from water pockets that under certain conditions act as a restriction in pipe size.

Equivalent Length[3] of Run

All tables for the flow of steam in pipes, based on pressure drop, must allow for pipe friction, as well as for the resistance of fittings and valves. These resistances are generally stated in terms of straight pipe; i.e., a certain fitting produces a drop in pressure equivalent to the stated length of straight run of the same size of pipe.[4] In all pipe sizing tables in this chapter the *length of run* refers to the *equivalent length of run* as distinguished from the *actual length* of pipe.[5] A common and practical sizing method is to assume the length of run and to check this assumption after pipes are sized. For this purpose the length of run is usually assumed to be double the actual length of pipe.

Notes

①用于干燥蒸汽或近于干燥蒸汽流动的蒸汽管道中的压力损失受 General Principles 一节中的方程支配。
②（3）有一个不变的初始压力（专门设计有变化初始压力的系统除外）如大气压的，这样的系统一般是在控制的部分真空条件下运行。（4）对重力回水系统来说，压降引起的水位上升可超过蒸汽管道、采暖装置或单一回路管道最低点和锅炉水位线之差。
③Equivalent Length 当量长度。
④这些阻力一般要按直管来表达，即一定长度管道产生等于相同管径该长度直管的压降。
⑤actual length 实际长度。

Reading Material B

Hot and Chilled Water Pipe Sizing

The theoretical basis for calculating pressure drop in hot and chilled water piping is discussed in the previous section.

The Darcy-Weisbach equation with friction factors from the Moody chart or Colebrook equation (or alternatively, the Hazen-Williams equation) is fundamental to these calculations; however, charts calculated from these equations provide easy determination of pressure drops for specific fluids and pipe standards. ①In addition, tables of pressure drops can be found in Ref. 1 and 2.

Most tables and charts for water are calculated for properties at 15℃. Using these for hot water introduces some error, although the answers are conservative; i. e., cold water calculations overstate the pressure drop for hot water. Using 15℃ water charts for 90℃ water should not result in errors in Δp exceeding 20%.

Range of Usage of Pressure Drop Charts

General Design Range. The general range of pipe friction loss used for design of hydronic systems is between 100 and 400 Pa/m. A value of 250 Pa/m represents the mean to which most systems are designed. Wider ranges may be used in specific designs, if the precautions described below are considered.

Piping Noise. The designer should also consider velocity. Close loop hydronic system piping is generally sized below certain arbitrary upper limits, such as a velocity limit of 4 fps for 50 mm pipe and under, and a pressure drop limit of 1.2m/s per 400Pa/m for piping over 50mm dia. Velocities in excess of 1.2m/s can be used in piping of larger size. This limitation is generally accepted, although it is based on relatively inconclusive experience with noise in piping. It is apparent that water *velocity noise* is caused, not by water, but by free air, sharp pressure drops, turbu-lence, or a combination of these, which in turn cause cavitation or flashing of water into steam.② Therefore, it seems practical to use higher velocities if proper precautions are taken to eliminate air and turbulence.

Air Separation

Because piping noise can be caused by free air, the hydronic system must be equipped with air separation devices to minimize the amount of entrained air in the piping circuit. Air should be vented at the highest point of the system.

In the absence of such venting, air can be entrained in the water and carried to separation units at flow velocities of 0.5 to 0.6 m/s or more in pipe sizes 50 mm and under. Minimum velocities of 0.6 m/s are therefore recommended. For pipe sizes 50 mm and over, minimum velocities corresponding to a head loss of 75 kPa/m are normally used. Pay particular attention to maintenance of minimum velocities in the upper floors of high rise buildings when the air tends to come out of solution because of the reduced pressures. Higher velocities should be used in *down-comer* return mains feeding into air separation units located in the basement.③

Valve and Fitting Pressure Drop

Valve and fitting pressure drop can be listed in elbow equivalents, with an elbow being equivalent to a length of straight pipe.

Tee Fitting Pressure Drop. Pressure drop through pipe tees varies with flow through the branch.

Notes

①从莫迪图或柯列勃洛克方程（或者从哈森-威廉方程）得出的带有摩擦因子的达西-维兹勃克方程，对于这些计算是基本的，然而根据这些方程所计算出来的图表则很容易地确定给定流体和管子规格的压降。

②很清楚，水速噪声不是由水而是由游离气体、明显的压降、扰动或这些因素综合作用而引起。而这些又会引起气蚀或者水溅入蒸汽。

③在向地下室里的空气分离设备注水的下降回水干管中，应使用较高的速度。

UNIT FOURTEEN

Text Operation and Maintenance of the Airconditioning Plant

Hand-over and documentation

[1] Designers and contractors can help to ensure adequate maintenance by stressing its importance to the client. The client should be advised about the personnel required and provided with the requisite information for maintenance.

[2] For plant to continue working properly throughout its life it is necessary for the maintenance and operating staff to be familiar with the principles and methods of running the plant. In addition to a full set of record drawings, two manuals should be available, one for the operating staff (e.g. office manager, caretaker) and another for the maintenance staff. The former should describe such things as the design principles, the method of operation, details of alarms and safety precautions. The latter, larger service manual, should contain the information listed by BS 5720: 1979 and reproduced below.

List of documentation required for system maintenance engineer

-the designer's description of the installation, including simplified line flow and balance diagrams for the complete installation;

-as fitted installation drawings and the designer's operational instructions;[1]

-operation and maintenance instructions for equipment, manufacturer's spare parts lists and spare ordering instructions;

-schedules of electrical equipment;

-schedules of mechanical equipment;

-test results and test certificates as called for under the contract, including any insurance or statutory inspection authority certificate;

-copies of guarantee certificates for plant and equipment;

-list of keys, tools and spare parts that are handed over.

[3] British Standard 5720: 1979 provides further advice regarding the organization and content of maintenance manuals. These should be available in draft form for checking at the commissioning stage, in addition to as fitted drawings. This will assist those concerned in setting the plant to work efficiently and, at the same time, the manual can be revised to suit any operational changes that may have been necessary, before they are issued to the client.

[4] Before the plant is handed over, it is necessary that the staff responsible for operating the plant are given verbal instruction and demonstrations on the principles and operation of the systems.[2] Any such verbal instructions should be given in addition to the documentation.

Maintenance organization

[5]　Once the client has accepted an installation from the contractor, the maintenance of a plant of any complexity should be organized to ensure continued efficient operation of the plant, aiming to protect the capital investment at a minimum economic cost.

[6]　The basis of any planned maintenance scheme is a filing system whereby the checks and services to be carried out on any piece of plant come to light at the appropriate time. ③ This can be done by a card index system or by using a computer. When staff complete a piece of maintenance they ought to note down anything which they see to be in need of attention or likely to be in need of attention in the near future, such as a bearing running hot which would eventually fail. This enables the repair to be carried out at a convenient time, rather than in a period when everything seems to fail at once.

[7]　Contract maintenance by specialist firms is often used as an alternative to directly employed labour, either for a part or the whole of the service.

Frequency of servicing

[8]　Routine maintenance includes inspections, cleaning, water treatment, adjustment and overhaul. The frequency at which these should be made is normally given in the manufacturers'manuals but these are average values which are best modified by the actual site conditions and in the light of operating experience.

[9]　The frequency at which plant is serviced depends on the following:

-plant and system efficiency and hence efficient energy consumption;

-effect on reliability of service;

-routine maintenance costs;

-fault repair costs;

-safety inspection;

-hours of system operation.

[10]　As part of the routine maintenance inspections, standby and emergency plant must be checked but not necessarily brought on-line for long operating periods.

　　Following shut-downs for repairs and plant modifications it may be necessary to re-commission the system or part thereof, in which case the appropriate procedures should be followed. ④

　　It is particularly important to include insurance inspections of pressure vessels and the testing of fire alarms in routine maintenance.

Fault-finding

[11]　Fault-finding procedures may be included in the service manual. Though these procedures for individual plant items will often be available from manufacturers, they should also relate to the system in which the plant item is placed.

Maintenance support

[12]　In support of maintenance, it is recommended that consideration be given to the following:

-engineer's office;
-workshop with appropriate tools;
-equipment spare parts;
-maintenance materials;
-instruments;
-site tools.

New Words and Expressions

hand-over *	n.	移交，交接
documentation [ˌdɔkjumen'teiʃən]	n.	提供的文件；文件（或证书等的）提供；文件（或证书等的）利用
client ['klaiənt]	n.	委托人；买方，顾客
requisite ['rekwizit]	a.	需要的，必不可少的
	n.	必需品
caretaker * ['kɛəteikə]	n.	看管人
statutory * ['stætʃutri]	a.	法定的，规定的
comissioning * [kə'miʃəniŋ]	n.	试运转，使用
demonstration * ['deməns'treiʃən]	n.	示范
complexity [kɔmp'leksiti]	n.	复杂性，复杂的物
filing * [failiŋ]	n.	（文件的）整理汇集
filing system *		档案制度
whereby [hwɛə'bai]	ad.	由此，从而
come to light *		被人发现
note down *		记录下，摘下
overhand [əuvəhænd]	n.; vt.	大修，仔细检查
in the light of *		依据，按照
effect on *		操作
standby * ['stændbai]	n.	备用设备
	a.	备用的
on-line *	n.	（与主机）联机，在线，机内
modification [ˌmɔdifi'keiʃən]	n.	更改，改装，修改
thereof ['ðɛər'ɔf]	d.	它的，其
fault-finding *	n.a.	检查故障（的）

Notes

①as fitted (installation) drawing 安装图。
②It is necessary that … are given … two systems. 句中因necessary 的要求，从句中是虚

拟语气，应该是 be given。

③ ··· a filing system whereby the checks and service ··· at the appropriate time. 句中 whereby＝by which 是关系副词引出的定语从句修饰 a filing system；to be carried out on any piece of plant 动词不定式被动式短语作定语修饰 the checks and services。

④ Following shut downs ··· should be followed. 句中 thereof＝of that；of it，所以 part thereof＝part of the system；in which case 引出定语从句，which 这里是指 to recommission the system or part thereof。

Exercises

Reading Comprehension

Ⅰ. Say whether the following statements are True (T) or False (F) according to the text, making use of the given paragraph reference number.

1. For the airconditioning plant to go on working properly throughout its life it is necessary for the maintenance and operating staff to be familiar with the principles and methods of running the plant. (para. 2)   (   )
2. In addition to as fitted drawings, these maintenance manuals should be available in draft form for checking at the test running stage. (para. 3)   (   )
3. Before the plant is handed over, it is necessary that the staff responsible for operating the plant should only be given the documentation. (para. 4)   (   )
4. Any planned maintenance scheme is based on a filing system whereby the checks and services to be carried out on any piece of plant come to light. (para. 6)   (   )
5. As part of the routine maintenance inspections, it is necessary to check standby and emergency plant and bring them on-line for long operating periods. (para. 10)   (   )

Ⅱ. Skim through "Hand-over and documentation" and complete the following table.

	List of documentation required for system maintenance engineer
1.	the designer's description of the installation
2.	
3.	operation and maintenance instructions,
	and
	spare ordering instructions
4.	
5.	schedules of mechanical equipment
6.	
7.	copies of guarantee certificates
8.	

Ⅲ. Fill in the blanks with the information given in the text.

1. The client should provide the requisite information for maintenance. In addition to a full set of record drawings, two manuals should be available, one _____ and another _____ .
2. Once the client has accepted an installation from the contractor, the maintenance of a plant of any complexity should be organized to ensure continued efficient operation of the plant, aiming _____ .
3. When staff complete a piece of maintenance they _____ which they see to be in need of attention or likely to be in need of attention in the near future.
4. Specialist firms often use contract maintenance _____ , either for a part or the whole of the service.
5. It is especially important to include _____ and the testing of fire alarms in routine maintenance.

vocabulary

I. Fill in the blanks with the words and expressions given below. Change the forms if necessary.

| complexity | in the light of | requisite | overhaul |
| thereof | come to light | whereby | modification |

1. With some _____ your composition will do for the college paper.
2. Fresh air is the prime _____ of life.
3. Is there any way _____ he can be saved?
4. _____ the new evidence, it was decided to take the manufacturers to court.
5. How long will it take to _____ the airconditioning plant?

II. Find the words in the text which almost mean the same as the following:
1. para. 1: transfer
2. para. 2: fixed, required by statute
3. para. 6: become visible or known
4. para. 10: sth. that one may depend upon or use in an emergency
5. para. 10: of that; from that source

III. Now use the words you have found to complete the following sentences. Change the form if necessary.
1. In support of maintenance, it is recommended that consideration be given to emergency plant and _____ .
2. It has recently _____ that a second person was implicated in the affair.
3. The time had now come for a _____ of power. The outgoing Minister handed over his department to his successor.
4. Test results and test certificates include any insurance or _____ inspection au-

  thority certificate.
5. After repairs or plant modifications it may be necessary to re-commission the system or part _____, in which case the right procedures should be followed.

Writing Abstract Writing

Directions: Read the text of Unit Fourteen again and write an abstract of the text using the words and phrases given below. (key words and phrases)
maintenance, air-conditioning, designer, contractor, frequency of serving, fault-finding

Reading Material A

Design Factors Affecting Outdoor Air Quantity

  The underlying design of the HVAC system has a major impact on the OA quantity that can delivered to the building occupants[①]. For instance, in the late 1970s many buildings were designed and built with an overriding emphasis on energy conservation and minimization of first costs. Many buildings constructed at this time therefore have HVAC system that can provide only a constant, minimum OA quantity. In contrast, please note that there are also other buildings whose designers recognized the energy-saving potential of air economizers. The buildings with fixed minimum outdoor air control can either be without or with a return air fan. For systems without return fans, the outdoor air damper is interlocked to open only when the supply air fan operates. The actual OA quantity entering will be a function of the damper opening and the pressure difference between the mixed air plenum and the outdoors[②]. For buildings where there is not a direct provision for building relief, or exhaust at the AHU (air handling unit), the OA quantity entering the building will ultimately only be equal to the quantity of air leaving the building due to exhausts (such as for the bathrooms) and exfiltration less the infiltration at other locations.

  For buildings with fixed minimum outdoor air control with return fans, the situation becomes more complex because the outdoor air quantity, minimum or otherwise, also depends on the airflow difference between the supply and return fans, as well as the OA damper position, the other building exhausts, and amount of exfiltration and infiltration.

  Another design approach for controlling the OA quantity entering the HVAC equipment is called "economizer control", where the OA quantity can increase as a function of the outdoor air temperature and thereby provide "free cooling". There are two types of economizer systems: temperature economizer and enthalpy economizer. With temperature-based economizers, the OA quantity to be introduced is based on the dry-bulb, or sensible, temperature of the OA stream. Typically, this latter system operates with an outdoor air control regime based on achieving a constant mixed air temperature. In this control regime, if the outdoor air temperature is below a high-temperature limit, typically anywhere between 65 F and the temperature of the return air (RA) stream, the return, exhaust, and OA dampers modulate to maintain a mixed air temperature close to the desired delivery temperature for the building. There will, of course, be a temperature rise of a few degrees as the mixed air passes by the supply air fan, picks up heat from the fan motor, and becomes the supply air. When the outdoor air temperature exceeds the high-temperature limit setpoint, the OA damper reverts to its fixed minimum position and the return air damper goes to full open[3].

Example 14-1. For a HVAC system operating with a return air temperature of 75 F an economizer high-temperature limit of 75 F, a minimum outdoor setting of 20%, and a mixed air goal of 58 F, the resulting relationship that can be expected to exist between the outdoor air temperature and the percentage of outdoor air is presented in Table 14-1.

Table 14-1   Estimate of % OA as a Function of Outdoor Air Temperature

Outdoor Air Temperature F	%OA
>75	20
70	100
65	100
60	100
55	85
50	68
45	57
40	49
35	43
30	38
25	34
20	31
15	28
10	26
5	24
0	23

As can be observed from the data in Table 14-1, economizer controls have the dual advantage of being able to help maintain good indoor air quality and minimize energy costs at the same time.

When evaluating buildings with economizer capability, the OA quantity entering the HVAC equipment can therefore vary during the day as the outdoor air conditions change. Therefore, to maximize the usefulness of the IAQ evaluation data, it is recommended that the controls of the system be overridden or reset to achieve the minimum outdoor air conditions even when they might not otherwise be expected to occur. One way of achieving the minimum outdoor air condition would be to reset the economizer high-temperature sensor/controller to a set point below the outdoor air temperature. The results will then indicate a "worst case" condition for the building, as opposed to a condition that can merely be described as typical or even "those conditions that existed on the day of testing". This situation is a perfect example of the need to understand the operating conditions of the HVAC systems before IAQ measurements are taken.

Notes

①暖通空调系统的基础设计对供给建筑物居住者的室外风量产生主要影响。OA：outdoor Air。

②对于没有回风风机的系统来说，室外空气风门被联锁，只有在送风风机运行时才打开。实际的室外进风量将是风门孔口和混流空气室和室外空气压力差的函数。

③当室外空气温度超出高温限定值时，室外空气风门回复到其固定的最小位置，而回风风门全部打开。setpoint：设定值，给定值。

Reading Material B

Methods of Varying Fan Volume

There are a number of different methods of varying fan volume in order to be proportional to the demand of the VAV terminals, to maintain proper duct pressure and to save energy.①

The only true way power can be saved in a VAV system is by a reduction in BHP requirements at the fan. This is achieved by reducing the volume of air flowing through the fan.

The amount of BHP savings are contingent on a number of factors-the method of fan volume control, the effectiveness of its application, fan performance curves, and the minimum amp draw of the motor.

Fan CFM's can be reduced in a number of ways: by riding the fan curve of a forward curve fan, with intake or discharge dampers, motor inverters, automatic variable pitch sheaves, and variable pitch vane axial fans.

When selecting a method of fan volume control, initial costs and the amount of savings are factors in the selection and evaluation.

Fan performance must be examined as to the CFM, SP, percent minimum/maximum flows desired, the maximum and minimum load efficiencies, partial loads stability, and the effect on fan sound loads.

Suitability of the method in terms of operation, maintenance and reliability must also be considered.

Methods of Varying Fan Volume
1. Riding the fan curve of a forward curve fan with terminal throttling.
2. Riding the fan curve on a forward curve fan with a discharge damper and terminal throttling.
3. Inlet vane dampers on air foil centrifugal fans

4. Motor inverters (variable frequency motor speed controllers)
5. Variable pitch vaneaxial fans
6. Variable pitch motor pulleys②
7. Two-speed eddy current coupling③
8. Automatic centrifugal fan wheel shroud
9. Fan bypass

Percent Horsepower Saved

The percent break horsepower saved varies with the type of fan volume control and the minimum BHP draw possible on the particular fan motor.

The motor inverter, which reduces motor and fan rpms, saves the highest percentage and is the most efficient. Second in line is a forward curve fan with inlet vanes. The method with the least savings, but nevertheless still of great value, is the backward incline centrifugal fan with a discharge damper. ④

Minimum Motor Amp Draws

There is a certain minimum amount of energy required to run a constant rpm motor at its rated speed regardless if there is an external load on the motor or not.

The higher the horsepower, the lower the minimum energy draw required. Motors from 20HP to 100HP generally can go down to 40% to 35% of full load amps. Motors in the range of 5HP to 20HP can generally reduce to 60% to 40% of full load amps. One to 5HP motors can reduce to around 60% to 80% and fractional HP motors save negligible amounts of energy.

If a centrifugal fan motor is only running at 50% of its load already, there would be very little if any energy savings made available on the motor by adding a fan volume control device, if the device is a constant rpm type such as a damper or riding the fan curve. ⑤ An inverter or some other method of reducing motor rpms would be required for further gain.

The closer the actual load on the motor is to the full load amps, the greater the potential savings with a fan volume controller.

Notes

①有若干变化风机流量的不同方法来与 VAV 终端需求匹配，以保持适当的管道压力和节能。
②可变间距的电机皮带轮。
③双速涡流联结器。eddy current：涡流。
④节能最少但是仍然具有很大价值的方法是带有排气风门的后倾离心式风机。
⑤如果离心式风机电机只是以 50% 负荷运行，那么增加一个流量控制装置，（如果这个装置是转速不变型的如风门或按风机曲线运行的）电机上能量的节约即使有也是极少的。

UNIT FIFTEEN

Text   Gas Gathering and Transport

I. Introduction

[1]   Natural gas produced from several wells in a given area is collected and brought to field separation and processing facilities via a system of pipes known as a gathering system. Processed or partially processed gas is then sent to the trunk lines that transport the gas to consumers. Gas is often distributed via pipeline grids that introduce a lot of complexity into the flow computations. This chapter briefly describes gathering systems and the transport of gas through pipeline networks, building upon the concepts for steady state flow through single pipe. Some basic elements of unsteady state gas flow, encountered quite often in pipeline practice, are introduced in another chapter.

II. Gathering Systems

[2]   The surface flow gathering system consists of the section of pipe and fittings that serve to transmit the produced fluid from the wellhead to the field treatment facilities (generally, the oil-water-gas separators). Production systems with extremely high capacity wells may provide individual separation, metering, and possibly treatment, facilities to each of the wells. Because these single well systems are seldom economical, it is quite common to design gathering and separation facilities that enable combined handling of several wellstreams.

[3]   The two basic types of gathering systems are radial, and axial. In the radial system, flowlines emanating from several different well-heads converge to a central point where facilities are located. Flowlines are usually terminated at a header, which is essentially a pipe large enough to handle the flow of all the flowlines. In the axial gathering system, several wells produce into a common flowline.

[4]   For large leases, these two basic systems are modified a little. The well-center gathering system uses a radial gathering philosophy at the local level for individual wells, as well as at the global level for groups of wells. ① The common-line or trunk-line gathering system uses an axial gathering scheme for the groups of wells that, in tarn, use a radial gathering scheme. The trunk-line gathering system is more applicable to relatively larger leases, and to cases where it is undesirable or impractical to build the field processing facilities at a central point. ②

[5]   It is obvious that very complex metering facilities are required to measure the production of individual wells simultaneously. Generally, a test header is used to route fluids from a single well through the metering system. This well test header also provides the means to control the production from individual wells and to conduct well tests on individual wells.

[6] The choice between the gathering systems is usually economic. The cost of the several small sections of pipe used in the well-center system is compared to the cost of a single large pipe for the trunk-line system. Technical feasibility may be another criterion. The gathering system may have to be buried a few feet beneath the surface, favoring one system over another in terms of cost and ease of maintenance.③ The production characteristics of the field are also important to consider. These include current and estimated future production distribution over the wells in the field, wellhead flowing pressures, future development of the field, and the possibility of the development of underground storage operations.

Ⅲ. Steady-State Flow in Simple Pipeline Systems

[7] The term "simple" is used here to indicate the gas pipeline systems that can be handled with minor modifications to the flow relationships presented in another chapter. The one feature for simplicity is that gas flows in at one end, and flows out at the other end; no flow occurs at any other point in the piping system. Such a scheme is often used for increasing the throughput of a pipeline while maintaining the same pressure and pressure drop (such as when new gas wells have been developed that must use the existing pipeline) or for operating a pipeline at a lower pressure (pressure-deration) while maintaining the same throughput. The latter may be required when the pipeline has "aged" or corroded.

[8] The three possible ways of handling these requirements are to replace a portion of the pipeline with a large one (pipelines in series), place one or more pipelines in parallel along the complete length of the existing line (pipelines in parallel), or place one or more pipelines in parallel only partially along the length of the existing line (series-parallel or looped lines). For each of these systems, relationships will be derived here, based upon the basic equation by Weymouth for steady-state flow of gas through pipes, that reduce the set of pipelines to a single pipeline that is equivalent to the set in terms of the pressure drop and flow capacity.

New Words and Expressions

computation [ˌkɔmpjuːˈteiʃən]	*n.*	计算
wellhead * [ˈwelhed]	*n.*	井口
meter * [ˈmiːtə]	*v.*	用表测量
wellstream * [ˈwelstriːm]	*n.*	井流量
radial [ˈreidjəl]	*a.*	径向的
axial [ˈæksiəl]	*a.*	轴的
emanate * [ˈeməneit]	*v.*	散发
converge [kənˈvəːdʒ]	*v.*	会聚
terminate [ˈtəːmineit]	*v.*	使结束
header [ˈhedə]	*n.*	集流管

flowline	['fləulain]	n.	管道
lease *	[li:s]	n.	出租（土地等）
well-center	['wel'sentə]	n.	气井中心
simultaneously	[ˌsiməl'teinjəsli]	ad.	同时发生地
route *	[ru:t]	v.	给…定线
trunk-line	['trʌŋklain]	n.	干线
deration *	[di:'ræʃən]	n.	减少
looped *	[lu:pt]	a.	环形的
corrode *	[kə'rəud]	v.	腐蚀
throughput	['θru:put]	n.	通过量

Notes

①a radial gathering philosophy 一种径向采集原理。

②The trunk-line gathering system is more applicable to relatively large leases, and to cases where it is undesirable or impractical to build the field processing facilities at a central point. 句中第一和第二个"to"都是介词，第三个"to"是动词不定式在从句子中做状语；where 引导的是定语从句修饰它前面的词 cases。

③in terms of：根据。

Exercises

Reading Comprehension

I. Fill in the gap with the information you have got from the text.

Production systems with extremely high capacity wells may provide individual separation, __1)__ , possible __2)__ , __3)__ to each of the wells. It is quite common to design __4)__ and separation facilities that enable __5)__ handling of several __6)__ .

For large leases, there are two basic system. One is the __7)__ gathering system which uses a __8)__ gathering philosophy at the local level to individual well, as well as at the globe level for groups of wells. The other is the __9)__ gathering system which uses an __10)__ gathering scheme for the groups of wells.

II. Find out the three possible ways of handling the requirement for steady-state flow in simple pipeline systems.

The first one is to __1)__ .

The second one is to __2)__ .

The third one is to __3)__ .

135

Vocabulary

Ⅰ. Fill in the blanks with the words given below. Change the forms if necessary.

| looped   trunk   emanate   route   meter   lease   deration   corrode |

1. Light and heat _____ from the sun.
2. The incorrect _____ string has thrown the toy off balance.
3. Salt water _____ the iron.
4. A pressure differential meter is used to _____ the volumes of electricity, water, ect.
5. I have a ten year _____ of this house.

Ⅱ. Find words in the text which mean approximately the same as the following.
1. Para. 3: of a straight line from the center of a circle or sphere to any point on the circumference
2. Para. 3: cause to come towards each other and meet at a point
3. Para. 3: put an end to
4. Para. 5 happening or done at the same time
5. Para. 7: an amount of material put through a process

Ⅲ. Now use the words you have found to complete the following sentences. Change the forms if necessary.
1. All the people in the auditorium burst into applause _____.
2. In the gas gathering system the gas flowlines usually _____ at a header.
3. All of the town _____ upon the election.
4. The pipeline with minor modifications can operate at a lower pressure while maintaining the same _____.
5. This new _____ drilling machine (旋臂钻机) saves more time than the old one when it works.

Writing   Abstract Writing

Directions: Read the text of Unit Fifteen again and write an abstract of the text in about 120 words.

　　The paper briefly describes _____
_____
_____
_____
_____
_____
_____

Reading Material A

Gas-Water Systems and Dehydration Processing

I. Introduction

Water vapor is the most common undesirable impurity found in natural gas. By virtue of its source, natural gas is almost associated with water, usually in the range of 400-500 lb water vapor/MMscf gas. The primary reason for the removal of water from gas is the problem of gas hydrate formation. Liquid water with natural gas may from solid, ice-like hydrates that plug flowlines and lead to sever operational problems. Other reasons for removing water are: (1) liquid water promotes corrosion, particularly in the presence of H_2S and CO_2; (2) slugging flow may result if liquid water condenses in the flowlines; and (3) water vapor reduces the heating value of the gas. For these reasons, pipeline specifications for natural gas restrict the water content to a value not greater than 6-8 lbm/MMscf.

Because most gas sweetening processes involve the use of an aqueous solution, dehydration is often done after desulfurization. Nevertheless, partial dehydration, or hydrate inhibition, are commonly necessary at the wellsite itself.

II. Water Content of Natural Gases

In order to design and operate dehydration processes, a reliable estimate of the water content of natural gas is essential. The water content of a gas depends upon:

1. Pressure—water content decreases with increasing pressure.
2. Temperature—water content increases with increasing temperature.
3. Salt content of the free water in equilibrium with the natural gas in the reservoir—water content decreases with increasing salt content of the associated reservoir water.[①]
4. Gas composition—higher gravity gases usually have less water.

The terms dew point and dew-point depression are widely used in dehydration terminology. Dew point indirectly indicates the water content of a natural gas, and is defined as the temperature at which the gas is saturated with water vapor at a given pressure. The difference between the dew-point temperature of a gas stream before and after dehydration is called the dew-point depression. Consider a gas saturated with water at 500 psia and 100℉. Its dew point is 100℉, and its water content is approximately 100 lbm/MMscf gas. The gas is to be transported in a pipeline at 60℉. Under pipeline conditions of 500 psia and 60℉, the water vapor content of the gas is only about 30 lbm/MMscf. Thus, 70 lb water per MMscf of gas exist as free water in the pipeline. If the dew point of the inlet gas to the pipeline is reduced to 60℉, no free water will exist in the pipeline at the pipeline flow conditions. In other words, the dehydration facility should give a dew point depression of 100−60=40℉. In practice, although a dew point depression of 40℉ is just sufficient, a 50℉ dew point depression may be desirable for operational safety.

The methods available for calculating the water content of natural gases fall into three categories: (1) partial pressure approach, valid up to about 60 psia (gases exhibit almost ideal behavior up to 60 psia in most cases); (2) empirical plots[2]; and (3) equations of state.

Ⅲ. Partial Pressure Approach

Assuming ideal gas and ideal mixture behavior, the partial pressure of water in the gas is given by $p_w = py_w$ and also by $p_w = p_v x_w$. Thus,

$$py_w = p_v x_w$$

where p = absolute pressure of the gas

y_w = mole fraction of water in the vapor (gas) phase

p_v = vapor pressure of water at the system temperature

x_w = mole fraction of water in the aqueous (liquid water) phase associated with the gas phase under equilibrium conditions

Since water is almost immiscible in the liquid phase with oil, x_w is usually as-sumed to be equal to unity. Thus, the water mole fraction in the gas, y_w, can be calculated as:

$$y_w = p_v/p$$

This simple approach has limited applicability at the pressure and temperature of interest in most natural gas production, processing and transport systems.

Ⅳ. Empirical Plots

For engineering calculations, empirical plots are widely used Numerous inves-tigations have resulted in several plots, such as by McGarthy et al. (1950), McKetta and Wehe (1958), the Gas Processors Suppliers Association (GPSA), Camp-bell (1984a), Robinson et al. (1978), and others. Since the real danger in design is to underestimate the water content, all correlations assume the gas to be completely saturated with water, and most correlations are designed to slightly overestimate the water content. Nitrogen holds about 6-9% less water than methane (Campbell, 1984a). Therefore, nitrogen is frequently included as a hydrocarbon, providing a small safety factor.[3]

Notes

①Salt content of the free water in equilibrium with the natural gas in the reservoir—water content decreases with increasing salt content of the associated reservoir water. 与容器中天然气相平衡的游离水含盐量——含水量随着相应容器中水的含盐量的增加而减少。

②empirical plots 按经验画的曲线。

③nitrogen is frequently included as a hydrocarbon, providing a small safety factor 氮常常

作为一种碳氢化合物被计入，提供了很小的安全系数。

Reading Material B

Gas and Liquid Separation

Ⅰ. Introduction

Only rarely does a reservoir yield almost pure natural gas.① Typically, a produced hydrocarbon stream is a complex mixture of several hydrocarbons, intimately mixed with water, in the liquid and gaseous states. Often, solids and other contaminants are also present. The produced stream may be unstable, with components undergoing rapid phase transitions as the stream is produced from a several hundred feet deep reservoir with a high temperature and pressure to surface conditions.② It is important to remove any solids and contaminants, and to separate the produced stream into water, oil, and gas, which are handled and transported separately. Gas and liquid separation operations involve the separation and stabilization of these phases into saleable products. Generally, intermediate hydrocarbons in the liquid state fetch a higher price;③ therefore, it is desirable to maximize liquid recovery.

Field processing of natural gas includes:
1. Gas and liquid separation operations to remove the free liquids-crude oil, hydro-carbon condensate, and water, and the entrained solids.
2. Recovery of condensable hydrocarbon vapors. Stage separation, or low temperature separation techniques are used.
3. Further cleaning of the gas and oil streams after separation.
4. Gas dehydration processing to remove from the gas condensable water vapor that may lead to the formation of hydrates under certain conditions.
5. Removal of contaminants or otherwise undesirable components, such as hydrogen sulfide and other corrosive sulfur compounds, and carbon dioxide.

This chapter describes gas-liquid separation and gas cleaning techniques.

Ⅱ. Separation Equipment

Separators operate basically upon the principle of pressure reduction to achieve separation of gas and liquid from an inlet stream. Further refinement of the gas and liquid streams is induced by allowing the liquid to "stand" for a period of time, so that any dissolved gas in the liquid can escape by the formation of small gas bubbles that rise to the liquid surface; and removing the entrained liquid mist from the gas by gravity settling, impingement, centrifugal action, and other means.④ Turbulent flow allows gas bubbles to escape more rapidly than laminar flow, and many separators therefore have sections where turbulence is induced for this purpose. On the other hand, for the removal of liquid droplets from the gas by gravity settling, turbulence is quite detrimental to removal efficiency. Thus, the design of a separator comprises different modules assembled to achieve different functions in a single vessel. Equilibrium is attained in the piping and equipment just upstream of the separators, the separator itself serving only as a "wide" spot in the line to refine the vapor and liquid streams resulting from this basic separation.⑤

To efficiently perform its separation functions, a well designed separator must:

1. Control and dissipate the energy of the wellstream as it enters the separator, and provide low enough gas and liquid velocities for proper gravity segregation and vapor-liquid equilibrium. For this purpose, a tangential inlet to impart centrifugal motion to the entering fluids is generally used.
2. Remove the bulk of the liquid from the gas in the primary separation section. It is desirable to quickly achieve good separation at this stage.
3. Have a large settling section, of sufficient volume to refine the primary separation by removing any entrained liquid from the gas, and handle any slugs of liquid (usually known as "liquid surges")
4. Minimize turbulence in the gas section of the separator to ensure proper settling.
5. Have a mist extractor (or eliminator) near the gas outlet to capture and coalesce the smaller liquid particles that could not be removed by gravity settling.
6. Control the accumulation of froths and foams in the vessel.
7. Prevent re-entrainment of the separation gas and liquid.⑥
8. Have proper control devices for controlling the back-pressure and the liquid level in the separator.
9. Provide reliable equipment for ensuring safe and efficient operations. This includes pressure gauges, thermometer, devices for indicating the liquid level, safety relief valves to prevent blowup in case the gas or liquid outlets are plugged, and liquid discharge ("dump") valves.

Notes

①只是在极为罕见的情况下,气池才产生几乎是纯的天然气。
②产生的气流可能是不稳定的,组成的成分经历着迅速的相变,因为气流是从几百英尺的深处产生的——对地表来说是高温和高压状态。
③intermediate hydrocarbons in the liquid state fetch higher price …,中间(馏分)的液态碳氢化合物售价较高…。
④对气体和液体的进一步精加工是通过以下方式实现的:使液体"停顿"一段时间;这样液体中任何未溶解的气体全由于小气泡的形成和上升到液体表面而逃逸;通过重力沉降、碰撞、离心作用和其他手段,从气体中除掉所挟带的液雾。
⑤平衡仅在分离器上游的管道系统和设备中实现。在输送管线中,分离器本身仅提供一个宽的场所来精制由该基本分离产生的汽和液流。
⑥Prevent re-entrainment of the separation gas and liquid. 防止已分离的气体和液体重新被挟带。

UNIT SIXTEEN

Text   The Volumetric Behavior of Natural Gases Containing Hydrogen Sulfide and Carbon Dioxide

Introduction

[1]　　Although a relatively accurate method for predicting compressibility factors of pure material is provided by charts based on reduced properties and the assumption that the compressibility factor is a unique function of T_r, P_r and v_{cr}, the determination of the correct values of compressibility factors for gas mixtures is somewhat difficult.

[2]　　Two general methods of dealing with gaseous mixtures have been proposed. The first assumes a direct or modified additivity of certain properties of the mixture in terms of the properties of the individual components. Examples of this method are based on the familiar laws of Dalton and Amagat.[①] The second method averages the constants of an equation of state applicable to the pure components. Both of these methods are of limited value in engineering calculations because the first usually provides reliable answers only over narrow ranges of pressure and temperature and the second is cumbersome to handle.

[3]　　In petroleum engineering practice accurate estimations of the volumetric behavior of natural gases are frequently required. To fulfill this need, several generalized compressibility charts have been developed. Of these, the one prepare by Standing, et al is widely used at present.[②] In the construction of charts of this type a third method for dealing with mixture has been followed. It is based on correlation of pseudo-critical properties as outlined by Kay and calculated from the critical properties of the individual components in a mixture. Although these charts provide relatively accurate information on the compressibility of dry or wet sweet natural gases, they are less reliable when used for gases containing high concentrations of hydrogen sulfide or carbon dioxide or both. Thus, an experimental program, although time consuming, is the best means now available for the determination of the volumetric behavior of sour or acid gas mixtures.

[4]　　An increased interest in the behavior of these gas mixtures, particularly in connection with some of the fields in Western Canada where the acid gas concentration of the reservoirs may be as high as 55 per cent and where hydrogen sulfide alone may be as high as 36 per cent, provided the incentive for this study. It was the purpose of the investigation to determine the volumetric behavior selected mixtures of methane, hydrogen sulfide and carbon dioxide over a range of temperature from 40 to 160 F and at pressures up to 3,000 psi.

Experimental Method

[5] The apparatus used in this investigation was basically the same as that described by Lorenzo. The amount of each pure component used in preparing the gas mixtures was measured over mercury in a glass-windowed pressure vessel. The pure components were then transferred individually in the desired amounts to a second glass-windowed pressure vessel where the volumetric behavior of the mixture was determined. Volume was varied by mercury injection or with drawl. The capacity of the cell was about 125 cc.

[6] Temperatures in the cells were measured with copper-constant an thermo-couples and a Leeds Northrup semi-precision potentiometer.[3] The temperature was held to within ± 0.5 °F of the desired value during the runs. Pressures above 1,000 psi were determined by a Heise bourdon tube gauge to ± 3 psi and below 1,000 psi by the same type of gauge to ± 1 psi. Both gauges were calibrated against a dead-weight piston gauge and were used with suitable calibration curves.

[7] A 100-cm cathetometer was used to measure the sample volume and determine the hydrostatic heads contributing to measured pressures. The reproducibility of length measurements was about 0.05 mm, corresponding to a precision in volume measurements of about 0.01 per cent for the largest volumes and 0.1 per cent for the smallest volumes. Volume calibration of the cells was made by filling each of the cells with mercury and weighing the outflow between levels determined by the cathetometer. Thus calibration curves were constructed.

[8] A check on the calibration was made by determining the compressibility of the pure components methane, carbon dioxide and hydrogen sulfide in both cells. An amount of the single component was introduced into either of the equilibrium or measuring cell at relatively low pressure. After the desired temperature was established, the number of moles of the gas was calculated using experimental compressibility factors reported in the literature. The pressure was then increased stepwise to the desired maximum and volumes were recorded at each stage. Using the number of moles at the initial condition and the measured variables, a compressibility factor was calculated for each pressure. These were then compared to the values reported in the literature. For a variety of temperatures in both the equilibrium cell and for about 30 different samples of the individual gases at pressures up to 2,500 psia, the error encountered was less than ± 2.5 per cent.

[9] An additional check was provided by making similar measurements on an approximately 50 : 50 mixture of methane and carbon dioxide for which experimental data were available. The agreement obtained was better than ± 1 per cent for pressures up to 3,000 psia. In all cases measurements were made for both increasing and decreasing pressure. The methane, carbon dioxide and hydrogen sulfide used in the experimental work all had a guaranteed minimum purity of 99 mol per cent.

New Words and Expression

compressibility	[kəmpresi'biliti]	n.	压缩性
additivity *	[ædi'tiviti]	n.	相加性
applicable	['æplikəbl]	a.	可适用的
cumbersome	['kʌmbəsəm]	a.	麻烦的
volumetric	[ˌvɔlju'metrik]	a.	容积的
correlation	[kɔri'leiʃən]	n.	相关
pseudo-critical *	[psjuːdəu'kritikəl]	n.	准临界
hydrogen sulfide *	['haidridʒən 'sʌlfaid]		硫化氢
sour *	['sauə]	a.	含硫的
methane *	['miːθein]	n.	甲烷
withdrawal	[wið'drɔːəl]	n.	取出
constantan	['kɔnstəntæn]	n.	康铜
thermocouple	['θəːməuˌkʌpl]	n.	热电偶
potentionmeter *	[pətenʃi'ɔmitə]	n.	电位计
bourdon * tube gauge			布尔登管式压力计
calibrate	['kælibreit]	vt.	校准
deadweight *	['dedweit]	n.	自重,净重
piston	['pistən]	n.	活塞
cathetometer *	[kæθi'tɔmitə]	n.	高差计
hydrostatic	[haidrɔ'stætik]	a.	静水力（学）的
reproducibility	[riːprədjuːs'biliti]	n.	可再现性
mole * =mol	[məul]	n.	摩尔
stepwise *	['stepwaiz]	ad.; a.	逐步（的）

Notes

①laws of Dalton and Amagat 道尔顿定律和阿曼加特定律。
②et al [缩][拉]，以及其他等等 (=and other)。
③a Leeds Northrup semi-precision potentiometer 一个利兹·诺思拉普半精密电位差计。

Exercises

Reading Comprehension

Ⅰ. Match Column A with Column B according to the text.

	A		B
1.	A semi-precision potentiometer, together with copper-constantan thermocouples	(a)	was used to measure the sample volume and to determine the hydrostatic heads
2.	Heise bourdon tube gauge	(b)	is used to measure the amount of each pure component used in preparing the mixture
3.	A 100-cm cathetometer	(c)	is used to measure the temperatures in the cells
4.	A glass windowed pressure vessel containing mercury	(d)	is used to measure the pressure above vessel 1,000 psi to ± 3 psi and below 1,000psi to ± 1 psi

II. Fill in the chart with the information given in para. 4.

Behavior of the Some Gas Mixtures

acid gas concen-tration	the concentration of hydrogen sulfide	the range of temperature	pressures up to
1) _____ %	2) _____ %	3) from ___ to ___	4) _____ psi

III. Fill in the blanks with the information given in the text.

There are three methods of dealing with gaseous mixture proposed:

The first one is to _____ 1) _____.

The second is to _____ 2) _____.

The third is _____ 3) _____.

Vocabulary

I. Fill in the blanks with the expressions given below. Change the forms if necessary.

mole additivity sour methane stepwise weight potentiometer dead-weight

1. Milk _____ quickly when it is left in the hot sun.
2. The _____ of the goods is 3,000 ton except the package.
3. "You should use the _____ computation when you calculate in these equations", said the mathematic teacher to the student.
4. The acid in this liquid has the purity of 45 _____ per cent.
5. A _____ is an instrument which is used to measure electro-motive force.

II. Find words in the text which mean almost the same as the following.

1. para. 1 capability of compression

2. para. 2 that can be applied or suitable
3. para. 2 burdensome,
4. para. 4 of or relating to the measurement of volume
5. para. 8 test the accuracy of

III. Now use the words you have found to complete the following sentences:
1. Is the rule _____ to this case?
2. A soldier today would find old-fashioned armour very _____ .
3. The _____ measurement of this store-room is 400 cubic meters.
4. A civil engineering should know about _____ of building material.
5. The mechanician _____ the scale of barometer now.

Writing   Abstract Writing

Directions: Read the text of Unit Sixteen again and write an abstract of the text in about 120 words.
   This paper, starting from _____
_____
_____
_____
_____
_____
_____
_____

Reading Material A

How to Estimate Size Cost of Producing Equipment

Detailed design and cost analysis of flow lines, manifolding, LACTs and crude storage is sometimes impossible in the field. What is needed are straight forward, reasonably accurate estimates for budgets, management decisions, etc. Methods described below will give field personnel tools to provide quick answers with a minimum of reservoir data.

Flow Lines   Sizing and costing of flow lines requires preliminary information such as:
   * EXPECTED PRODUCTION RATES FROM INDIVIDUAL WELLS
   * FULL WELL STREAM FLUID PROPERTIES

* WELLHEAD FLOWING PRESSURES
* ESTIMATED LATER LIFE PRESSURES
* PROCESSING PRESSURE OR ALLOWABLE FLOW LINE PRESSURE DROP
* INDIVIDUAL FLOW LINE LENGTHS
* KNOWLEDGE OF TERRAIN, ESPECIALLY FOR TWO-PHASE FLOW.

Methods for Sizing There are many methods for predicting pressure drop in flow lines. The method presented in NGPSA Data Book, Eighth Edition, is suggested for single-phase gas pressure drop. For single-phase liquid pressure drop, the Humble Pipe Line Hydraulics Manual is recommended.

Three commonly used methods for predicting two-phase pressure drops are Baker, Lockhart and Martinelli and Duckler.

All of these require detailed calculations, almost exclusively by computer. The easiest to use by hand is the Lockhart and Martinelli. All methods give acceptable results.

For flow lines crossing hilly terrain, the Flannigan method is suggested for predicting effect of elevation changes on two-phase pressure drop.

Determining Cost Flow line costs are generally developed on installed cost basis. Since several things influence cost of flow lines-above ground, buried, internal and/or external corrosion protection it is usually necessary to modify available cost data to suit particular needs.

Flow line costs are thousands of dollars per mile versus line diameter. The cost is for material and labor for laying in continental United States, above ground, on reasonably dry and level terrain. The cost curve is also acceptable for most overseas locations as lower cost of pipe manufactured outside the United States tends to offset higher installation costs.

Multiplers for alternative methods and locations for laying flow lines also are given in the other chapter. These factors were developed from contractor quotations and closely parallel actual job costs. [1]

MANIFOLDS Because many factors influence manifold design, it is difficult to generalize costs. Such factors include pressure rating, type of valves, number of headers and well connections per manifold. The following data considers some of these variables to allow rapid costing for several alternatives.

The base design includes connections for pigging if required. All wells are assumed to have 2-inch adjustable chokes with production capabilities into either test or production headers. Manifold rating is 600-lb. ASA.

Costs for the base design using 2, 3 and 4-inch laterals are tabulated in figure shown in the other chapter. Also given is cost of adding ligaments (header connection) to the base design. Multiplication factors allow cost estimation of 300-lb. or 900-lb. ASA designs. Skid and header costs are averaged for each lateral and are included in the base cost. Therefore, these costs should be used for manifolds with a minimum of five well connection.

LACT Cost estimated for LACT units can be readily developed knowing: initial and future maximum crude production, purchaser requirements, government regulations and working pressure.

Cost Determinations   Costs estimated for LACT capacity were developed for units equipped with:
- Flanged connections
- Explosion-proof motors and panels
- Positive displacement meters with ticket printers[②]
- Centrifugal pipe line delivery pumps, 25-30 psig
- Air eliminators and strainers
- 38&W monitors and probes
- Automatic samplers
- Sample containers with electric mixing pumps
- Three-valve prover loops
- Spring loaded back pressure valve
- Control panels, fused, totalizing and allowable counters, on-off-manual switches, etc.
- Three-way diverting valves
- Warning beacons

Specifically not included are: pump start-step controls, lease shut-in equipment and electric lease equipment transformers, fuses, conduits, cable etc.

Cost approximations can be made with figure shown in the other chapter, assuming low pressure transfer pumps are used. Generally this is true as high pressure equipment (meters, probes, pumps, valves, etc.) costs can be excessive.

Weights and deliveries range from 1,500 pounds and 6-8 weeks for a 2500-bpd unit to 10,000 pounds and 16-18 weeks for a 50,000-bpd unit.

Notes

①这些指标根据承包商报价单得出并紧密与工程成本相对应。
②带有票签打印机的容积计量仪器。

Reading Material B

Foam Insulation Reduces Gathering system Costs

Installation and operating costs were reduced significantly by use of a polyurethane foam insulated gathering and production system in East Calgary field, Alberta.

The insulated system was selected over other types of headed systems because of lower fuel gas requirements to maintain line temperature above 85 °F. With ambient temperature as low as −30 °F, this design has resulted in significant savings.

SOUR GAS PRODUCTION

Gas is produced from three zones in this field: the Elkton, Basal Quartz and Wabamun. These zones are produced separately due to widely varying compositions. However, all gas is processed for sulfur and liquid removal in the Petrogas Processing, Ltd. plant owned by a consortium of 26 companies[①].

Production and gathering of Elkton and Basal Quartz gas presents few problems since total acid gas content is only 6% and both contain substantial liquid hydrocarbons. However, Wabamum gas contains 32% H_2S, 10% CO_2 and only 1-3 barrels/MMcf liquid hydrocarbons. Gas in place contains 110 pounds of elemental sulphur/MMcf which precipitates with temperature and pressure reduction. Production and gathering of this gas involves unusual problems.

Air Pollution   Prior experience in producing similar gas in Okotoks field, south of Calgary. This system used vertical field separators and glycol contactors which stripped H_2S from the glycol with high pressure sweet plant gas and regenerated the glycol in the field. [②]Sweet gas stripping was necessary to avoid air pollution from glycol regenerators.

The pollution problem was also present in East Calgary field. Since this field is considerably larger than Okotoks field, a similar system as used, with glycol pumped from the plant to the wells and H_2S rich glycol returned to the plant for regeneration. The gathering system was conventionally wrapped 5LX-42 pipe in 4-inch, 6-inch and 8-inch diameters.

EXPANSION PROGRAM

When it was decided to expand the system and double Wabamum gas production, four design alternatives were analyzed:

1. Further extension of the glycol dehydration system.
2. A conventional line header system to maintain additional gas in the new system above its hydrate point of 85 °F.
3. A hot-water traced, heated gathering system.
4. A heated system using polyurethane pre-insulated pipe to reduce heat loss.

Polyurethane Insulation   To investigate the insulated system, similar calculations were made with a revised over-all coefficient of 0.116 Btu/hr./sq.ft./°F. It was apparent that few line heaters would be required for such a system, all heat being supplied by the required wellhead heaters.

As proposed new wells were located, rigorous evaluation and design was made for each type of system. Expansion of the glycol system was eliminated completely at this point. It was further established that any heated system must:

  * Maintain a main-line temperature above 85 °F.

* Have sufficient capacity to relieve existing glycol system capacity limits and carry proposed volumes at future field pressure of 500 psig.
* Provide main-line operating continuity in the absence of production from any or all wells.
* Permit well shut down for tubing sulfur removal for at least four hours without hydrate blockage in the well lateral.
* Supply wellhead gas to laterals at 160℉.

Final economic analysis showed a slightly lower cost for the insulated system over the hot-water traced system, with only slightly reduced operating flexibility. However, fuel gas requirement was substantially higher for the traced system. Since contracts were available for sales of all gas, the insulated system was finally selected.

Damage Resistance Tests　　Typical installations used one inch of polyurethane foamed on the pipe in permanent molds with a layer of butyl mastic over the insulation and 0.060-inch polyethylene "Yellow Jacket" outer wrap extruded over the exterior.

Before specifying the polyethylene covering thickness, tests to determine resistance to rock penetration were made. Double-thick 0.060 polyethylene with mastic between was selected to prevent any possibility of water damage.

To insulate joints cold mastic primer was used on the pipe and exposed insulation to prevent water penetration in case of joint covering failure. Pre-molded sections of polyurethane insulation were then covered with heat-shrinkable polyethylene sleeves.

Notes

① 所有燃气都在 26 家联合公司所拥有的液体丙烷有限公司加工厂进行脱硫除液处理。
② 该系统使用垂直现场分离设备和乙二醇接触器，乙二醇接触器利用高压无硫气体从乙二醇中除去硫化氢并回收油田中的乙二醇。

Appendix I Vocabulary

absorbant * n. 吸收剂	(11)
absorption n. 吸收	(11)
absorptivity * n. 吸收率	(03)
accessibility n. 可及性	(01)
accumulate * v. 累积，存储	(12)
accumulation * n. 聚集（物）	(02)
accumulator n. 贮液器；收集器	(05)
actuate vt. 开动，驱使	(06)
additivity n. 相加性	(16)
advent n. 出现	(07)
adventitious a. 外来的	(03)
advocate * vt. 提倡	(04)
aesthetic * a. 审美的，美学的	(03)
agglomerate * n. 附聚物，大块	(08)
aggregate a. 集合的，合计的	(10)
alumina * n. 氧化铝，矾土	(03)
ambient * a. 周围的	(06)
apex * n. 顶（点，尖）	(02)
applicable a. 可适用的	(16)
aqueous a. 水的，水状的	(11)
assend * v. 上升，上浮	(02)
augment vt. 增加，扩大	(02)
availability n. 可得到，可获得	(12)
axial a. 轴的	(15)
azimuth * n. 方位角	(03)
back-drop * n. 背景	(12)
baffle-plate n. 缓冲板	(10)
baghouse * n. 集尘室	(08)
bearing n. 轴承	(05)
bituminous a. 沥青的	(04)
blast n. （气）流，（气）浪	(09)
blister * v. 气泡，结疤	(10)
blowdown n. 排污	(10)
blowoff 排污管	(10)
boil off 汽化	(11)
boost * vt. 升高，增加	(11)
bourdon tube gauge 布尔登管式压力计	(16)
break down 分解	(05)
brim * n. 边缘	(02)
bristle * v. 充满；被充满	(13)
bronze n. 青铜色，青铜	(03)
budge v. 动（一动），挪动（一下）	(09)
bulging n. 膨胀，凸部	(10)
bushing n. 加固垫	(10)
calcium * n. 钙	(01)
canopy * n. （排气）罩	(02)
capacious * a. 容量大的，宽敞的	(02)
caretaker * n. 看管人	(14)
casement n. 窗扉	(02)
cat-like a. 像猫一样的	(07)
catch 难题	(04)
caulk vt. 填隙	(10)
cellar * n. 地道	(13)
charge 注入，装填	(05)
check with 与…联系	(05)
circulation n. 循环，环流	(02)
circumferential a. 圆周的	(10)
clatter n. （发出）卡搭声	(05)
client n. 委托人；买方，顾客	(14)
coefficient n. 系数	(11)
coil n. 蛇［盘，旋］管	(05)
combustor n. 燃烧室（器）	(04)
come * to light 被人发现，为人所了解	(14)
comissioning * n. 试运转，使用	(14)
compartment * n. 间隔；隔室	(08)
compartmentalize * vt. 把…分成区，隔开	(08)
compatibility n. 兼容器	(06)

compatible *a.* 配伍的，适合的		(07)
compensate *vt.* 补偿		(06)
complexity *n.* 复杂性，复杂的物		(14)
compressibility *n.* 压缩性		(16)
computation *n.* 计算		(15)
concentrated * *a.* 浓缩的		(11)
conception *n.* 构思，设想		(09)
concession * *n.* 让步，妥协		(04)
conductivity * *n.* 传热系数		(13)
conduit * *n.* 导管		(13)
conical *a.* 圆锥形的		(02)
constantan *n.* 康铜		(16)
contaminant *n.* 污染物		(05)
contaminate *vt.* 污染		(02)
contamination * *n.* 污染，污染物		(02)
contractor *n.* 承包商		(12)
controversy *n.* 争论		(04)
convector *n.* 对流散热器		(07)
converge *v.* 会聚		(15)
corrode * *v.* 腐蚀		(15)
corrosion *n.* 腐蚀		(10)
cost-effective *a.* 划算的，经济的		(11)
coverage *n.* 有效范围		(05)
crankcase *n.* 曲轴箱		(05)
criterion *n.* 标准，准则		(07)
crop up *vt.* 暴露		(04)
cross-current * *n.* 逆流		(02)
cuddle * *v.* 蜷缩着身子躺（或睡）		(07)
cumbersome *a.* 麻烦的		(16)
cyclone * *n.* 旋风分离器		(04)
damper * *n.* 风门，风挡		(08)
daunt * *v.* 吓倒，使胆怯		(13)
deadweight *n.* 自重，净重		(16)
debris * *n.* 岩屑		(12)
debug * *vt.* 排除		(04)
deflect *v.* （使）偏转，偏离		(02)
deliverability *n.* 供应能力		(12)
demo * =demonstration *n.* 示范		(04)
demonstration * *n.* 示范		(14)
deration * *n.* 减少		(15)
detrition * *n.* 耗损		(04)
differential *n.* 差别		(07)
diffuser * *n.* 散流器		(09)
dilute *v.* 变稀薄		(02)
diluted *a.* 稀释的		(11)
dislodge * *vt.* 移去，除去		(08)
displacement *n.* 排水量，移置		(06)
documentation *n.* 提供的文件		(14)
dominate *vt.* 支配		(04)
droplet *n.* 微滴		(05)
ductwork * *n.* 风道		(09)
effect * on 操作		(14)
emanate *v.* 散发		(15)
emissivity * *n.* 辐射率，辐射能力		(03)
enhance *vt.* 提高，增强		(08)
entrain * *v.* 吸入，卷入		(02)
envisage *v.* 想象		(13)
erosion *n.* 侵蚀		(04)
executive * *n.* 主管企业的人		(04)
exhilaration * *n.* 高兴		(07)
extract *vt.* 提取		(11)
extraction *n.* 抽出，排出		(02)
fault-finding * *n.* ; *a.* 检查故障（的）		(14)
feed-water *n.* 给（供）水		(10)
felt * *v.* 把…制成毡		(08)
filing * *n.* （文件的）整理汇集		(14)
filing * system 档案制度		(14)
filter * *n.* 过滤器		(08)
flat *a.* 平坦的，平缓的		(12)
flex * *v.* （使）挠曲，褶曲		(08)
flexibility *n.* 机动性		(12)
flexibility *n.* 适应性，机动性，灵活性		(09)
flexion *n.* 弯曲，褶曲		(08)
float-glass 浮法玻璃		(03)
flowline *n.* 管道		(15)
flowrate * *n.* 流量		(06)

151

fluctuate * v. 增减，（使）起伏	(09)	
flue a. 烟道	(11)	
flue gas a. 烟气，废气	(11)	
fluidize * vt. 使流化	(04)	
flush a. 齐平的，同高的	(02)	
foam n. 泡沫	(01)	
freevent n. 通风	(13)	
freon * n. 氟利昂	(03)	
frigid a. 寒冷	(09)	
fusion n. 溶化	(10)	
gale n. （一）股，（一）阵	(09)	
gall v. 咬住，卡死	(05)	
gasket n. 衬圈，衬垫	(05)	
glaze * v. 装（配）玻璃于	(13)	
glob n. 团块	(09)	
gradient * n. 梯度	(07)	
greenhouse effect 温室效应	(03)	
grid n. 线路网，管网	(01)	
groove vt. 开槽	(10)	
gush * v；n. 涌（喷）出	(09)	
hand-over n. 移交，交接	(14)	
header n. 集流管	(15)	
heartache n. 痛心，伤心	(04)	
hefty * a. 异常大的，很高的	(12)	
hit v. 查到，偶然找到	(12)	
hood * n. 罩，挡风板（罩）	(02)	
hopper * n. 料斗	(08)	
horizontal a. 卧式的	(10)	
hum * v. （发出）嗡嗡声	(09)	
hybrid a. 混合式的	(04)	
hydrogen sulfide 硫化氢	(16)	
hydrostatic a. 静水力（学）的	(16)	
illumination n. 照明，照明度	(03)	
in essence 本质上，大体上	(12)	
in the light of 依据，按照	(14)	
inaccessible a. 不可达到的	(07)	
inception n. 开始，开端	(09)	
incidence n. 发生（率），入射（角）	(03)	

incorporate v. 合并，纳入	(06)	
induce vt. 引起，导致	(08)	
infill n. 补充	(12)	
infrastructure n. 下部（低层）结构	(01)	
initiate vt. 启动，开始	(08)	
inject v. 罐入	(12)	
innovative a. 变改的，革新的	(06)	
integral a. 整体的，一切的	(07)	
interface v. 连接	(01)	
intermittent a. 间歇的，断断续续的	(08)	
interstate a. 州际的，州之间的	(12)	
inertial * a. 惯性的，惯量的	(12)	
irradiance n. 辐射（度）	(03)	
knuckle * n. 万向接头	(10)	
laminated a. 分层的，叠层的	(03)	
laten heat 潜热	(11)	
latent a. 潜在的	(11)	
lease n. 出租（土地等）	(15)	
life-cycle n. 整个使用周期	(11)	
likelihood n. 可能性	(06)	
lime * n. 氧化钙，石灰	(03)	
limestone n. 石灰石	(04)	
liquefy * v. 液化，溶解	(03)	
logarithm n. 对数	(13)	
logging n. 阻塞	(05)	
logistics * n. 后勤工作，后勤学	(12)	
longitudinal a. 纵向的	(10)	
looped * a. 环形的	(15)	
louver * n. （通风用）气窗，天窗	(09)	
lubricating n. 润滑	(05)	
lubrication n. 润滑	(05)	
magnesia * n. 氧化镁	(03)	
main * n. 总管道	(13)	
malfunction n. 机能失常，发生故障	(05)	
mandated a. 命令的，下令的	(12)	
manhole n. 检查孔，人孔	(10)	
mesmerize vt. 陶醉	(04)	
metallic a. 金属（性）的	(03)	
meter * v. 用表测量	(15)	

microprocessor * n. 微处理器	(06)
migration n. 流动	(05)
military-grade n. 军事级别的	(12)
minimize vt. 使…成极小	(01)
modulation * n. 调节器	(09)
mole=mol n. 摩尔	(16)
multiplication n. 乘，乘法，倍增	(03)
Naperian logarithms （那皮尔）自然对数	(13)
non-aqueous a. 非水的	(13)
note * down 记录下，摘下	(14)
notification * n. 通知	(06)
occupant n. 居住者	(03)
odorant * n. 加臭	(06)
odorization * n. 加臭，加臭剂	(06)
odorizer * n. 加臭器	(06)
odorometer * n. 臭味计	(06)
off-line 脱机	(08)
on-line 联机	(08)
operability * n. 操作	(04)
option n. 选择，任选项	(12)
orifice n. （管子的）口，孔	(03)
oscillate v. 振荡，震动	(08)
overfilled * a. 过满的	(02)
overhand n.；vt. 大修，仔细检查	(14)
overspill * n. 溢出物	(02)
pane * n. 窗格玻璃	(03)
parameter n. 参数，系数	(13)
peak-demand n. 需求高峰期	(12)
pedestrian n. 步行者，行人	(01)
perimeter * n. 边长，周长	(02)
photosensitive * a. 光敏的，感光的	(03)
pick up 吸收	(05)
pigment * n. 颜料	(03)
pit vt. 使凹下，挖坑于	(10)
plotting n. 绘制	(13)
plunger * n. 活塞	(06)
pneumatically * ad. 风动地，气动地	(06)
polyurethane * n. 聚氨酯	(01)
porosity n. 气孔	(10)
porous a. 疏松的，多孔的	(08)
positive displacement pump 容积式泵	(06)
potentionmeter n. 电位计	(16)
pre-fabricated a. 预制的	(01)
precipitate n. 沉淀	(10)
preliminary * a. 前期的，预备的	(12)
preprogram（me）* vt. 预先规定，预先安排	(06)
procedure n. 程序，工序	(05)
progressively * ad. 逐渐地	(03)
prohibitive a. 禁止 过高的	(01)
pseudo-critical n. 准临界	(16)
psig=pounds per square inch gauge 表压（磅/英寸^2）	(04)
pull on （用力）拉，拽	(09)
pyramidal * a. 金字塔形的	(02)
pyropower * 火（热）力	(04)
radial a. 径向的	(15)
reap * from v. 从…获得	(12)
recipe * n. 配方	(06)
recondition v. 修理，检修	(12)
rectangular a. 矩形的	(02)
reed n. 簧片	(05)
reflectivity * n. 反射率	(03)
regression * n. 退回	(13)
regulatory a. 调节的，调整的	(06)
reheat vt. 再热，	(04)
render * v. 打底，初涂	(03)
reproducibility n. 可再现性	(16)
requisite a. 需要的，必不可少的	(14)
restructuring n. 调整	(12)
retrofit * n. 重建	(01)
rig vt. 安装	(12)
rivet v. 铆接	(10)
route * v. 给…定线	(15)
rumble * v. （发出）隆隆声，噪声	(09)

saturate	*vt.* 使饱和	(13)
scale	*n.* 水锈，锅垢	(10)
scramble *	*v.* （急忙）抢，夺	(09)
screw *	*vt.* 拧（紧），螺旋	(10)
scrutinize *	*v.* 仔细检查，核对	(12)
seam	*n.* 缝	(10)
segregate *	*vt.* 使分离，使隔离	(06)
selenium *	*n.* 硒	(03)
sensation *	*n.* 感觉（知）	(07)
series-connected	*a.* 串联的	(11)
setting	定位，调整	(05)
shaft *	*n.* 竖井	(09)
shudder *	*v.; n.* 发抖，打颤	(09)
silica *	*n.* 氧化硅	(03)
silicate	*n.* 硅酸	(01)
simultaneously	*ad.* 同时发生地	(15)
slugging	*n.* 缓动	(05)
sniff *	*vi.* 以鼻吸气，嗅	(06)
soda *	*n.* 苏打，氧化钠	(03)
sour	*a.* 含硫的	(16)
spot-market	*n.* 销售点	(12)
spray *	*v.* 喷射	(11)
stagnant	*a.* 停滞的，滞止的	(09)
stale	*a.* 陈旧的；不新鲜的	(09)
standby *	*n.* 备用设备，备用品	(14)
startup *	*n.* 开动，启动	(09)
stash *	*v.* 储存；*n.* 储存处	(12)
static *	*a.* 静止的，静态的	(09)
statutory *	*a.* 法定的，规定的	(03)
stepwise	*ad.; a.* 逐步（的）	(16)
stifle *	*v.* （使）感到窒息，气闷	(09)
stratify	*v.* 分层	(05)
stride	*v.* 跨过	(07)
sturdy *	*a.* 坚实的	(01)
sub-routine	*n.* 子程序	(13)
suck out	抽出	(02)
supplement *	*vt.* 增补，增添	(08)
tamper *	*vi.* 损害	(07)
tanh	*n.* =hyperbolic tangent 双曲正切 (13)
terminate	*v.* 使结束	(15)
terrain	*n.* 地形	(01)
thereof	*ad.* 由此，因此	(14)
thermocouple	*n.* 热电偶	(16)
thermostatic	*a.* 热力学的，恒温的	(01)
throb *	*v; n.* 震动，跳动	(09)
throttle	*vt.* 节流	(11)
throughput	*n.* 通过量	(15)
tin *	*n.* 锡	(03)
tinted	*a.* 染（上，涂）了色的	(03)
totalizer *	*n.* 累加器	(06)
toughened	*a.* 坚韧的，有硬度的	(03)
toupee *	*n.* （指头顶上的）一缕头发 (09)
trade-off	*n.* 权衡，折衷（办法，方案）选择 (08)
transact *	*v.* 处理，办理，进行（交易等） (09)
transition	*n.* 变革	(04)
transmissivity *	*n.* 透射率	(03)
transmittance *	=transmissivity	(03)
transparent	*a.* 透明的	(03)
trunk-line	*n.* 干线	(15)
tube bundle	管束	(11)
tubular	*a.* 管（状、型）的	(10)
tug	*v.* 吃力的拉	(09)
turbine	*n.* 涡轮机	(01)
typically *	*ad.* 一般，有代表性地	(08)
unbounded *	*a.* 不受限制的	(02)
uniformity	*n.* 均匀	(02)
utilisation	*n.* 利用	(07)
valve	*n.* 阀门	(01)
vandal *	*a.* 破坏性的	(07)
vaneaxial fan	翼式轴流风扇	(09)
ventilate	*vt.* 使通风	(02)
ventilation	*n.* 通风	(02)
verification	*n.* 验证	(06)

verify *	vt. 证实，检验	(06)
versatile	a. 通用的，万能的	(09)
via	prep. 经过，通过	(11)
viable	a. 有生存力的	(01)
volumetric	a. 容积的	(16)
weave * (wove, woven)	v. 编织	(08)
well-center	n. 气井中心	(15)
wellhead *	n. 井口	(15)
wellstream *	n. 井流量	(15)
whereby	ad. 由此，从而	(14)
withdrawal	n. 提取，回采	(12)
withdrawl	n. 取出	(16)
wrist pin	n. 销	(05)
yonder	a.; ad. （在）那边（的）	(09)

Appendix II Translation for Reference

第1单元

热传输和分配系统

热通过输热管道从热厂输送到需热中心，中心可能在一定的距离以外。传输系统费用是距离和传输热量的函数，传输热量又是由温差和传热介质的流速所决定。管道的质量（厚度）是水压的函数，而一定热负荷的管道直径是流速和温差的函数。

很多大电厂由于经济、环境保护、燃料（如煤）可及性和贮存等原因而远离人口居住中心。这样，虽然从大电厂可得到的热量从技术角度可以回收来供区域供热使用并可以适应大城市的供热需求，但是输热管线的成本却可能大到不能这样做的地步。目前，从经济角度讲，可达到的最大输送距离，根据热负荷和燃料价格而定，热水可达30km，蒸汽3～5km。一些研究报告已经表明热水输送距离大于30km，从经济意义上讲，可能是有吸引力的。但由于上面已经提到的负荷和热量需求的局限性，从经济角度讲，潜在的使用场合数量是有限的。在很多场合下，在离需热中心近距离处建新的热厂要比建造长输送管线更为经济。

根据输水管线所经过的地形，可以要求通过泵站来保持送水管与回水管之间的压降。在可能的地方，管线可以建在地面以上以降低成本。

目前，最常见的管道系统是钢管埋设在混凝土管道沟里，不过钢管套钢管或塑料套钢管已在很多专用场合使用。用聚氨酯泡沫做保温材料的预制管，成本上是可行的，但必须在一定的温度范围内使用。保温材料可以是岩棉、矿棉或玻璃棉、玻璃纤维、聚氨酯泡沫（有时和玻璃棉结合使用）或硅酸钙。

热量从输热干管分配到用户，有时候是直接到达用户室内热分配系统的，有时候是通过热交换器而到用户室内分配系统的。在有些场合，一次分配网通过热交换器与二次分配网连接，二次分配网直接馈入用户设备。

热水供热分配网的成本（包括泵以及局部热网的控制系统）取决于一系列因素，包括需热密度、供水和回水温度、地形特征和当地基础设施以及供热系统是新建还是改造翻新等因素。

管道系统的温度对于单位长度的配热成本有重要的影响。一般来说，系统运行的温度范围越低，管道成本越低。这种情况是因为这只需要成本低的管道和保温材料。同时，成本在很大程度上取决于需热密度。热负荷密度越大，（供热）分配成本就越低。

通过房间供热和热水装置采用串联连接、使用低温供热装置，尤其是在室内供热装置上使用恒温阀可以实现较低的回水温度。恒温阀控制离开散热器或其他供热装置的热水温度。不过，对于这些场合，室内供热装置表面积要增加，要增加一定的成本。

供水温度和压力的增加就会要求管壁更厚，管道阀门更耐用，保温程度更高，因此成本就会增加。安装成本往往也会更高。进一步影响到涡轮机抽出系统的因素是，电量输出会随着抽出温度（即，区域供热温度）的增加而减少，这就导致了同样的能量输出却需要更大的燃料消耗。在判断联合生产系统的全面经济效益时这是一个重要因素。

最重要的因素之一是区域供热系统是新建的还是翻新改造的。对前者来说，成本要低得多，而且交通、行人过往中断可降到最低程度。对于翻新改造而言，（尤其是在较老的城镇），成本可能大到不可行的程度，而且交通中断程度也可能大。

第 2 单元

排 风 罩

排风罩是局部排风系统的收集装置，通常为金字塔形或锥形，安装在污染源的上方或侧旁。应用非常广泛，其实有些场合并不适用，这是因为在使用过程中难以找到十分有效的其他方式。

对于排风罩来说，在污染源和罩本身之间总存在一个不受限制的空间，因此周围的空气能流过污染源，而在某些条件下周围的空气能使污染气流偏离排气罩，所以排气罩比通风柜要耗费更多的空气量。

各种排气罩可分为简易的，活动的，独体的和组合的（从天花板悬吊装有玻璃的框架结构罩）。图 2-1 所示的分别为简易独体罩（a），加热炉装料口上方罩（b），周边有狭长口的活动罩（c），工作台两侧设有送风的排气罩（d）和装有玻璃窗扉的复式罩（e）。其他类型的排气罩在有关除尘用局部排气罩中介绍。排风系统可以是自然排风或机械排风，无论那种方式都要尽可能使排风罩靠近污染源。设在污染源上方的排风罩通常距地面1.8至2米，形成无障碍净空区，同时（排气罩）也可以尽可能靠近呼吸区域。

当聚积在排风罩下的污染空气量比能被排走的量大时，多余的气体会从罩下边缘流出，污染工作区。在这种情况下，如果没有排气罩反而更好些，因为如果污染空气的密度低于周围空气的密度值，那么这些气体就会上升，并且在由于循环作用最终返回到工作区后，会比留在过满的排气罩时稀薄而污染程度小。

当污染源与罩之间空间的吸入速度足够吸收罩下所有污染气体时，排气罩是有效的。吸入速度必须克服室内空气交叉流动的影响，交叉流动会使污染气流偏离排气罩。吸入速度在罩口的整个平面应相当均匀。因此排气罩的效果基本上取决于其形状。

在长矮形罩中要获得均匀吸入速度是不可能的。在另一章中已证实：为了使吸入速度均匀，罩的顶点角度不应超过 60 度。

当污染空气的上升气流在污染源上方形成时，会卷入大量的周围空气一道进入排气罩。对于有效的运行情况来说，排出的空气量不应少于上升的气流量，否则污染空气肯定会从罩下流入房间。

我们可以根据下面的例子进行说明，它也可说明排气罩和排气柜之间的实际差别，图2.2 所示的是内装一个排风罩的矩形柜，抽气风机与管道 2 相连接，通过开口 1 进入的空气与通过管道 2 被抽出的空气一样多。如果排风罩的底边与孔 1 齐平,那么所有通过孔 1 进入的空气便全部进入罩内并被排出。

假定我们现在移动该罩离开进口 1 一定的距离,由于卷入了一些周围的空气,通过口部进入罩内的空气增多,但是由于管道 2 仅可以排出固定的空气量,即由进口 1 进入的空气量,与卷入的那部分等量的空气就会流出罩口进入柜内。

与自然通风配合使用的排气罩,只有当室内的全面通风布局合适才能有效进行,否则,从外面流进罩内的可能是空气而不是需排出的污染空气。

悬吊于顶棚、装有玻璃窗扉的复式罩的优点是比独体排风罩容量大。由于有较大的体积,与独体罩相比也较少受到交叉气流的影响。它们在外观上更令人满意而且不致使室内变暗。在最大污染量时,它们往往大得足以用很短时间容纳这些污染气体而不外溢。这些聚集起来的污染气体最终能被按平均污染速度设计的排风系统排出。

第 3 单元

通过玻璃的热传递

玻璃是由 70% 的氧化硅(SiO_2)、15% 的苏打(Na_2O)、10% 的氧化钙(CaO)、2.5% 的氧化镁(MgO)、2.5% 的氧化铝(Al_2O_3)或其他使其具有特定性能的金属元素,例如能使玻璃感光的金(Au)和硒(Se)的混合物熔化所形成的。燃油炉在 1590℃ 以上时可使这些成分液化,然后漂浮在熔化的锡槽上并逐渐地冷却,这就是现在使用的浮法玻璃方法。玻璃纤维和玻璃丝是使热玻璃液通过微细的小孔而制成的(Encyclopaedia Britannica 1980)。玻璃以 4mm、6mm、10mm 和 12mm 厚的规格生产成透明的浮法玻璃、变性浮法玻璃,钢化玻璃和夹层玻璃,取决于类型、安全要求和风负荷。透明的浮法玻璃是最普通的,但由于美学、日光和热的原因,可以选择本体着色为灰色、青铜色、蓝色或者绿色。在熔化阶段加入着色颜料,玻璃的全部厚度被着色。生产过程中处于流体阶段时将金属粒子加到表面上则在玻璃的一边形成反射表面。反射光底色可能是银色,但透射光却可能呈青铜色。低辐射率表面改进了玻璃的热绝缘性能。

玻璃对高温、高频太阳辐射射线是可以透射的,但对来自于建筑物内低温表面的长波辐射传递很少,因而产生了温室效应。具有反射层的玻璃表面为保护常常设置在双层玻璃窗的内表面上。本体着色的玻璃吸收太阳辐射能力强而减少了进入到建筑物的热流量,然而,使玻璃温度增高,引起热膨胀。在密封的双层玻璃窗内可用氟利昂气体充满空间,因为其较低的 U 值降低了的对流热传递能力。

出于能源保护原因,所使用的玻璃面积可通过法定规章来限制。玻璃窗面积是大还是小更为有利取决于每年外来的太阳得热以及来自于人体、照明和设备的内部散热与各种热损失间的平衡。随着用于人工照明电能的减少,通过玻璃窗的天然内部照明的可用性是能量平衡的一个重要部分。大玻璃面积有利与否可从以每月和每年为基础的整个建筑物的净能量消耗得以分析。

图 3-1 表明通过玻璃太阳能的比例随其透射率 T、吸收率 A、反射率 R 的三个特性而改变。对于直射和漫射，玻璃具有不同的透射率。由玻璃吸收的某些辐射被射入房间，给出了总的透射率值，这些特性保持不变直到太阳入射角超过大约 45°，当入射角在 90°时其迅速地减少到零。双层玻璃窗可以由着色的或反射的玻璃作为外层和透明的浮法玻璃作为内层构成。外部玻璃由于与较冷的建筑物内部绝热而上升到一个较高的温度并且承受较大的热膨胀。全部的直接太阳透射率将是两种玻璃类型的透射率乘积（如透明玻璃 0.86，反射玻璃 0.23，等于 0.2）。外部视野通过着色玻璃并未受严重影响，并且这种影响可能几乎注意不到。对建筑物的居住者来说，反射玻璃提供了高度的内部私秘性。

玻璃的性能数据 表 3-1

玻璃类型	光	太阳直射			总计
	T	T	A	R	T
4mm 透明	0.89	0.82	0.11	0.07	0.86
6mm 着色	0.5	0.46	0.49	0.05	0.62
6mm 反射	0.1	0.08	0.6	0.32	0.23

例外是在夜晚，当内部照明和外部黑暗造成视线方向相反时，从大街上看内部是清晰可见的。典型的数据在表 3-1 中给出。

例 3-1

一窗户面朝西南方向，3m 长，2.75m 高，阴影面积 0.2m²，太阳高度角 43.5°，太阳方位角南偏西 66°，垂直于太阳射线的直接辐射度是 832W/m²，漫射辐射度是 43W/m²，直射和漫射的透射率是 0.85 和 0.8，计算通过玻璃传递的太阳得热。

玻璃方位角南偏西 45°，因此，

玻璃与太阳的方位角 = 66° − 45° = 21°

$I_{DVd} = I_D \cos A \cos D$

$= 823 \text{W/m}^2 \times \cos 43.5 \times \cos 21 = 563.4 \text{W/m}^2$

直射辐射度 $Q_D = 0.85 I_{DVd} \times$ 日照面积 W

漫射辐射度 $Q_d = 0.8 \times 43 \times$ 玻璃面积 W

$Q_D = 0.85 \times 563.4 \times [(3 \times 2.75) - 0.2] = 3855.1 \text{W}$

$Q_d = 0.8 \times 43 \times 3 \times 2.75 = 283.8 \text{W}$

总共传递得热 = $Q_D + Q_d = 3855.1 + 283.8 = 4138.9 \text{W}$

第 4 单元

转化中的流化床技术

EPRI 的 Kurt Yeager 说：流化床是在商业转化阶段中盛行的。他称："对一项新技术，那是一个危险阶段"。他要求那些开发者和使用者,不要因流化床燃烧技术在商业上的成功而"迷惑"。Yeager 又说:仍然还需要很大的技术发展,他提到诸如操作、维修方法、腐蚀和耗损等问题。许多新装置中已经暴露出操作方面的问题,虽然多数供应商和用户对排除故障充满信心,但这些问题在有些场合已经很严重了。

一位厂商代表说:现在流化床燃烧方面,令人头痛的事情就象 70 年代初烧西部煤的锅炉一样多。他在回顾用了几年的时间才解决了那些操作问题以后,预言流化床燃烧技术也会有同样的经历。

关于流化床锅炉的设计还存在着明显的根本问题。尽管循环床技术有明显优势,仍有人倡导用泡床设计。传统的理论似乎认为泡床方法更适用于小型新设备或锅炉改造,而循环床对多数新装置最适合。

Gilbert/Commonwealth 的 Nick Gaglia 为循环床与泡床的争论作了有趣的概述。泡床在石灰石和燃料层中有热传递管束。流化气体流速为 4~12ft/sec。只有很少的物质离开泡床,每燃烧 1 磅燃料大约有 2 到 4 磅的物料进行再循环。

循环床的设计使更多的固体颗粒从炉膛飞出去,大部分热传递在燃烧区外进行。一些循环床装置甚至有外部换热装置。循环床中的流化速度 12~30ft/sec,每燃烧 1 磅燃料,有 50~100 磅的再循环物料。

两种形式的炉膛温度大体是相同的,但循环床却被认为有更好的钙硫利用比,流化床的钙硫比为 1.5:1 而泡床则为 3.2:1。

循环床设计中的难题是要求有一个大的机械旋风分离器来截获物料并使其再循环,而且对锅炉高度也有要求。无论设备容量是大是小,在流化速度为 20ft/sec,燃料在炉中停留 3 到 5 秒的情况下,燃烧室都必须约 100ft 高。循环床设计导致较大的设备尺寸。Gaglia 提出的临界点是每小时产蒸汽 50000~100000 磅之间。

FBC 设计的下一步是 CFB 与 BFB 的结合形式。B&W 的 Bob Jonh 说:他期待着 W&B 能提供一种结合形式的设计,他说需要一种折衷:比现在 CFB 的再循环率低,但是要取消 BFB 所需的床内管子。

Foster-Wheeler 在 ASME 会议上介绍了正在进行的 BFB 与 CFB 结合型设计,这种设计的特点是完全采用了泡床设计的双室结构,而第三室是使整套装置显示循环床设计一些优点的再循环室。NSP 的 Jensen 说,目前 NSP 没有受托建造这样的设备。没有场地、许可证和设计的燃料。他又补充说:然而,到 1987 年底这套装置将已运行四年半,如果负荷确有增长,公用事业部门将进行投标。一位企业官员说:具有 NSP 产品运行的两个州的州长说他们将为此铺平道路——完全不同于上次公用事业部门接受计划建造核电站的态度。

在其示范性的项目中,有一个现在正在克罗拉多州的 Ute 核电站开工。这个项目中,把一台由 Pyropower 提供的新的无再热 AFBC 循环床锅炉与一台新的 75MW 汽轮机安装在现有的电厂内。现存的三台 12MW 的汽轮机被新的汽轮机排出的蒸汽所驱动,总功率是 110MW。锅炉的设计容量是压力为 1510psig,温度为 1005°F 时,每小时生产蒸汽 925000 磅。燃烧的是当地含硫和灰分分别为 0.7% 和 26% 热值为 9700Btu/lb 的烟煤。

第 5 单元

压缩机故障

许多压缩机出现故障是由于一个或几个下列情况的原因：(1) 缓动，(2) 液体满流，(3) 润滑油损缺，(4) 杂质，(5) 不良配管，(6) 不恰当的恒温膨胀阀过热定位，(7) 满液启动。

(1) 缓动。缓动通常发生在压缩机启动时，只持续很短的时间。然而当压缩机运转时，在系统运行工况迅速改变期间，缓动有可能发生。这种缓动伴随格噻格噻的噪声产生，很像汽车发动机在重力下发出的声音。这种噪声是由液体制冷剂和/或油的压缩而产生的。按设计压缩机只压缩气体而不压缩液体。当液体通过压缩机被压缩时，在汽缸内会产生超过 1000psig（6890kPa）的液压。

缓动能够毁坏端盖和/或阀板密封垫，折断阀门弹簧片、活塞和损坏活塞销。如果这些情况中任何一项被发现，就应检查产生缓动的情况。一经发现就应纠正。

(2) 液体满流。液体满流是指制冷剂液滴连续不断地流到压缩机。液体制冷剂进入压缩机后，就进入曲轴箱，在曲轴箱里油被稀释。液体制冷剂是一种很好的清洗剂，会从压缩机表面洗去油。在多数情况下，油会起泡沫，从而降低了润滑价值和导致轴承表面过热。这种情况发生在空气冷却式压缩机上要比在制冷剂冷却式压缩机上更为可能。

在液体严重满流的情况下，活塞、气门和活塞环的损坏可能是由于缺少润滑。也有可能部件已损坏而外表却看不出什么磨损。通常，液体满流是通过离油泵最远的部件磨损较多而显示出来的。

(3) 润滑油损缺。润滑油损缺会导致压缩机损坏。磨损面将被卡死，发生过热，结果损坏。压缩机电机会过热，可能会被烧坏。随着曲轴箱油量的减少，剩油的温度就上升。压缩机油在 310～320°F（136.66～142.22℃）时开始汽化，这就减少了对汽缸的润滑，造成活塞环和汽缸的过量磨损。油在 350°F（158.89℃）时彻底分解，产生杂质，并完全失去润滑性能。

(4) 杂质。系统中的污染物包括空气、湿气、尘土和其他异物。这些杂质会引起系统的几种故障，如排气压力高、系统性能差，流量控制装置中水分结冰、油污染和酸。

(5) 不良配管。不良配管也能促使油离开压缩机。系统中如果允许有不必要的存油弯时，油就会在存油弯处沉积，从而使压缩机缺油运行。吸气管线的尺寸对合适的油回路极其重要。如果使用贮液器，大小必须适合于该系统。贮液器应当能储备大约是较小系统制冷剂注入总量的二分之一。一般来说，最理想的是要与贮液器和设备生产厂家接洽征求他们的建议。此外，在非循环期间，贮液器将不保护压缩机免使制冷剂回流。

(6) 不恰当的恒温膨胀阀过热定位。在检查和调整恒温膨胀阀过热定位时，程序应当是在蒸发器盘管处开始。如果膨胀阀多于一个，它们必须全部保持同样的过热定位，如果过热定位不一致，很可能会发生油阻塞，特别是在低温场合。

(7) 满液启动。一般说来，满液启动是在非循环期间制冷剂流到压缩机而引起的。当压缩机比系统其余部分温度低时，制冷剂就流入压缩机曲轴箱并与油混合。当压缩机启动时，液体制冷剂迅速蒸发，造成油起泡沫。

油所吸收的制冷剂量由油温和曲轴箱的压力所决定。温度越低、压力越高，油所吸收的制冷剂就越多。在一定的条件下，制冷剂和油的混合物将分离和分层，液体制冷剂沉降到曲轴箱底部，在那里被油泵首先吸入，压缩机启动时，油泵把液体制冷剂注入到轴承，那里的全部油会被洗掉。

第 6 单元

喷射加臭系统的设计

数年来，人们已研究出了几种方法并已用于天然气加臭。常用的一种加臭系统是喷射型加臭器，这种加臭器有规则地将少量加臭剂喷入天然气流。这种系统已在喷射工艺方面有了改进。

有几个在系统运行中要考虑的基本因素，在设计中计入这些基本因素时，就会使得系统有价值。这些因素包括：

· 加臭剂的选择
· 流量比例调节
· 流量和喷射率特征
· 基本系统设计
· 运行验证
· 系统监控
· 故障断定和报警
· 失效防护

要使加臭剂配方与管线中的天然气相匹配涉及到了解化学成分、管道系统布局和所需加臭程度。建议向加臭剂制造厂家咨询。

选择一种按流量调节比例的系统。所有加臭系统应该使用一种使喷射率与测得流量相关联的比率来作为主要操作方法。一般来说，这个比率用测得的磅（喷射的加臭剂）/百万立方英尺（天然气）来表示。加臭器不是评价天然气中臭量是否合适的判断装置。这要由人鼻来测定。经常使用仪器输送少量燃气供技术人员去嗅。如果技术人员觉察有燃气存在时。加臭级别就用该仪器来鉴定。这种装置常称为臭味计。这种喷射系统使得一定比例的加臭剂能被喷射，这里所说的一定比例是指达到一定级别臭味，已能被觉察并超过规定要求。

系统必须具有在范围很广的可能流量时按规定比例喷射的能力，一般取决于环境温度或工业负荷。流量可低达 100 千立方英尺/天或高达 300 百万立方英尺/天。此外，系统必须在喷射率变化范围大的情况下操作。喷射率可以低达 0.3 磅/百万立方英尺到有时候高达

3～4磅/百万立方英尺，取决于系统中要达到适当臭味所需的量。必须保证系统在预定流量的整个范围内按所需的喷射率运行。

系统应该具有每次能喷射已知量的、可变量的和不可变量加臭剂的设备。这个量应该在系统内被考虑，以证实系统操作成功。

因为系统是全机械性的而且耐磨，因此主要关注是故障。新型泵的设计已大大减少了所需的维修。然而，系统内没有一个零件可以始终保持无故障。因此新设计采用了重要的、变革性的想法，例如屏上系统监控，故障报警输出来作为标准故障报警信号。这两种新的功能缩短了从故障发生到通知公司人员来修理之间的危险时间段，从而减少了燃气带有不适当加臭剂的可能性。

典型的喷射型加臭器组成部件是：
- 喷射泵
- 喷射率控制器
- 喷射率检验系统
- 监控和报警系统

喷射泵是最重要的组成部分之一，一般是容积式泵。新型泵设计考虑了内密封和工作零件与加臭剂化学特性的相容性，是一种分离设计的方法。在这个方法中，泵中的活动部件和主要密封在含有液压流体的环境中工作。这种流体的可压缩性使得密封隔离室内加臭剂排出成为可能。泵可以调节每次喷射排出可变量（0.1～1.0mL/喷射）。事实上，一切喷射泵都是由压缩空气启动，活塞型。在系统控制器确定需要喷射时，就向泵传送压缩空气。

喷射率控制器从电子测量装置利用微处理器接收流量信息，并按照与预先设计的喷射率（磅/百万立方英尺）相匹配的频率自动启动泵。这种跟踪流量并使喷射频率与之相匹配的能力叫做按比例调节流量喷射。控制器可供关键数据的简单程序控制之用：

1. 所需喷射率（磅/百万立方英尺）；
2. 加臭剂的化学密度；
3. 所需的泵排量/行程；
4. 失效喷射率（min/喷射）

检验系统用仪表计量泵所消耗的流体。然后进行计算并在液晶显示器上显示。实际的泵排量不但显示而且得到补偿以保持稳定喷射率。温度对加臭剂密度的影响也予以考虑。

加臭剂消耗可以现场监控也可以摇控。每当0.01磅被消耗时，内累加器作为转换闭路被适时修正。该闭路由监控和数据测取装置实现。如果系统中有什么部件失灵报警器就接通。

负荷下降证明正在进行适量加臭操作。

对安全、清洁和廉价燃料供应的要求提高了各种对天然气加臭的技术。随着新喷射系统的发展，大众对于使用天然气安全性的信任程度也随着提高。可提供24小时检验、监控和报警能力的加臭技术对提高信任程度起重要作用，而当需要维修时减少必要的反应时间和修理时间。

第7单元

地板供热系统：实现人工环境中的热舒适性

现代人们要求，在人工环境中有高水平的热舒适性。与之相联系的是，减少对地球储存能消耗的国际压力日益增长。现代技术在发展新型变革性热源方面迈出了巨大步伐。然而，在热舒适和能源保护相结合方面，最大的进展还是现代地板供热加湿系统。高质量塑料管的出现使得在地板供热系统中用低温水成为可能。地板供热加湿系统完全可以和新热源技术配伍。地板供热系统已完全发展成为适合于各种地板结构，把传导、辐射、对流等所有传热结合起来，从而适应整个建筑物内理想温度梯度的要求。这种安全、隐蔽、节约空间，并且防破坏和防受损的系统既敏感又具有节能意识，提供了被动的自动调节。

热舒适性可定义为，人们对热环境感到满意时的精神状态。研究表明，脚比头略微温暖时，人感觉更舒服。单独进行的实验表明，人可接受的最佳室内气候条件是19℃至29℃的地板温度范围和20℃至24℃的头部位置的空气温度。

然而，由于个人兴趣爱好是一切人类活动必不可少的，因此不可能规定一套满足各种情况的环境条件。我们能够达到的最佳结果取决于5%的不满意因素。不存在使每个人都高兴的温度。但是，我们可以以建立一个舒适区域为目标，使最大数量的处于这个区域的人感到满意。

在辐射散热器或对流散热器的供热系统中，产生竖向温度梯度，地板处比头部位置冷。现代室内气候条件无疑需要一种与人类热舒适条件相匹配的供热系统，即，热效应均匀分配在地面而不是头部。我们已经看到，温暖的脚部会产生良好的感觉，因此，让我们来考察一下，如果把整个地面加热到恰当的温度，将对室内气候产生什么影响。

我们已经涉及到对建筑物标准的改进，然而无论怎么保温也不能改变物理学的规律——热仍然上升。但是有效的绝热会把热量截留在对舒适无帮助的头部以上区域，要解决这个问题涉及到仔细研究我们可利用的三种热。辐射热提供了最令人愉快的舒适感觉。有助于增加人们在春天阳光下散步的情趣，虽然环境空气温度只比冰点高几度。我们对传导热反应良好，给人一种好象抱着热水瓶或依偎在别人怀中而得到的象猫似的愉快感觉。最后还有一种使空气温暖并使空气上升的辐射和传导效应而引起的对流热。通过综合使用这三种热，就可达到高水平的热舒适程度。供热系统设计的正常标准是要获得指定的气温，这个指定的气温是指在一定的室外气温下，抵消建筑物一定热耗后的气温。在设计地板供热系统时，由于全面辐射程度较高以及温暖便利的地板导热的好处，较低空气温度也是可以接受的。

在现代保温好的建筑物中，地板表面温度只需略高于空气温度就可以获得所需舒适因素。这些小的温差在整个建筑物中引起了轻微的低速对流。与其他形式的供热形式相比较，低速对流减少了空气中的灰尘量。不存在那种象辐射散热器或对流散热器后面那样的灰尘或污垢能聚集而（清扫工具）不能达到的地方。而且运行成本也较低。消除高速对流意着在人头部空间将没有聚集的高温空气团。

加热地板是一个辐射面，面上的物体将受到全方位辐射的益处。

高水平的辐射舒适意味着用地板供热系统时，其室内空气温度实际上可以略低于采用其他供热方法通常所需的温度。辐射、传导和对流综合起来，为健康和舒适创造了理想的热环境。

第 8 单元

织 物 过 滤 器

织物过滤器是工业环境中碰到的最普通型过滤器，也是用于局部排风系统中最可靠的过滤器。过滤器本身是由安装在一个壳体中的用织物缝制的若干圆筒或封套组成。在运行中，排风被风机吸入通过织物，尘粒被织物捕集或者以尘饼的形式附在织物表面，尘粒就这样从排风气流中除掉。

像其他过滤器一样，织物过滤器最终必须清灰。事实上，清灰是如此重要，以至织物过滤器是由所采用的清灰方法来分类的。三种最常用的清灰方法是振打、反向吹风以及脉冲喷吹。每种清灰方法都有不同的用途，这里将简单予以叙述。

振打是清洁织物过滤器最老式最简单的方法。在滤袋的顶部沿水平方向或者垂直方向振动，振动使织物挠曲，使聚积的尘饼剥离并落入料斗。振打清灰的滤袋通常是机织织物制成，捕集的灰尘在其表面形成饼块，这种饼块在织物挠曲时能容易除掉。

振打机械通常由电机驱动，电机起动可以是自动的（如感应过量的压降）或在操作人员判断有清灰必要时手工起动。小型设备清灰可以不使用电机而是通过摇动外操作杆振动滤袋来进行。振打滤袋前必须关闭排风气流以使除下的灰尘落进料斗。这意味着在清洁集尘室时或者采用停止运行的方法，或者将滤袋室分为若干间隔，以便当其余间隔继续过滤排气时，一个间隔能通过风门隔开而清灰。第一种可以用于间歇生产或者生产过程产尘很少，能在生产班次结束时进行清灰的场合，然而绝大多数场合，则需要分成间隔的集尘室。

在一些情况下，滤袋振动辅以轻度的反吹气流通过织物，反吹气流帮助把脱落的灰尘带离织物而落入灰斗。反吹气流清灰需要一个风门系统来关闭主气流和开放反吹气流，这样往往使得滤袋室设计和运行复杂化，并增加投资额和运行费用。因此反吹风清灰通常只出现在滤袋室相当大，过滤灰尘只采用振打难以清除的场合。

高温过滤需要使用能经受这种恶劣环境的专用织物，如玻璃纤维，机织的玻璃纤维不能承受振打，因此使用这些织物的滤袋室采用不带振打的轻度反吹风方式清灰。这样的系统通常需要经过特殊表面处理的滤袋以增强灰尘与织物表面的分离。

最后一种主要的织物过滤器清灰方法是使用高压空气喷吹来清除收集到的灰尘。这种方法称为脉冲喷吹清灰。从滤袋顶部输入一高压压缩空气短脉冲，脉冲沿袋向下传播，临时产生的反向气流流经织物并使滤袋向外挠曲。这种突然的挠曲从滤袋外表面除去块团形式的灰尘，使之落入料斗。清灰脉冲可以通过安装定时器以规则的时间间隔来施加或者通过测量织物内外过量压降来起动。

脉冲喷吹清灰需要使用毡状制品，不使用机织品，以经得起脉冲引起的剧烈运动。毡状制品是在整个厚度上收集灰尘，而不是在表面上把灰尘以饼状形式收集，这种疏松状灰尘沉积比表面沉积更难除去，因此脉冲喷吹清灰方法在效率上低于其他方法，在典型工况下应更经常地使用。

对滤袋施加脉冲可以是"联机"方式，即系统在清灰过程中保持正常的气体流动；也可以是"脱机"方式，即清灰过程中有一个分隔间与排风气流隔离。绝大多数脉冲喷吹系统采用联机清灰方式。这种系统构成了最简单的织物型过滤器。因为不需要诸如隔离风门或振打机械之类的运动部件。从维护保养的角度出发这是一个大优点，但自然也涉及权衡问题。联机清灰在清除积尘方面不如脱机清灰有效，因为排风气流会使清除的灰尘在脉冲过后再沉积到织物滤袋上。脱机清灰可以在过滤重新开始前使清除掉的灰尘落入料斗，但这又增加了需要隔离风门的复杂性和费用。

第 9 单元

变风量系统介绍

变风量系统是当今现有的供热通风空调系统中最有前途和通用的型式，它是在应用上没有局限性，而只是由于缺少知识和过去的习惯，应用才受到限制的一种令人振奋的方法。

除了有助于解决能量问题外，在建筑能量的成本方面，变风量系统比传统的定风量系统能够节能 20%～30%。通过使用较小的设备如风机、水泵、锅炉、冷却器、造价较低的风道和管路分布系统，变风量系统也能减少初期投资。

此外，如果设计、维护和操作得当，变风量系统能够提供极好的舒适。在分区方面，变风量系统可提供良好的机动性并且能够容易地增容、压缩、调整、或关闭部分设备而对中央设备无任何程度的影响。

自从变风量系统被构思和开始应用以来，在过去几年中，令人麻烦的是变风量系统一直就存在着问题，这些问题并非已经全部 100% 地被解决或能很容易地控制。

举一个在过去十年里暖通空调工业遇到的各类问题的例子。请来想象一下，你要在你的城市或家乡的一幢新的多层建筑物中，处理一些业务。让我们来看看当你在建筑物里走动的情况吧。

在门口，你拉门，但门一动也不动。你用双手用力拉门，门突然开了。走进建筑物时，一股风随你一起冲入。

来自于头上天花板散流器的空气噪声使你烦恼，气流或气浪吹乱了你的头发，你急忙把头发整理好。在另一个散流器下方，空气停滞而静止，再往里走，在第三个散流器下方，一股冷空气沉下来使你冷得打颤。

在你逗留的第一个办公室里，热得令人窒息，你脱掉上衣，松开领带。在第二个办公室里，你竖起衣领还发抖，感觉象初冬一样寒冷。

总的说来，建筑物内使人感觉空气不新鲜——好象没有通风。

一个金属板制的人模站在梯子上，头伸进顶棚里。这告诉你，他肯定是在忙于对一个理论上讲是自我平衡的系统进行大量的测试和调节。他把其他问题说给你那意气相投的耳朵听：这个箱操作的压力不够，那个箱压力太大。在那边，末端调节器没有保持最大的风量（立方英尺/分）。

你坐电梯到机械房去调查那里的情况，你听到空气涌上竖井。

在设备间里，你看到纸板盖住了助燃空气百叶窗。建筑工程师抱怨早晨启动时没有足够的热量，风道发出隆隆声并震动。他在为要换掉那台装在翼式轴流风机上的发热的嗡嗡响的电机而发愁。

我们能够将这个故事继续讲下去，但观点已经阐明：尽管变风量系统可以使用而且有效率，但在过去并没有总是完全正确地运行。

在过去十年里所解决的问题
1. 风机风量调节被改进；
2. DDC 控制使得更精确的风机控制成为可能；
3. 每一个末端装置单独的微信息处理机控制；
4. 在变风量末端装置上要求较低的进气压力来使之运行；
5. 使用能达到最大变风量节能的转换器；
6. 风道的计算机计算静压复得设计，减少了的风道压力波动和噪声；
7. 变风量系统的恰当启动；
8. 适当的测试和平衡；
9. 用于风机风量控制的风道静压传感器的更有效的安装位置和设定值；
10. 变风量末端装置更有效的设定值和实际控制。

第10单元

卧式多程火管锅炉

卧式多程火管锅炉现常由熔焊成圆柱形的锅筒和浸在水中且直径相同并穿过锅筒全长的管子组成的。水面以上的空间主要用来分离和储存蒸汽。为了获得较大干度的蒸汽，目前，通常在蒸汽出口附近设置挡板（或干管）。

这种锅炉结构简单，初次费用少，是一种性能良好的蒸汽发生器。经济性比立管式或机车型锅炉好，但是正在被苏格兰船用锅炉所代替。卧式多程火管锅炉的缺点是管束间水表面的污垢难以清除。另一个缺点是如果水侧的锅筒板上形成污垢或污泥沉积物，就存在着锅筒被烧坏的危险。从管子清除污垢与其他类型火管锅炉一样是困难的。

排污管的连接：因为没有足够的连接螺纹数来给予适当的支撑，排污管不能只用螺纹拧在锅筒上，而是要在锅筒底部铆或焊一块加固垫板，然后将排污管拧在上面。

对于超过10马力（hp）（100平方英尺受热面）的锅炉来说，排污管的最小直径为1英寸。对于小于10马力的锅炉，多数州允许的最小管径是3/4英寸。在任何情况下，排污管的最大直径为5/2英寸。

给水入口：给水应从锅筒的顶部或前端进入，应该避开任何铆接的缝隙或暴露于辐射热和高温的锅炉部分。

如果锅炉的直径超过40英寸，锅筒上要设置检查孔。进水管可通过锅筒壁加固垫进入锅炉中。进水管应该向从最热一端——一般从前端算起大约3/5的锅炉长度上进水。这样进水中含的固性物不会沉淀在前端受热强的锅炉板上，因为那儿可能产生过热和损坏。

循环：在操作温度下，卧式多程火管锅炉里的水是按如下情况循环的：锅筒上炉火的辐射热使水沿锅筒的两侧上升。由于管子温度稍低，水从管子间向下返回。水的循环因其（管子）纵向位置不同而有某些差异。热烟气进入管子的后端，随着烟气向前移动，一些热量被锅炉水吸收。虽然锅炉后端的烟气温度可能超过1000℉，但前端出口温度可能是500℉了。因此，在纵轴上的循环，在锅炉后部管子之间趋于上升，前端趋于下沉。

额定功率：确定卧式多程火管锅炉额定功率的常规方法是根据受热面来计算。多数权威机构接受锅炉每马力为 10 ft^2 水受热面这一标准。这种锅炉的水受热面被认为是二分之一的锅筒面积加上所有管子（按内径计算）的总面积，再加上三分之二后管板面积减去管孔总面积。

检验：由于锅筒暴露在火里，火管锅炉要求认真检查内部的水垢、凸胀、鼓泡。

检查时，卧式多程火管锅炉上要仔细检查的一些部分如下：内部：管束上方部分，检查管子腐蚀和凹点。认真检查封头、锅筒、焊接、铆接点、和管子连接处的沟槽。检查裂缝、铆钉断裂、气孔以及锅筒板水线附近有无变薄。检查所有支撑物的固定和张力情况。检查内给水管的固定和支撑物情况，并注意管子不是部分堵塞。检查水位计、安全阀、压力表的孔口处是否有污垢堵塞。还必须检查锅筒和管子表面是否有污垢堆积。随后同步检查管子下面积垢。然后检查排污管连接孔口，并确保锅筒底部向排污管倾斜并且没有凸胀或鼓泡。

外部：拆开水位计接管上的旋塞，确保其中没有污垢。检查排污管垫和排污管确保管子防火并且完好，而且要确保排污阀处于良好状态。检查管端和铆固处或焊接处是否有开裂，检查管与管板连接处是否有疲劳。检查缝隙周边是否有爆裂以及堵缝边缘是否有泄漏。然后检查定位和支座是否良好。

第11单元

吸 收 式 热 泵

1. 吸收式热泵的功能

吸收式热泵从低温热源（如废热或地表水）取热，在较高的温度下输出热量用于冬天供热或其他场合，其效能系数大于1。

在日本和瑞典，吸收式热泵已经安装于使用工业废热的工业和区域供热工厂来提供热水(代表性的温度是165℉),用于冬天供热或其他用途,其COP(效能系数)在1.4到1.7之间。

吸收式热泵或用于冬天供热或用于夏天供冷冬天供热。

对于吸收式热泵来说,可计算供冷的效能系数COP_c,对于双级吸收式热泵而言,供热的效能系数COP_{hp}计算如下:

$$COP_{hp} = \frac{Q_{ab} + Q_{con}}{Q_{lg}}$$

式中　Q_{ab}＝从吸收器排出的热,Btu/h;

　　　Q_{con}＝从冷凝器排出的热,Btu/h;

　　　Q_{lg}＝输入到第一级发生器的热,Btu/h;

除了溴化锂水溶液,还有几种吸收剂,即工作流体正在得以发展,例如,$LiBr/ZnCl_2$ 和 $LiBr/ZnBr_2/CH_3OH$,在吸收式热泵中,溴化锂水溶液($LiBr/H_2O$)仍然是最广泛使用的。

2. 吸收式热泵和蒸汽压缩式热泵的比较

尽管对离心式热泵来说,供热效能系数COP_{hp}值在4～4.5之间,而对吸收式热泵来说,供热效能系数COP_{hp}仅仅为1.3至1.7,但是离心机使用的电能比吸收机使用的热能远远昂贵得多。

在选择过程中,应该对整个使用周期的成本进行分析。在考虑单位电价对天然气价比率时,特别应该考虑消耗费用和用电高峰时较高的电耗,在许多场合中,吸收式热泵可能是更经济的。

3. 串联吸收式热泵

串联吸收式热泵由两个单级吸收式热泵组成,每一级带有一个蒸发器,吸收器,发生器,冷凝器,热交换器和溶液泵。

液体水制冷剂在蒸发器内蒸发,水蒸气由吸收器内的浓溶液提出,传递到吸收器内热水中的吸收热用于区域供热。稀溶液通过热交换器从吸收器用泵打到发生器。在发生器中,来自工厂的蒸汽使稀溶液中的水汽化,汽化的水蒸气被排到冷凝器而冷凝成液体形式。冷凝潜热又传给区域供热的热水中。

来自发生器的浓溶液通过热交换器从发生器流到吸收器。冷凝液体水通过节流孔进入蒸发器,并且被喷射到管束上,在管束里,流入来自工厂的烟气冷却水。在吸收了来自烟气冷却水的汽化潜热之后,液体水在蒸发器内蒸发成水蒸气。

在这种串联吸收热泵中,第一级吸收式热泵在较高的温度下运行,而第二级热泵在较低的温度下运行。

在运行期间,来自区域供热的热水回水在第二级吸收式热泵的吸收器和冷凝器中从144℉被加热到152℉,并且在第一级吸收式热泵的吸收器和冷凝器中,从152℉被加热到160.5℉在蒸发器内,热从低温热源,即烟气冷却水中释放出来,废气冷却水在97.7℉的温度下进入吸收式热泵并且在75.2℉的温度下离开。高温热源——蒸汽在320℉下以66000lb/h的流量从焚烧工厂供应,串联吸收式热泵的平均效能系数COP_{hp}大约是1.6。

4. 运行特性

吸收热传递装置在两个压力水平上运行:高压,包括蒸发器和吸收器;低压,包括发生器和冷凝器。

输入和输出流体有三个温度水平：
- 带有热输出的来自吸收器的流体在最高的温度水平。
- 热源（输入到蒸发器和发生器的废热）在中间的温度水平。
- 冷凝器中的冷却水在最低的温度水平。

吸收热传递装置的用途是使输入废热流体的温度上升。吸收式热泵的功能是从较低的温度热源中获得一个较高的效能系数（COP）。

第12单元

天然气储存技术显身手

储存天然气的能力一直为用户和燃气公司提供着额外的机动性。不过，目前随着联邦政府关于对工业进行结构调整的636号令，储气服务业的存在已经显得更为重要。地方公用事业公司和其他用户对合同储气服务的需求正在上升。

因此，州际管道公司，如ANR和CIG，根据合同协议，储存了更多的燃气以迎合那些希望能够储气来供销售点售气要求的客户。

此外，据ANR公司的一位销售主任Dave Dowhan介绍，近年来储气工作已经越来越重要，因为地方公用事业公司占了ANR29个公司——储气服务客户的大部分，经验不足，但更困难的是最高负荷需要日期，因为他们的市场现在是由那些对温度敏感的住户和商业"核心"用户所统治。Dowhan特别指出，多数大的工业客户因为在全年中用气负荷状态相对平稳，正通过他们自己的供气安排，充分利用新的工业规定来获利。

纯效应就是ANR的传统储气季节(11月1日到3月31日)已压缩到了约70天的狭窄时间范围内。

根据这种情况，ANR1989年开始探索能够从本公司范围极广的储气业务中获取最大利润的方法。Gengtes回忆时说："因为这些发生在这个行业里的变化，我们感到成为利润中心的机会正在出现。"

Gentges和他的同事，包括Nowaczewski和Man Miron（另一个项目地质师）开始考察ANR的15个密执安地下储气池的运行情况，在那里1930亿立方英尺的天然气储存在多孔岩层中以在用气高峰期间回采。

在检查多年来气井和储气田运行数据时，他们发现在40多年的服务过程中，一些ANR公司的旧储气田已经损失了相当大的回采能力，即，24小时内从气田中可以抽出的燃气量。Gentges说回采能力损失是多年正常运行而造成的岩层破坏而引起的。

为扭转这种趋势和恢复储气能力，Gentges，Nowaczewski，Miron和Bob Scheid（气井维护和钻探经理）考虑了几种选择，其中包括钻更多的井。一个选择就是扩大现有的气井检修维护方案。

储存的燃气经过几百口储气井注入和回采。与行业的其他公司一样，ANR一般每年检修一定数量的井来作为它常规维修计划的一部分。若不进行检修，经过一定时间后，堆积的岩霄就会限制燃气的流动，从而减少燃气从储气池中回采的气量。

　　Rick Gengtes 解释说："在把扩大井检修方案和钻另外的气井的费用及后勤保障加以比较后，我们感到向内插入钻井方案——在生产于同一储气源现有的井之间打井——是最经济的。"

　　与此同时，燃气研究所（GRI）公布了一项燃气储存业调查报告的结果，表明被调查的美国储气经营者中有85％每年平均损失5％的送气能力。要恢复这部分送气能力，储气行业每年耗巨资1亿美元。

　　燃气研究所（GRI）建议储气经营者考虑水平钻井，因为在恰当的条件下，这可能比常规的竖井产量多得多。

　　1990年7月，部分是受到GRI研究报告的启发，Gentges 和他的同事们查找书本，翻阅了一切能找到的有关水平钻井的资料。

　　"在过去的8～10年中该技术有了很大的进展，它从一项技术变为一门科学"，Gentges 说："最大的进展在于控制钻井过程的惯性制导系统。实质上，目前的水平钻井承包商用的是类似于导弹上所采用的军事级别的技术。"

　　高技术制导系统的关键部分位于钻头后38英尺。在钻井过程中，这种装置向钻塔上的计算机输送电信号，这样，操作者就能调节钻头的角度和方向来保持钻井方向。钻头在地表下1200～1500英尺的水平方向上前进时是由装置在钻管上的下行钻孔电机和稳定器来提供动力的。

　　在与水平钻探顾问和承包商磋商后，Gentges 的同事开始前期研究，使用一种专用的计算机计算模型来帮助确定水平钻探能产生最佳效果的位置。

　　在现场调查和进一步分析后，他们决定在ANR的里德市和在密执安的林肯储气场打三口试验水平井，这三口井是为了恢复那些气田送气能力而补打25口井计划的一部分。

　　在以后的几个月中，Gentges 和他的同事们努力攀登陡峭的知识坡峰，其中很重要的细节之一就是为水平钻井测试和选择适当的钻头。在经过了广泛的测试后，他们首先选定了一种天然的金刚石钻头。一年以后，他们发现人造金刚石钻头结果更好。

　　1991年7月5日，在经过了近两年的准备后，在里德市开始第一口水平钻井。最初两口井在40天里完成，并且双双测试成功。第一口井有840英尺"开放孔"，第二口井有920英尺而常规的竖井只有15英尺。

第13单元

区域供热管网设计

　　本文中笔者将叙述三个计算机程序，这些程序既能用于区域供热管网设计又能用于民用和工业采暖区域的较为基础的场合。

　　这些程序是：

　　NO.1 PIPELINE；

NO.2 BURIED，和

NO.3 CONDUIT

PIPELINE 程序：该程序用来确定管道垂直或水平悬吊时，来自热水管道或蒸汽管道的热损失。热从介质传递到外边是经过下列各层的：

(a) 从介质传递到管壁，然后通过管子。

(b) 从管外壁层穿过各保温层等，以及

(c) 通过对流将热传给管外空气。

这个程序当然能成功地用于工厂、公共建筑物等中需要为蒸汽管道或热水管道保温或者确实需要保温绝热的烟囱、烟道等一般场合。在管道要穿过铁路隧道、地道等的区域供热场合，这个程序特别有用。PIPELINE 程序的结果也需要输入到 BURIED 和 CONDUIT 程序中。

BURIED 程序：直埋供热管道问题已经由瑞典建筑研究所和德国格雷弗林（Grafeling）热传输研究所进行了研究。在这些研究所中，为解决这个问题而形成的数学公式令人望而生畏。作者必须承认，虽然自己在数学方面有合情合理的大学（毕业）合格证书，但在运用这类数学方面也非常困难。

例如，即使是在所有系统里最简单的系统中，有一根裸管，外径为 d 米，被埋在深为 h 米的土中，土的导热系数为 k（W/m·K），也必须用如下方程表示：

$$R = (1/2\pi k) \times \text{arcosh}(2/hd)$$

式中 $\text{arcosh} x = \ln[x + (1-x^2)^{1/2}]$

想象一下更复杂的系统，即，在使用保温管或者埋两根不同温度管子时（区域供热系统中的供、回水主管），方程将变得更加复杂。因为其中包含了许多 Naperian 对数、双曲正切和更多的及双曲余统等。

就管道和它们的保温层而言，由于使用的数学能把涉及到的所有关系式考虑进去。得出的结果 100% 是可靠的。但仅有一项是不能确定的，那就是土的传热系数，如果它能被精确地测出来，计算结果就会与实验完全吻合。但是实际上土的导热系数全年在变化，与土的潮湿程度有关。

为了解决这个问题，笔者努力通过把一个专用的子程序引入到 BURIED 程序中来，确定要埋设管线的土的 K 值。

土被细分为四类：

(a) 沙和沙质的土。

(b) 轻粘土。

(c) 重粘土。

(d) 颗粒或松散的岩石。

假如给计算机前三种土壤的近似湿度值和最后一种的密度值，计算机就会给出能够用于计算的近似 K 值。很明显，这个 K 值绝不会完全精确，因为土的湿度随测量的深度而变化，而且在不同的时期变化幅度也很大。

程序能够处理保温和不保温管道的问题。

CONDUIT 程序：顾名思义，这个程序用来处理管沟内管道热损失问题。

设想五种不同的系统：

(a) 一对供水和回水管道保温后悬吊在地下的圆形管沟中。

(b) 类似的两根相同保温管道被自由支撑在地下的矩形截面管沟中。

(c) 两根相同保温管道埋在圆形截面管沟内的保温材料中。

(d) 两根相同未保温管道埋在圆形截面管沟的保温材料中。

(e) 两根相同未保温管道埋在没有固定管沟的长方形槽的土中。

最后一种类型是把管子放在松散的土中。对于上述管沟方式的每种选择，程序都有相应的子程序来计算出可靠的结果。

附录：由作者开发的计算机程序的全部目录：

1：U-VALUE（所有墙和屋顶结构U值的计算）。
2：DAMPNESS（建筑物接缝及表面防止冷凝的计算）。
3：SOLAR（通过玻璃窗面进入的太阳得热计算）。
4：LIVING（使用期间房屋的得热和失热计算）。
5：FLOOR（地板周边及区域的热损失计算）。
6：WINDOW（不同条件下，各类型窗户U值的计算）。
7：TOTAL（年均热负荷的计算）。
8：ECONOMY（多层玻璃窗最佳隔热层厚度及经济性的计算）。
9：HEATTRANS（不同类型热交换的计算）。
10：PIPELING（不保温和保温热管线的热损失计算）。
11：BURIED（区域供热和集中供热的热损失计算）。
12：CONDUIT（区域供热和集中供热的热损失计算）。
13：WATERPIPE（泵扬程和流量的计算）。
14：REGRESSION（用数据制作曲线图的数学分析）。
15：STEAM（过热和饱和蒸汽的热计算）。
16：FREEVENT（交换空气量及热损失的计算）。
17：GASPIPE（燃气及供气管线的尺寸计算）。
18：RADSIZE（建筑物散热器的尺寸计算）。
19：OILPIPE（所有非水管线的压头损失）。
20：RHLIMIT（建筑物内未出现冷凝时的最大相对湿度计算）。
21：CONDCURE（为避免冷凝所需空气量的计算）。
22：SUNHEAT（通过墙、窗、屋顶进入室内的太阳辐射热计算）。
23：HEATPUMP（设备容量的评价）。
24：COAL（确定燃煤炉设计各种参数）。
25：OIL（决定不同类型油的燃烧参数）。
26：GAS（19种不同燃气燃烧参数的研究）。
27：VENTAIR（公共区域所需通风参数的计算）。
28：AIRCOND（冷负荷和冷量的确定）。
29：AIRDUCT（组合通风系统的压头损失计算）。
30：DUCTSIZE（热风和冷风管道系统的尺寸计算）。
31：PIPESIZE（液体输送管线的尺寸计算）。

32：OFFICE（包括两个功能的组合程序：(a)：通讯地址；(b)：开户银行）。

33：HEATBAL（全部建筑热特性的估算软件包）。

第 14 单元

空调设备的运行和维修

移交和文件

设计者和承包商通过对当事人强调维修的重要性而保证足够的维修，应该向当事人建议所需的人员并向当事人提供必要的信息以进行维修。

为使设备在其整个使用期限内连续正常工作，维修和操作人员必须熟悉设备运转的原理和方法。除了全套资料图纸外，还应该有两本手册，一本供操作人员使用（如办公室经理，设备管理员），另一本供维修人员使用。前者应叙述这样的内容：设计原理、操作方法、报警细节和安全预防措施；后者是较大的服务手册，应包含 BS 5720：1979 中所列的资料，复述如下：

系统维修工程师所需要的文件单：

-设计者的安装说明，包括整套安装所需要的直线流程图和对照示图；

-安装图和设计者的操作说明书；

-设备操作和维修说明书、厂商的备件表和备件定货说明；

-电气设备明细表；

-机械设备明细表；

-合同所要求的测试结果和检测证书，包括任何保险或法定检查机关的证书；

-机器和设备的保证书副本；

-移交的钥匙、工具和备件单；

英国标准 5720：1979 对维修手册的编排和内容提出了进一步的建议。除了安装图外，这些材料应该以草稿形式在试运转阶段提供以便核对，这将帮助有关人员安装设备并使其有效运转，同时，手册在发到买方之前，可以进行修改，以适合可能需要的任何操作变化。

设备移交前，有必要对负责操作设备的人员就该系统的原理和操作给予口头说明和示范。除了提供文件之外，还应该有这样的口头说明。

维修组织

一旦当事人接受了承包商的安装，就应组织对设备的维修以确保设备连续有效地运行，不管这些设备复杂程度如何，目的是以最低的经济成本来保护投资。

任何有计划的维修方案的基础是档案制度，凭此对任何一件设备在适当的时候要进行的检查和服务就一目了然。这可以通过一个卡片检索系统或使用计算机来完成。当工作人员完成了一项维修时，他们应该记录下他们认为需要注意的或在不远的将来可能需要注意的事情，例如，会引起轴承最终失灵的过热运转。这能使维修在方便的时候进行，而不是在一切都似乎立即要失灵的时候才进行维修。

通过专业厂商承包维修，常常被用来作为直接雇佣劳力进行部分或全部服务的可供选择的措施。

服务的频率

常规维修包括检查、清理、水处理、调试和大修。对这些维修的频率通常在制造厂商的手册中给出，但这只具有一般意义，最好由实际现场情况和根据运行经验进行修改。

设备服务的频率取决于下列因素：
- 设备和系统效率以及由此而产生的有效的能量消耗；
- 对服务可靠性的影响；
- 常规维修费用；
- 故障修理费用；
- 安全检查；
- 系统运转的时数。

作为常规维修检查的一部分，必须对备用设备和应急设备进行检查，但不必使它们联机长时间运行。

在修理和设备改装停机后可能需要对系统或系统某一部分再次进行试运行。这种情况下应遵循适当的程序。

在常规维修中，尤其重要的是应包括对压力容器的安全检查和火警检测。

故障检查

故障检查程序可能包括在服务手册中。尽管从制造厂家常常可以得到每个设备的运行程序，这些程序也与设备所在的系统有关。

维修支持

为了保障维修，建议对下列因素予以考虑：
- 工程师办公室；
- 有适当工具的车间；
- 设备备件；
- 维修材料；
- 仪表；
- 安装工具。

第15单元

燃气采集和输送

I 引言

从一给定区域内的若干口井生产的天燃气通过称为采集系统的管道系统汇集并送到油田分离和处理设备。然后，经处理或部分经过处理的燃气被送到负责将燃气送到用户的干线管道。燃气常常通过管网进行分配，管网给流动计算带来很多复杂的问题。本章简要叙述燃气的采集系统和通过管网输送燃气，管网是根据单管稳定流动概念建立的，这些概念在另一章叙述。对在管道实践中相当常见的不稳定状态燃气流动的一些基本内容在另一章作介绍。

Ⅱ 采集系统

地面流动采集系统由把生产的流体从井口输送到油田处理装置（一般为油-水-燃气分离器）的管道及附件组成。具有极高生产能力气井的生产系统可对每口井提供单独的分离、计量、和合理的处理及设备。因为这些单井系统很少是经济的，因此常常设计成能组合控制若干口井流量的采集及分离设备。

采集系统的两种基本形式是径向型和轴向型。在径向系统中来自几口不同井的流送管汇集到设备所在的中心点。流送管常常在集合管终止，集合管实质上是足以输送所有流送管流量的大管道。在轴向采集系统内，若干口气井汇入公共管线。

对于大的油田，这两种基本系统要稍加修改。井中心区采集系统对局部区域的每口井和整个区域的井群使用径向采集系统。公共管道或干管管道采集系统对于几组气井使用轴向采集方案，然后再用径向采集方案。干管管道采集系统更适应于油田相对来说较大以及在中心区建造油田处理设备不理想或行不通的场合。

显而易见，同时测量各气井产量需要非常复杂的仪表设备。一般采用测试集流管来引导流体从单井通过计量系统。这种气井测试集流管也提供控制单口井的生产以及对各气井实施测试的手段。

采集系统之间的选择通常是考虑经济的。在井中心系统中使用几根小截面管道的成本与干管式系统中单根大管道的成本相似。技术上的可行性可以是另一个标准。采集系统可能要埋到地表以下几英尺，从成本和维护容易性方面前者比另一种系统有利。气田的生产特性也很重要，应予以考虑。这些包括了现在的和估算未来的油气田所有气井的产量分布、井口流动压力、油气田未来发展以及地下储备实用的可能性。

Ⅲ 简易管道系统中的稳态流动

"简易"一词用在这里是指对流动关系稍加改变就能讨论的燃气管道系统。流动关系在另一章中叙述。"简易"的一个特点就是燃气从一端流入，另一端流出，管道系统内的任何其他点没有流动出现。这种系统常常用于在保持原来的压力和压力降的情况下（比如新气井已被开发但必须使用原有管道的场合），增加管道流量，或者用于在维持原有流量条件下，以较低压力（压力降）使管路运作。当管道已老化或腐蚀时需用后者。

运用这些条件的三种可行方法是用较大的管道替换部分管道（管道串联）；沿现有管道的整个长度并列布置一根或多根管道（管道并联）；或沿现有管道部分长度局部并列布置一根或多根管道（串并联或环形线路）。对于这些系统中的每一种都将依据威莫斯关于气体流经管道的稳态流动的基本公式导出关系式，这儿气体流经的管道是指已把管道组简化为在压力降和流量都与之相等的单根管道。

第16单元

含有硫化氢和二氧化碳天然气的容积特性

引言

尽管预测纯物质气体压缩系数的相对准确方法已由图表提供，这些图表是以简化性质以及假设压缩系数是 T_r，P_r 和 v_{cr} 单值函数为根据的，但确定气体混合物压缩系数准确值是稍有困难的。

处理气体混合物的两种普通方法已被提出。第一种方法是依据各组成成分的性质而假定混合气体的某些性质具有直接的或修正的相加性。这种方法的例证基于熟悉的道尔顿和阿曼加特定律。第二种方法是求出适合于纯物质状态方程常数的平均值。在工程计算中这两种方法都有局限性，因为第一种方法通常仅在窄的压力和温度范围内提供可靠的答案，而第二种方式使用起来麻烦。

在石油工程实践中常常需要准确判断天然气的容积特性。为满足这个需求，已经提出了几个具有普遍性的压缩系数图表。其中由斯坦丁等人提出的图表目前广泛使用。在制作这类图表时，遵循了处理混合气体的第三种方法。该方法是建立在由凯论述的准临界性质基础上并通过混合物中各个组成气体的临界性质来进行计算的。尽管这些图表对于干式或湿式无硫天然气的可压缩系数提供了相对准确的数据，但当用于含有高浓度的硫化氢或二氧化碳或二者兼含的燃气时还缺乏可靠性。这样，实验图表是现行的可得到的确定含硫或酸性气体混合物容积特性的最好方法，但要耗费时间。

在这些气体混合物的特性、特别是与加拿大西部油田有关的天然气方面，人们所表现的兴趣为这些研究提供了动因。加拿大西部油田里的酸性气体浓度可高达55%，仅硫化氢的浓度就高达36%。试验的目的就是确定所选择的甲烷、硫化氢和二氧化碳混合气体在 40～160°F 温度范围、压力达到 3000 磅/英寸^2 条件下的容积特性。

实验方法

这个试验所用的装置基本上与洛伦佐所描述的相同。配制气体混合物时所用的每一种纯气体成分的量通过带玻璃孔口的压力容器水银面高度来计量。然后纯气体组分按要求的量被逐一输送到另一个确定混合气体容积特性的带有玻璃孔口的压力容器。通过水银的注入或抽出实现体积变化。容器的容量约为 125 立方厘米。

容器中的温度由铜-康铜热电偶配合利兹·诺思拉普半精密电位计来计量。操作时温度保持在所需要温度的 ±0.5°F 范围之内。压力值高于 1000 磅/英寸^2 时采用海斯布尔登管式压力计测定，精确值在 ±3 磅/英寸^2 之内，压力低于 1000 磅/英寸^2 时采用精确到 ±1 磅/英寸^2 的同类仪表。两种仪表参照自重活塞式仪表校验并配合相应的校准曲线使用。

曾经用 100 厘米的高差计来测量所取样本的体积并确定影响测定压力的静水压头。长度测量的可再现性（精度）约为 0.05 毫米，这与体积测量的精度在最大体积时为 0.01% 及最小体积时为 0.1% 相对应。容器体积的校准通过用水银注满每一容器并对由高差计所测定的两水平面间流出的水银进行称重。这样就建立了校准曲线。

校准的检验通过确定纯气体的组分甲烷、二氧化碳和硫化氢在两个容器中的压缩性来进行。单一组分的量在相对低压下被输入平衡容器或测量容器中。在要求的温度被建立以后，用文献中报告的试验压缩系数来计算气体的摩尔数。然后逐级增加压力到所要求的最大值，记录每一级的体积。利用初始状态的摩尔数和测得的变化量计算每一压力下的压缩系数，然后用这些结果与文献中的报告值相对比。因为两个平衡容器中温度的变化以及在压力达 2500 磅/英寸^2 时各单独气体的约 30 个不同的取样样本，所出现的误差低于 2.5%。

对近似 50：50 的甲烷和二氧化碳混合气体进行类似的测量为可得到的试验数据提供了补充的检验。在压力达到 3000 磅/英寸^2 时，所获得结果的吻合程度优于±1%。就所有情况而论，测量应在增加压力和减小压力的条件下进行。试验工作中所使用的甲烷，二氧化碳和硫化氢都要保证最低纯度为 99% 摩尔。

Appendix Ⅲ Key to the exercises

UNIT ONE
Reading Comprehension

Ⅰ. 1. F 2. F 3. T 4. T 5. F

Ⅱ. 1. distance and the quantity of heat transmitted
  2. the water pressure
  3. the flow rate and the temperature difference

Ⅲ. 1. the heat demand density
  2. the supply and return temperature
  3. the characteristics of the terrain
  4. the local infrastructure
  5. a new development or a retrofit development

Vocabulary

Ⅰ. 1. accessibility 2. viable 3. valve 4. minimize 5. prohibitive

Ⅱ. 1. minimized 2. accessibility 3. viable 4. valve 5. prohibitive

Ⅲ. 1. d 2. b 3. d 4. a 5. d

Writing   Selecting the key words

1. heat transmission
2. distribution system
3. district heating
4. transmission line
5. heat demand

UNIT TWO
Reading Comprehension

Ⅰ. 1. T 2. T 3. F 4. T 5. F

Ⅱ. 1. C 2. A 3. C 4. B 5. D

Ⅲ. 1. 1) a rectangular chamber 2) is connected to 3) is flush with hole 1; and is removed

  2. 1) is moved some distance; is then augmented by some of the surrounding air which is entrains

    2) equal to that entrained; out of the entry; into the chamber

Vocabulary

Ⅰ. 1. extraction 2. perimeter 3. dilute 4. deflect 5. ascending 6. sucked out
Ⅱ. 1. unbounded 2. brim 3. entrain 4. flush 5. augment 6. accumulation
Ⅲ. 1. accumulation 2. flush 3. unbounded 4. brim 5. entrain 6. is augmented

Writing   Selecting the Key Words (2)

exhaust hood, source of impurity, circulation, rates of suction, rate of contamination

UNIT THREE

Reading Comprehension

Ⅰ. 1. F 2. T 3. T 4. T 5. F
Ⅱ. 1. Daylight transmittance 89%   2. Transmissivity 82%   3. Absorptivity 11%
    4. Reflectance 7%
Ⅲ. 1. metallic particles   2. increased glass temperature and thermal expansion
    3. freon gas   4. the net energy consumption   5. hardly noticeable

Vocabulary

Ⅰ. 1. toughened 2. illumination 3. irradiance 4. multiplication 5. aesthetic
Ⅱ. 1. tint 2. render 3. transparent 4. adventitious 5. occupant
Ⅲ. 1. tinted 2. occupants 3. adventitious 4. rendering 5. transparent

Writing   Outline Writing (1)

A) par. 2   B) par. 3   C) par. 1   D) par. 4

UNIT FOUR

Reading Comprehension:

Ⅰ. 1. T 2. F 3. T 4. F 5. F
Ⅱ. 1. 4-12 2. 12-30 3. about 2-4 4. 50-100 5. 1.5∶1 6. 3.2∶1
Ⅲ. 1. 925000 2. steam 3. 1005 4. 0.7 5. 26 6. 9700
Ⅳ. 1. operability 2. erosion 3. detrition 4. bubbling 5. small 6. circulating
    7. dominating 8. hybrid 9. recycle 10. elimination 11. cells 12. bubbling
    13. cir-culating

Vocabulary:

Ⅰ. 1. fluidized 2. advocate 3. cyclone 4. concession 5. executive
Ⅱ. 1. transition 2. dominate 3. controversy 4. combustor 5. hybrid
Ⅲ. 1. transition 2. dominate 3. controversy 4. combustor 5. hybrid

Writing   Outline Writing (2)

para. 1 Prediction of the operational problems of the fluidized bed combustion.

para. 2 The present situation and future of fluidized bed combustion.

para. 3 Conventional viewpoints on the bubbling bed and the circulating bed.

para. 4 An interesting overview of the circulating vs bubbling bed controversy.

para. 5, 6 Main characteristics and parameters of the circulating bed.

para. 7 The catch in the circulating bed design.

para. 8 Next step in FBC designs.

para. 9 A brief description of combined BFB/CFB design.

para. 10 A demonstration of the combined BFB/CFB design.

UNIT FIVE

Reading Comprehension

I. Say whether the following statements are True (T) or False (F) according to the text.

1. (F)   2. (T)   3. (T)   4. (F)   5. (F)

II. Skim through the (1) - (7) conditions and complete the following table:

1. liquid flooding 2. damage to the pistons, valves and rings, also broken parts which show very little wear 3. damage to the compressor 4. oil leaving the compressor 5. set to maintain different superheat settings 6. oil clogging, especially on low-temperature applications 7. flooded starts 8. causing the oil to foam

III. Fill in the blanks with the information given in the text.

1. is associated with a clattering noise

2. more likely on air-cooled compressors

3. reduces the amount of lubrication the cylinders receive

4. high discharge pressure, poor system performance, moisture freezing

5. to check with the accumulator and equipment

Vocabulary

I. Fill in the blanks with the words and expressions given below. Change the forms if necessary.

1. breaks down   2. pick…up   3. checks with   4. malfunctions   5. droplets

II. Find the words in the text which almost mean the same as the following:

1. slugging   2. clatter   3. lubricate   4. migration   5. stratify

III. Now use the words you have found to complete the following sentences. Change the form if necessary.

1. lubricating   2. migration   3. stratified   4. clattering   5. slugging

Writing Outline writing (3)

1—A, 2—D, 3—F, 4—B, 5—C, 6—G, 7—H, 8—E

UNIT SIX

Reading Comprehension

Ⅰ. 1. T   2. F   3. F   4. T   5. T

Ⅱ. 1. ②Flow proportional operation
   ③Flowrate and injection rate capabilities
   ⑥System monitoring
   ⑦Determination of malfunction and alarm

2. ②Injection rate controller
   ④Monitoring and alarm system

3. ②Chemical density of the odorant
   ③Pump displacement/stroke desired

Ⅲ. 1. knowledge of the chemical composition, the physical layout of the pipeline system, and the desired odorant level.

2. deliver a small amount of gas for the technician to sniff.

3. at a desired injection rate

4. on-board system monitoring, and alarm outputs upon malfunction

5. at a frequency to match a preprogrammed injection rate (lb./MMCF).

Vocabulary

Ⅰ. 1. verification   2. have been incorporated   3. segregates   4. compatibility
   5. actuated

Ⅱ. 1. malfunction   2. ambient   3. verify   4. likelihood   5. compensate

Ⅲ. 1. ambient 2. likelihood 3. compensated 4. was verified 5. malfunction

Writing Outline writing (4)

1) One commonly utilized style of odorization system is the injection style odorizer.

2) There are basic considerations of system operation.

3) Matching the odorant recipe to the natural gas in the stream involves a lot of knowledge.

4) Chose a system that will operate in proportion-to-flow.

5) The system must have the ability to perform a prescribed injection rate over a wide range of possible flowrates.

6) Systems should have a means of injecting a known, variable, and consistent amount of odorant with each injection.

7) A primary concern has to be malfunction.

8) A typical injection type odorizer consists of four components.

9) The injection pump is one of the most important components and is usually a posi-

tive displacement pump.

10) The injection rate controller receives flowrate information from an electronic measurement device.

11) The verification system meters fluid consumed by the pump.

12) Odorant consumption may be monitored both locally and remotely.

13) Downloading provides verification that proper odoration was taking place.

14) The requirement for a safe, clean and inexpensive fuel supply has given rise to various techniques of odorizing natural gas.

UNIT SEVEN

Reading Comprehension

I. 1.F 2.T 3.F 4.F 5.T

II. can be defined as the state of mind where satisfaction is felt with the thermal environment

III. 1. 19~20℃   2. 20 and 24℃

IV. 1. provides the most pleasurable sensation of comfort
   2. is the cat-like pleasure that comes from the warmth of a hot water bottle or just cuddling up to another person
   3. is caused by the effects of the radiation and conduction warming the air and causing it to rise

V. 1. match 2. required 3. principal 4. ground 5. head 6. dust 7. comparison

Vocabulary

I. 1. sensation 2. exhilaration 3. convector 4. strides 5. vandal

II. 1. compatible 2. gradient 3. advent 4. integral 5. cuddle

III. 1. cuddled 2. compatible 3. gradient 4. advent 5. integral

Writing Summary Writing (1)

1) thermal 2) comfort 3) radiant 4) gradient 5) subject 6) infloor 7) reduction 8) convectors

UNIT EIGHT

Reading Comprehension

I. Say whether the following statements are True (T) or False (F) according to the text, making use of the given paragraph reference number.

1.T 2.F 3.F 4.F 5.T

II. Choose the best answer.

1.C 2.A 3.D 4.B 5.D

Ⅲ. Fill in the blanks with the information given in the text:
1. pieces of fabric sewn into cylinders or envelopes
2. shaking, reverse air flow, pulse jet air
3. the oldest and simplest method
4. from the fabric and into the hopper
5. 1) normal airflow is maintained
   2) a compartment is isolated

Vocabulary
Ⅰ. Fill in the blanks with the expressions given below, change the form if necessary.
1. cylinder 2. hoppers 3. dislodge 4. incorporating 5. supplemented
Ⅱ. Find words in the text which mean almost the same as the following:
1. oscillate 2. initiate 3. enhance 4. induce 5. typically
Ⅲ. Now used the words you have found to complete the following sentences. Change the form if necessary.
1. enhances 2. has induced 3. typically 4. is oscillated 5. initiated

Writing Summary Writing (2)
1. cylinders or envelopes 2. Fabric filters 3. cleaning method 4. different applications 5. Shaking 6. is flexed 7. is dislodged 8. be initiated 9. Reverse flow cleaning 10. dampers 11. High-temperature filtration 12. specialized fabrics 13. Pulse-jet lean-ing/Cleaning pulse 14. regular intervals 15. sensing excess pressure drop 16. felted fabrics 17. on-line 18. off-line

UNIT NINE
Reading Comprehension
Ⅰ. 1. T 2. T 3. F 4. F 5. T
Ⅱ. 1. improved 2. more precise controls of fans 3. Separate microprocessor controls 4. Lower intake pressures 5. maximize VAV energy savings 6. fluctuating duct pressure and noise 7. Proper startup 8. Proper testing 9. for fan volume control 10. VAV terminal units
Ⅲ. 1. only by lack of knowledge and past habits
2. by using smaller equipment
3. has been involved with over the past decade
4. to set it back in place
5. changing the hot, humming motor

Vocabulary

I . 1. versatile   2. conception   3. stagnant   4. stifling   5. pulled on
II . 1. transact   2. gush   3. throb   4. rumble   5. fluctuate
III . 1. throbbed   2. fluctuating   3. had transacted   4. rumbling   5. gushing

Writing   Summary writing (3)

There have been problems over the past years, not all of which have been resolved. For an example of the kinds of problems, as you enter a multistory building a gale of air rushes in with you. The air noise from the ceiling diffuser disturbs you. Under another diffuse the air is stagnant and still and under a third diffuser a glob of cold air sinks down and chills you. The air of the building feels generally stale as if there is no ventilation. When you ride the elevator up you can hear air gushing up the shaft. Ductwork rumbles and throbs.

VAV systems haven't always operated altogether correctly in the past, but some problems have been resolved in last decade.

UNIT TEN

Reading Comprehension

I . 1. c   2. d   3. a   4. b

II . 1. simple   2. fairly low   3. good

III . 1. that hard deposits of scale are difficult to remove from water surfaces of inner rows of tubes.
2. the danger of burning the shell plates above the fire if thick scale or deposits of mud form on the waterside on these plates
3. 5/2
4. 1
5. rise
6. downward

IV . 1) the section above the tubes   2) the knuckles of heads, shells, welds, rivets, and tubes   3) seams   4) areas near the water-line of the shell plate   5) all stays   6) the internal feedpipe   7) the openings to the water-column connections   8) safety valve and pressure gauge   9) shell and tube surface 10) the above-mentioned parts be-low the tubes 11) the opening to the blowdown connections

vocabulary:

I . 1. (had) bulged   2. screwed   3. caulked   4. porosity   5. feeding water

II . 1. fusion   2. rivet   3. precipitate   4. longitudinal   5. aggregate

III . 1. precipitate   2. riveted   3. fusion   4. aggregates   5. longitudinal

Writing Summary Writing (4)

Horizontal-Return-Tubular-boilers (HRT) consist of a cylindrical shell, today usually fusion-welded, with tubes of identical diameter running the length of the shell thought the water space, with a baffle plate (or dry pipe) near the steam outlet. The HRT boiler is simple in construction, low in first cost and is a good steamer. It is more economical than the Vertical Tubular or Locomtive types, but it has two disadvantages which should not be ignored. For effective and smooth operations of the HRT boiler, the following pointed are mentioned and stressed. (1) The blowdown pipe cannot be merely screwed into the shell but into a pad which is riveted or welded to the bottom of the shell. (2) The feedwater should enter through the upper part of the shell or front head and it should discharge clear of any riveted seam or part of the boiler exposed to radiant heat or high temperature. (3) A manhole is provided above the tubes if the boiler is over 40 in. diameter. (4) The circulation both of water and of hot gases should take place smoothly. For water it is to rise around each side of the shell and then returns downwater between the tubers. For hot gases, the circulation in a longitudinal axis will tend to rise between the tubes at the real of the boiler and to be downwater at the front end. (5) The conventional means of rating an HRT boiler is according to its heating surface. The standard of 10 ft^2 of water heating surface per boiler horsepower is accepted by most authorities. (6) Careful inspection should be carried out both internally and externally.

UNIT ELEVEN
Reading Comprehension

    I. 1. F   2. F   3. T   4. F   5. T

   II. 2. water vapor; in the absorber

       3. is used; for district heating

       4. The diluted solution; is pumped

       5. The boiled-off water vapor; is extracted

  III. 1. the highest temperature level

       2. the lowest temperature level

       3. the intermediate temperature level

       4. high pressure

       5. low pressure

Vocabulary

    I. 1. concentrated   2. be sprayed   3. diluted   4. be extracted   5. boiled-off

   II. 1. cost-effective   2. via   3. bundle   4. latent   5. boost

  III. 1. via   2. cost-effective   3. boost   4. Latent   5. bundle

Writing   **Abstract Writing (1)**

    functions, absorption, coefficient, two-stage, pump, economy, series-connected, characteristics

UNIT TWELVE
Read Comprehension
  I . 1. F   2. F   3. F   4. F   5. T
  II . 1. c   2. a   3. d   4. e   5. b

Vocabulary
  I . 1. reaps from   2. scrutinized   3. was stashed   4. debris   5. inertial
  II . 1. flexibility   2. option   3. inject   4. recondition   5. deliverability
  III . 1. deliverability   2. options   3. reconditioned   4. is injected   5. flexibility

Writing Abstract (2)
  1. pipeline   2. storage   3. withdrawal   4. capability   5. comparison   6. drill
  7. maintenance   8. horizontally

UNIT THIRTEEN
Reading comprehension
  I . 1. b   2. c   3. a
  II . 1. external diameter of the pipe buried
     2. depth of the pipe buried in soil
     3. thermal conductivity
  III . 1. the wall of the pipe and through it
     2. the series of insulation layers
     3. convection to the outside air
  IV . 1. sand and sandy soil
     2. light clay
     3. heavy clay
     4. solid or loose rock

Vocabulary
  I . 1. glazed   2. is bristled   3. daunted   4. main   5. conduit
  II . 1. envisage   2. logarithm   3. conductivity   4. saturate   5. sub-routine
  III . 1. saturated   2. envisaged (envisage)   3. logarithms   4. conductivity   5. sub-routines

Writing   Abstract Writing (3)
  This paper, with the theory of mathematics and heat transmission, explains principles

of calculation for heat losses in pipeline networks of district heating, and based on them, a programs of calculation is developed, which is a package consisting of three subroutines. A brief introduction is given to the principles of the program design, its contents and function, and an example is given to prove that the programs solves complex calculation problems in the design of district heating networks. Besides, the paper makes a deep analysis of the effect on the thermal conductivity of soils with different structures.

UNIT FOURTEEN
Reading Comprehension
I. Say whether the following statements are True (T) or False (F) according to the text, making use of the given paragraph reference number.
1. T 2. T 3. F 4. T 5. F

II. Skim through "Hand-over and documentation" and complete the following table:

2.	installation drawings and operational instructions
3.	manufacturer's spare parts lists
4.	schedules of electrical equipment
6.	test results and test certificates
8.	list of keys, tools and spare parts that are handed over

III. Fill in the blanks with the information given in the text:
1. for the operating staff for the maintenance staff
2. to protect the capital investment at a minimum economic cost
3. ought to note down anything
4. as an alternative to directly employed labour
5. insurance inspections of pressure vessels

Vocabulary
I. Fill in the blanks with the words and expressions given below. Change the forms if necessary.
1. modifications 2. requisite 3. whereby 4. In the light of 5. overhaul

II. Find the words in the text which almost mean the same as the following:
1. hand-over 2. statutory 3. come to light 4. standby 5. thereof

III. Now use the words you have found to complete the following sentences. Change the form if necessary.
1. standby 2. come to light 3. hand-over 4. statutory 5. thereof

Writing   Abstract Writing
In the article, the importance of the maintenance of air conditioning plant is

stressed. For the plant to continue working properly throughout its life, it is necessary to ensure adequate maintenance. And many concrete requirements are advanced for the designers, contractors and maintenance and operating staff. It is pointed out that the basis of any planned maintenance scheme is a filing system. Furthermore, it explains frequency of serving, fault-finding and maintenance suppert, which may be referred to in the course of the maintenance of the air conditioning plant.

UNIT FIFTEEN
Reading comprehension
    I. 1. metering   2. treatment   3. facilities   4. gathering   5. combined
       6. wellstreams   7. center   8. radial   9. common-line   10. axial
    II. 1. replace a portion of the pipeline with a large one
       2. place one or more pipelines in a parallel along the complete length of the existing line
       3. place one or more pipelines in parallel only partially along the length of the existing line

Vocabulary
    I. 1. emanates   2. looped   3. corrodes   4. meter   5. lease
    II. 1. radial   2. converge   3. terminate   4. simultaneously   5. throughput
    III. 1. simultaneously   2. are terminated   3. converged   4. throughput   5. radial

Writing   Abstract Writing
    The paper briefly describes the basic conceptions of the gathering system and the transport of gas through pipeline network, makes a comparison between single well systems and gathering and separation facilities that enable combined handing of several well streams in terms of economy proposes detailed modifications to the two gathering systems which should be made in the case of large leases, and presents three factors that need consideration when a choice of systems is being made. The paper also makes a brief introduction to the steady-state flow in simple pipeline systems, and the comsumptions made for the convenience of study.

UNIT SIXTEEN
Reading comprehension
    I. 1. c 2. d 3. a 4. b
    II. 1. 55 2. 36 3. 40°to160°F 4. 3000
    III. 1. assumes a direct or modified additivity of certain properties of the mixture in terms of the properties of the individual components

2. average the constants of an equation of state applicable to the pure components
3. based on correlation of pseudo-critical properties as outlined by Kay and calculated from the critical properties of the individual components in a mixture

Vocabulary

I . 1. sours   2. dead-weight   3. stepwise   4. mole   5. potentiometer

II . 1. compressibility   2. applicable   3. cumbersome   4. volumetric   5. calibrate

III . 1. applicable   2. cumbersome   3. volumetric   4. compressibility   5. is calibrating

Writing   Abstract Writing

This paper, starting from analysing the limitations of two general methods of dealing with gaseous mixtures and being geared to the needs of engineering practice, proposes two methods to precisely determine the volumetric behavior of natural gas with or without sulfide. The paper also gives detailed descriptions of (1) the apparatus used in this investigation, (2) the method to determine the volume of gases, (3) the choise of meters with different pressure ranges, (4) the precision requirements of temperature and pressure, (5) the method and steps of experiment, (6) numbers of gases samples, (7) permissible allowance, and the purity of the gases used.

图书在版编目（CIP）数据

建筑类专业英语. 暖通与燃气. 第3册/周保强，张少凡主编. —北京：中国建筑工业出版社，1997
（2005重印）
高等学校试用教材
ISBN 978-7-112-03037-8

Ⅰ. 建… Ⅱ. ①周… ②张… Ⅲ. ①建筑学—英语—高等学校—教材②采暖—英语—高等学校—教材③通风—英语—高等学校—教材④燃料气—英语—高等学校—教材 Ⅳ. H31

中国版本图书馆CIP数据核字（2005）第114648号

高等学校试用教材

建筑类专业英语

暖通与燃气

第三册

周保强　张少凡　主编

师涌江　冀桂娥

陈星星　管继顺　编

颜景台

王　鸣　　　主审

*

中国建筑工业出版社出版、发行（北京西郊百万庄）
各地新华书店、建筑书店经销
北京建筑工业印刷厂印刷

*

开本：787×1092毫米　1/16　印张：12½　字数：300千字
1997年6月第一版　2012年7月第十三次印刷
定价：**22.00元**
ISBN 978-7-112-03037-8
（20970）

版权所有　翻印必究
如有印装质量问题，可寄本社退换
（邮政编码 100037）